Henry Du Pré Labouchere

Diary of the Besieged Resident in Paris

Henry Du Pré Labouchere

Diary of the Besieged Resident in Paris

ISBN/EAN: 9783337015299

Printed in Europe, USA, Canada, Australia, Japan

Cover: Foto ©ninafisch / pixelio.de

More available books at **www.hansebooks.com**

DIARY

OF

THE BESIEGED RESIDENT

IN PARIS.

REPRINTED FROM "THE DAILY NEWS,"

WITH

SEVERAL NEW LETTERS AND PREFACE.

IN ONE VOLUME.

LONDON:
HURST AND BLACKETT, PUBLISHERS,
13, GREAT MARLBOROUGH STREET.
1871.

LONDON:
BRADBURY, EVANS, AND CO., PRINTERS, WHITEFRIARS.

PREFACE.

The publishers of these letters have requested me to write a preface. In vain I have told them, that if prefaces have not gone out of date, the sooner they do, the better it will be for the public; in vain I have despairingly suggested that there must be something which would serve their purpose, kept in type at their printers, commencing, "At the request of—perhaps too partial—friends, I have been induced, against my own judgment, to publish, &c., &c., &c.;" they say that they have advertised the book with a preface, and a preface from me they must and will have. Unfortunately I have, from my earliest childhood, religiously skipped all introductions, prefaces, and other such obstructions, so that I really do not precisely know how one ought to be written; I can only, therefore, say that—

These letters are published for the very excellent reason that a confiding publisher has offered me a sum of money for them, which I was not such a fool as to refuse. They were written in Paris to the *Daily News* during the siege.

I was residing there when the war broke out; after a short absence, I returned just before the capitulation of Sédan—intending only to remain one night. The situation, however, was so interesting that I stayed on from day to day, until I found the German armies drawing their lines of investment round the city. Had I supposed that I should have been their prisoner for nearly five months, I confess I should have made an effort to escape, but I shared the general illusion that—one way or the other—the siege would not last a month.

Although I forwarded my letters by balloon, or sent them by messengers who promised to "run the blockade," I had no notion, until the armistice restored us to communications with the outer world, that one in twenty had reached its destination. This mode of writing, as Dr. William Russell wittily observed to me the other day at Versailles, was much like firing in the dark—and it must be my excuse for any inaccuracies or repetitions.

Many of my letters have been lost *en route*—some of them, which reached the *Daily News* Office too late for insertion, are now published for the first time. The reader will perceive that I pretend to no technical knowledge of military matters; I have only sought to convey a general notion of how the warlike operations round Paris appeared to a civilian spectator, and to give a fair and impartial account of the inner life of Paris, during its isolation from the rest of Europe. My bias—if I had any—was in favour of the Parisians, and I should have been heartily glad had they been successful in their resistance. There is, however, no getting over facts, and I could not long close my eyes to the most palpable fact—however I might wish it otherwise—that their leaders were men of little energy and small resource, and that they themselves seemed rather to depend for deliverance upon extraneous succour, than upon their own exertions. The women and the children undoubtedly suffered great hardships, which they bore with praiseworthy resignation. The sailors, the soldiers of the line, and levies of peasants which formed the Mobiles, fought with decent courage. But the male population of Paris, although they boasted greatly of their " sublimity," their " endurance," and their " valour," hardly appeared to me to come up to their own estimation of themselves, while many of them seemed to consider that heroism was a necessary consequence of the enunciation of advanced political opinions. My object in writing was to present a practical rather than a sentimental view of events, and to recount things as they were, not as I wished them to be, or as the Parisians, with perhaps excusable patriotism, wished them to appear.

For the sake of my publishers, I trust that the book will find favour with the public. For the last three hours I have been correcting the proofs of my prose, and it struck me that letters written to be inserted in separate numbers of a daily paper, when published in a collected form, are somewhat heavy reading. I feel, indeed, just at present, much like a person who has obtained money under false pretences, but whose remorse is not sufficiently strong to induce him to return it.

DIARY

OF THE

BESIEGED RESIDENT IN PARIS.

CHAPTER I.

PARIS, *September* 18*th*.

No one walking on the Champs Elysées or on the Boulevards to-day would suppose that 300,000 Prussians are within a few miles of the city, and intend to besiege it. Happy, said Laurence Sterne, in his "Sentimental Journey," the nation which can once a week forget its cares. The French have not changed since then. To-day is a fête day, and as a fête day it must be kept. Every one seems to have forgotten the existence of the Prussians. The Cafés are crowded by a gay crowd. On the Boulevard, Monsieur and Madame walk quietly along with their children. In the Champs Elysées honest mechanics and bourgeois are basking in the sun, and nurserymaids are flirting with soldiers. There is even a lull in the universal drilling. The regiments of Nationaux and Mobiles carry large branches of trees stuck into the ends of their muskets. Round the statue of Strasburg there is the usual crowd, and speculators are driving a brisk trade in portraits of General Uhrich. "Here, citizens," cries one, "is the portrait of the heroic defender of Strasburg, only one sou—it cost me two

—I only wish that I were rich enough to give it away." "Listen, citizens," cries another, "whilst I declaim the poem of a lady who has escaped from Strasburg. To those who, after hearing it, may wish to read it to their families, I will give it as a favour for two sous." I only saw one disturbance. As I passed by the Rond Point, a very tall woman was mobbed, because it was thought that she might be a Uhlan in disguise. But it was regarded more as a joke than anything serious. So bent on being happy was every one that I really believe that a Uhlan in the midst of them would not have disturbed their equanimity. "Come what may, to-day we will be merry," seemed to be the feeling; "let us leave care to the morrow, and make the most of what may be our last fête day."

Mr. Malet, the English secretary, who returned yesterday from Meaux, had no small difficulty in getting through the Prussian lines. He started on Thursday evening for Creil in a train with a French officer. When they got to Creil, they knocked up the Mayor, and begged him to procure them a horse. He gave them an order for the only one in the town. Its proprietor was in bed, and when they knocked at his door his wife cried out from the window, "My husband is a coward and won't open." A voice from within was heard saying, "I go out at night for no one." So they laid hands on the horse and harnessed it to a gig. All night long they drove in what they supposed was the direction of the Prussian outposts, trumpeting occasionally like elephants in a jungle. In the morning they found themselves in a desert, not a living soul to be seen, so they turned back towards Paris, got close in to the forts, and started in another direction. Occasionally they discerned a distant Uhlan, who rode off when he saw them. On Friday night they slept among the Francs-tireurs, and on the following morning they pushed forward again with an escort. Soon they saw a Prussian outpost, and after waving for some time a white flag, an officer came forward. After a parley Mr. Malet and his friend were allowed to pass. At three o'clock they arrived at Meaux. Count Bismarck was just driving into the town; he at once recognised Mr. Malet, whom he had known in Germany, and begged him to call upon him at nine o'clock. From Mr. Malet I know nothing more. I tried to "interview" him with respect to his conversation with Count Bismarck, but it takes two to make a bargain, and in this bargain he declined to be the number two. About half an hour afterwards, however, I met a foreign diplomatist of my acquaintance who had just come from the British Embassy. He had heard Mr. Malet's story, which, of course, had been communicated to the Corps Diplomatique, and being slightly demoralised, without well thinking what he was doing, he confided it to my sympathising ear.

Mr. Malet, at nine o'clock, found Count Bismarck seated before a table with wine and cigars. He was in high spirits and very sociable. This I can well believe, for I used to know him, and, to give the devil his due, he is one of the few Prussians of a sociable disposition. The interview lasted for more than two hours. Count Bismarck told Mr. Malet that the Prussians meant to have Metz and Strasburg, and should remain in France until they were obtained. The Prussians did not intend to dismantle them, but to make them stronger than they at present are. "The French," he said, "will hate us with an undying hate, and we must take care to render this hate powerless." As for Paris, the German armies would surround it, and with their several corps d'armée, and their 70,000 cavalry, would isolate it from the rest of the world, and leave its inhabitants to "seethe in their own milk." If the Parisians continued after this to hold out, Paris would be bombarded, and, if necessary, burned. My own impression is that Count Bismarck was not such a fool as to say precisely what he intended to do, and that he will attack at once; but the event will prove. He added that Germany was not in want of money, and therefore did not ask for a heavy pecuniary indemnity. Speaking of the French, Count Bismarck observed that there were 200,000 men round Metz, and he believed that Bazaine would have to capitulate within a week. He rendered full justice to the courage with which the army under Bazaine had fought, but he did not seem to have a very high opinion of the French army of Sédan. He questioned Mr. Malet about the state of Paris, and did not seem pleased to hear that there had been no tumults. The declaration of the Republic and its peaceful recognition by Paris and the whole of France appeared by no means to please him. He admitted that if it proved to be a moderate and virtuous Government, it might prove a source of danger to the monarchical principle in Germany.

I do trust that Englishmen will well weigh these utterances. Surely they will at last be of opinion that the English Government should use all its moral influence to prevent a city containing nearly two million inhabitants being burnt to the ground in order that one million Frenchmen should against their will be converted into Germans. It is our policy to make an effort to prevent the dismemberment of France, but the question is not now so much one of policy as of common humanity. No one asks England to go to war for France; all that is asked is that she should recognise the *de facto* Government of the country, and should urge Prussia to make peace on terms which a French nation can honourably accept.

General Vinoy, out reconnoitering with 15,000 men, came to-day upon a Prussian force of 40,000 near Vincennes. After an artillery combat, he withdrew within the lines of the forts. There have been unimportant skirmishes with the enemy at several points. The American, the Belgian, the Swiss, and the Danish Ministers are still here. Mr. Wodehouse has remained to look after our interests. All the secretaries were anxious to stay. I should be glad to know why Mr. Falconer Atlee, the British Consul at Paris, is not like other consuls, at his post. He withdrew to Dieppe about three weeks ago. His place is here. Neither a consul, nor a soldier, should leave his post as soon as it becomes dangerous.

Victor Hugo has published an address to the nation. You may judge of its essentially practical spirit by the following specimen:—" Rouen, draw thy sword! Lille, take up thy musket! Bordeaux, take up thy gun! Marseilles, sing thy song and be terrible!" I suspect Marseilles may sing her song a long time before the effect of her vocal efforts will in any way prevent the Prussians from carrying out their plans. " A child," says the evening papers, " deposited her doll this afternoon in the arms of the statue of Strasburg. All who saw the youthful patriot perform this touching act were deeply affected."

September 19th.

I don't know whether my letter of yesterday went off or not. As my messenger to the post-office could get no authentic intelligence about what was passing, I went there myself. Everybody was in military uniform, everybody was shrugging his shoulders, and everybody was in the condition of a London policeman were he to see himself marched off to the station by a street-sweeper. That the Prussian should have taken the Emperor prisoner, and have vanquished the French armies, had, of course, astonished these worthy bureaucrats, but that they should have ventured to interfere with postmen had perfectly dumbfounded them. " Put your letter in that box," said a venerable employé on a high stool. " Will it ever be taken out?" I asked. " Qui sait?" he replied. " Shall you send off a train to-morrow morning?" I asked.

There was a chorus of "Qui sait?" and the heads disappeared still further with the respective shoulders to which they belonged. "What do you think of a man on horseback?" I suggested. An indignant "Impossible" was the answer. "Why not?" I asked. The look of contempt with which the clerks gazed on me was expressive. It meant, "Do you really imagine that a functionary—a postman—is going to forward your letters in an irregular manner?" At this moment a sort of young French Jefferson Brick came in. Evidently he was a Republican recently set in authority. To him I turned. "Citizen, I want my letter to go to London. It is a press letter. These bureaucrats say that they dare not send it by a horse express; I appeal to you, as I am sure you are a man of expedients." "These people," he replied, scowling at the clerks, "are demoralised. They are the ancient valets of a corrupt Court; give me your letter; if possible it shall go, 'foi de citoyen.'" I handed my letter to Jefferson, but whether it is on its way to England, or still in his patriotic hands, I do not know. As I passed out through the court-yard I saw postmen seated on the boxes of carts, with no horses before them. It was their hour to carry out the letters, and thus mechanically they fulfilled their duty. English Government officials have before now been jeered at as men of routine, but the most ancient clerk in Somerset House is a man of wild impulse and boundless expedient compared with the average of functionaries great and small here. The want of "shiftiness" is a national characteristic. The French are like a flock of sheep without shepherds or sheep-dogs. Soldiers and civilians have no idea of anything except doing what they are ordered to do by some functionary. Let one wheel in an administration get out of order, and everything goes wrong. After my visit to the post-office I went to the central telegraph office, and sent you a telegram. The clerk was very surly at first, but he said that he thought a press telegram would pass the wires. When I paid him he became friendly. My own impression is that my twelve francs, whoever they may benefit, will not benefit the British public.

From the telegraph-office I directed my steps to a club where I was engaged to dine. I found half-a-dozen whist tables in full swing. The conversation about the war soon, however, became general. "This is our situation," said, as he dealt a hand, a knowing old man of the world, a sort of French James Clay: "generally if one has no trumps in one's hand, one has at least some good court cards in the other suits; we've got neither trumps nor court cards." "Et le Général Trochu?" some one suggested. "My opinion of General Trochu," said a General, who was sitting reading a newspaper, "is that he is a man of theory, but unpractical. I know him well; he has utterly failed to organise the forces which he has under his command." The general opinion about Trochu seemed to be that he is a kind of M'Clellan. "Will the Garde Nationale fight?" some one asked. A Garde National replied, "Of course there are brave men amongst us, but the mass will give in rather than see Paris destroyed. They have their families and their shops." "And the Mobiles?" "The Mobiles are the stuff out of which soldiers are made, but they are still peasants, and not soldiers yet." On the whole, I found the tone in "fashionable circles" desponding. "Can any one tell me where Jules Favre has gone?" I asked. Nobody could, though everybody seemed to think that he had gone to the Prussian head-quarters. After playing a few rubbers, I went home to bed at about one o'clock. The streets were absolutely deserted. All the cafés were shut.

Nothing in the papers this morning. In the *Figaro* an article from that old humbug Villemessant. He calls upon his fellow-citizens in Paris to resist to the death.

"One thing Frenchmen never forgive," he says,—"cowardice."

The *Gaulois* contains the most news. It represents the Prussians to be all round Paris. At Versailles they have converted the Palais into a barrack. Their camp fires were seen last night in the forest of Bondy. Uhlans have made their appearance at St. Cloud. "Fritz" has taken up his quarters at Ferrières, the château of Baron Rothschild. "William"—we are very familiar when we speak of the Prussian Royal family—is still at Meaux. "No thunderbolt," adds the correspondent, "has yet fallen on him." The Prussian outposts are at the distance of three kilomètres from St. Denis. Near Vitry shots have been heard. In the environs of Vincennes there has been fighting. It appears General Ambert was arrested yesterday. He was reviewing some regiments of Nationaux, and when they cried, "Vive la République" he told them that the Republic did not exist. The men immediately surrounded him, and carried him to the Ministry of the Interior, where I presume he still is. The *Rappel* finds faults with Jules Favre's circular. Its tone, it says, is too humble. The *Rappel* gives a list of "valets of Bonaparte, *ce coquin sinistre*," who still occupy official positions, and demands that they shall at once be relieved from their functions. The *Rappel* also informs its readers that letters have been discovered (where ?) proving that Queen Victoria had promised before the war to do her best to aid Germany.

Butler of a friend of mine, whose house is close by the fortifications, and who has left it in his charge, has just been to see me. The house is a "poste" of the National Guard. Butler says the men do not sleep on the ramparts, but in the neighbouring houses. They are changed every twenty-four hours. He had rather a hard time of it last night with a company from the Faubourg St. Antoine. As a rule, however, he says they are decent, orderly men. They complain very much that their business is going to rack and ruin; when they are away from their shops, they say, impecunious patriots come in to purchase goods of their wives, and promise to call another day to pay for them. On Saturday night the butler reports 300 National Guards were drawn up before his master's house, and twenty-five volunteers were demanded for a service of danger. After some time the twenty-five stepped forward, but having heard for what they were wanted, eighteen declined to go.

A British coachman just turned up offers to carry letters through—seems a sharp plucky fellow. I shall employ him as soon as the Post-office is definitely closed. British coachman does not think much of the citizen soldiers in Paris. "Lor' bless you, sir, I'd rather have 10,000 Englishmen than the lot of them. In my stable I make my men obey me, but these chaps they don't seem to care what their officers says to them. I seed them drill this morning; a pretty green lot they was. Why, sir, giving them fellow Chassepôts is much like giving watches to naked savages."

The Breton Mobiles are making pilgrimages to the churches. I hope it may do them good. I hear the curés of Paris have divided the ramparts between them, and are on the fortifications—bravo! curés. By-the-bye, that fire-eater, Paul de Cassagnac, has not followed the example of his brother Imperial journalists. He enlisted as a Zouave, fought well, and was taken prisoner at Sédan. He is now employed by his captors in making bread. I hope his bread will be better than his articles.

1.30 P.M.

Been sitting with a friend who commands a company of National Guards. The company is now outside the fortifications. Friend tells me that the men in his company are mostly small shopkeepers. At first it was difficult to get them to come to drill, but within the last few days they have been drilling hard, and he is convinced that they will fight well. Friend tells me that a large number of National Guards have run away from Paris, and that those who remain are very indignant with them. He requests me to beg my countrymen, if they see a sturdy Monsieur swelling it down Regent Street, to kick him, as he ought to be defending his country. I fulfil his request with the greatest pleasure and endorse it. I have just seen a Prussian spy taken to prison. I was seated before a café on the Boulevard des Capucines. Suddenly there was a shout of "un Prussien;" every one rushed towards the Place de l'Opéra, and from the Boulevard Haussmann came a crowd with a soldier, dressed as an artilleryman, on a horse. He was preceded and followed by about one hundred Mobiles. By his side rode a woman. No one touched them. Whether he and his "lady friend" were Germans I do not know; but they certainly looked Germans, and extremely uncomfortable.

3 P.M.

Been to Embassy. Messenger Johnson arrived this morning at 12 o'clock. He had driven to Rouen. At each post station he was arrested. He drove up to the Embassy, followed by a howling mob. As he wore an unknown uniform they took him for a Prussian. Messenger Johnson, being an old soldier, was belligerently inclined. "The first man who approaches," &c. The porter of the Embassy, however, dragged him inside, and explained to the mob who he was. He had great difficulty in calming them. One man sensibly observed that in these times no one should drive through Paris in a foreign uniform, as the mass of the people knew nothing of Queen's messengers and their uniforms. Messenger Johnson having by this time got within the Embassy gates, the mob turned on his postilion and led him off. What his fate has been no one has had time to ask.

When I went upstairs I found Wodehouse sitting like patience on a stool, with a number of Britons round him, who wanted to get off out of Paris. Wodehouse very justly told them that Lord Lyons had given them due notice to leave, and that they had chosen at their own risk to remain. The Britons seemed to imagine that their Embassy was bound to find them a road by which they might safely withdraw from the town. One very important Briton was most indignant—"I am a man of wealth and position. I am not accustomed to be treated in this manner. What is the use of you, sir, if you cannot ensure my safe passage to England? If I am killed the world shall ring with it. I shall myself make a formal complaint to Lord Granville," said this incoherent and pompous donkey. Exit man of position fuming; enter unprotected female. Of course she was a widow, of course she had lost half-a-dozen sons, of course she kept lodgings, and of course she wanted her "hambassader" generally to take her under his wing. I left Wodehouse explaining to her that if she went out of Paris even with a pass, she might or might not be shot according to circumstances. I will say for him that I should not be as patient as he is, were I worried and badgered by the hour by a crowd of shrieking women and silly men.

4 P.M.

Fighting is going on all round Paris. There are crowds on the Boulevard; every one is asking his neighbour for news. I went to one of the Mairies to hear the bulletins read. The street was almost impassable. At last I got near enough to hear an official read out a despatch— nothing important. The commanders at Montrouge and Vincennes announce that the Prussians are being driven back. "Et Clamart?" some one cries. "A bas les alarmistes," is the reply. Every one is despondent. Soldiers have come back from Meudon demoralised. We have lost a position, it is whispered. I find a friend, upon whose testimony I can rely, who was near Meudon until twelve o'clock. He tells me that the troops of the line behaved badly. They threw away their muskets without firing a shot, and there was a regular *sauve qui peut*. The Mobiles, on the other hand, fought splendidly, and were holding the position when he left. I am writing this in a café. It is full of Gardes Nationaux. They are saying that if the troops of the line are not trustworthy, resistance is hopeless. A Garde National gives the following explanation of the demoralisation of the army. He says that the Imperial Government only troubled itself about the corps d'élite; that the object in the line regiments was to get substitutes as cheaply as possible; consequently, they are filled with men physically and morally the scum of the nation. Semaphore telegraphs have been put up on all the high public buildings. There are also semaphores on the forts. I see that one opposite me is exchanging signals. The crowd watch them as though by looking they would discover what they mean. "A first success," says a National next to me, "was absolutely necessary for us, in order to give us confidence." "But this success we do not seem likely to have," says another. The attempt to burn down the forests seems only partially to have succeeded. The Prussians appear to be using them, and the French to the last carrying on war without scouts.

6 P.M.

Evening papers just out. Not a word about Clamart. The *Liberté* says the Minister of the Interior refers journalists to General Trochu, who claims the right to suppress what he pleases. When will French Governments understand that it is far more productive of demoralisation to allow no official news to be published than to publish the worst?

Rochefort has been appointed President of a Committee of Barricades, to organise a second line of defence within the ramparts.

7 P.M.

The cannon can be distinctly heard. The reports come from different quarters. Jules Favre, I hear from a sure source, is at the Prussian head-quarters.

7.30 P.M.

I live *au quatrième* with a balcony before my room. I can see the flashes of cannon in the direction of Vincennes. There appears to be a great fire somewhere.

12 P.M.

Have driven to the Barrière de l'Enfer. Nothing there. On the Champ de Mars I found troops returned from Clamart. They complain that they never saw their officers during the engagement, that there were no scouts in the Bois de Clamart, and that the Prussians succeeded by their old game of sticking to the cover. At first they fell back—the French troops pressed on, when they were exposed to a concentric fire. From the Champs Elysées I drove to the Buttes de Montmartre. Thousands of people clustered everywhere except where they were kept off by the Nationaux, who were guarding the batteries. The northern sky was bright from the reflection of a conflagration—as the forest of St. Germain was burning. It was almost light. We could see every shot and shell fired from the forts round St. Denis. At ten o'clock I got back to the Boulevard des Italiens. Every café was closed. It appears that at about nine o'clock the Café Riche was full of Gardes Mobiles, officers, and *lorettes*. They made so much noise that the public outside became indignant, and insisted on their giving up their orgie. The National Guard joined in this protest, and an order was sent at once to close every café. Before the Maison Dorée I saw a few *viveurs*, gazing at its closed windows as though the end of the world had come. This café has been opened day and night for the last twenty years. From my balcony I can no longer hear the cannon; the sky, however, is even brighter from the conflagration than it was.

September 20th.

The firing has recommenced. We can hear it distinctly. General Ambert has been cashiered. *Figaro* announces that Villemessant has returned. We are given a dozen paragraphs about this humbug of humbugs, his uniform, &c., &c. I do not think that he will be either killed or wounded. The latest telegram from the outer world announces that "Sir Campbell"—médecin Anglais—has arrived at Dieppe with despatches to the Ministers of Foreign Affairs and of Marine.

11 A.M.

Paris very quiet and very despondent. Few soldiers about. The Line is reviled, the Mobile extolled. From all accounts the latter seem to have behaved well—a little excited at first, but full of pluck. Let the siege only last a week and they will be capital soldiers, and then we shall no longer be called upon to believe the assertions of military men, that it takes years of drill and idling in a barrack to make a soldier.

My own impression always has been that Malet brought back a written answer from Bismarck offering to see Jules Favre. Can it be that, after all, the Parisians, at the mere sound of cannon, are going to cave in, and give up Alsace and Lorraine? If they do, I give them up. If my friends in Belleville descend into the streets to prevent this ignominy, I descend with them.

4 P.M.

I got, about an hour ago, some way on the road to Charenton, when I was turned back, and a couple of soldiers took possession of me, and did not leave me until I was within the city gate. I could see no traces of any

Prussians or of any fighting. Two English correspondents got as far as St. Denis this morning. After having been arrested half-a-dozen times and then released, they were impressed, and obliged to carry stones to make a barricade. They saw no Prussians. I hear that a general of artillery was arrested last night by his men. There is a report, also, that the Government mean to decimate the cowards who ran away yesterday, *pour encourager les autres*. The guns of the Prussians which they have posted on the heights they took yesterday it is said will carry as far as the Arc de Triomphe.

There have been two deputations to the Hôtel de Ville to interview the Government with respect to the armistice. One consisted of about 100 officers of the National Guard, most of them from the Faubourgs of St. Antoine and the Temple. They were of course accompanied by a large crowd. Having been admitted into the Salle du Trône, they were received by the Mayor of Paris and M. Jules Ferry. The reply of the latter is not very clear. He certainly said that no shameful peace should be concluded; but whether, as some assert, he assured the officers that no portion of French soil should be ceded is not equally certain. Shortly after this deputation had left, another arrived from the Republican clubs. It is stated that M. Jules Ferry's answer was considered satisfactory. The walls have been placarded with a proclamation of Trochu to the armed force. He tells them that some regiments behaved badly at Clamart; but the assertion that they had no cartridges is false. He recommends all citizens to arrest soldiers who are drunk or who propagate false news, and threatens them with the vigorous application of the Articles of War. Another proclamation from Keratry warns every one against treating soldiers or selling them liquor when they already have had too much. I went to dine this evening in an estaminet in the Faubourg St. Antoine. It was full of men of the people, and from the tone of their observations I am certain that if M. Jules Favre concludes an armistice involving any cession of territory, there will be a rising at once. The cafés are closed now at 10 o'clock. At about 11 I walked home. One would have supposed oneself in some dull great provincial town at 3 in the morning. Everything was closed. No one, except here and there a citizen on his way home, or a patrol of the National Guard, was to be seen.

September 21st.

I suppose that you in England know a good deal more of what is passing at the Prussian head-quarters than we do here. M. Jules Favre's departure was kept so close a secret, that it did not ooze out until yesterday. The "ultras" in the Government were, I understand on good authority, opposed to it, but M. Jules Favre was supported by Picard, Gambetta, and Keratry, who, as everything is comparative, represent the moderate section of our rulers. We are as belligerent and cheery to-day as we were despondent on Monday evening. When any disaster occurs it takes a Frenchman about twenty-four hours to accustom himself to it. During this time he is capable of any act of folly or despair. Then follows the reaction, and he becomes again a brave man. When it was heard that the heights at Meudon had been taken, we immediately entered into a phase of despair. It is over now, and we crow as lustily as ever. We shall have another phase of despondency when the first fort is taken, and another when the first shells fall into the town; but if we get through them, I really have hopes that Paris will not disgrace herself. Nothing of any importance appears to have taken place at the front yesterday. The commanders of several forts sent to Trochu to say that they have fired on the Prussians, and that there have been small outpost engagements. During the day the bridges of St. Cloud, Sèvres, and Billancourt were blown up. I attempted this morning to obtain a pass from General Trochu. Announcing myself as a "Journalist Anglais," I got, after some difficulty, into a room in which several of his staff were seated. But there my progress was stopped. I was told that aides-de-camp had been fired on, and that General Trochu had himself been arrested, and had been within an inch of being shot because he had had the impudence to say that he was the Governor of Paris. I suggested that he might take me with him the next time he went out, and pointed out that correspondents rode with the Prussian staffs, but it was of no use. From Trochu I went to make a few calls. I found every one engaged in measuring the distance from the Prussian batteries to his particular house. One friend I found seated in a cellar with a quantity of mattresses over it, to make it bomb-proof. He emerged from his subterraneous Patmos to talk to me, ordered his servant to pile on a few more mattresses, and then retreated. Anything so dull as existence here it is difficult to imagine. Before the day is out one gets sick and tired of the one single topic of conversation. We are like the people at Cremorne waiting for the fireworks to begin; and I really do believe that if this continues much longer, the most cowardly will welcome the bombs as a relief from the oppressive ennui. Few regiments are seen now during the day marching through the streets—they are most of them either on the ramparts or outside them. From 8 to 9 in the morning there is a military movement, as regiments come and go, on and off duty. In the courtyard of the Louvre several regiments of Mobiles are kept under arms all night, ready to march to any point which may be seriously attacked. A good many troops went at an early hour this morning in the direction of St. Cloud.

The weather is beautiful—a lovely autumn morning.

They say that Rochefort and his friends are busily employed at Grenelle.

1.30 o'clock.

The cannonade has been audible for the last half-hour. It is getting every moment louder. The people are saying that Mont Valérien *donne*. I am going up to the Avenue de l'Impératrice, where I shall be able to see what is going on.

2.30 o'clock.

Come back; heavy firing—but I could not make out whether it came from Mont Valérien. Jules Favre has returned. They say the Prussians will only treat in Paris. Just seen an American who tried to get with a letter to General Sheridan. He got into the Prussian lines, but could not reach headquarters. On his return he was nearly murdered by the Mobiles; passed last night in a cell with two drunkards, and has just been let out, as all his papers were found *en règle*.

CHAPTER II.

September 22nd.

I SENT off a letter yesterday in a balloon; whether it reaches its destination, or is somewhere in the clouds, you will know before I do. The difficulties of getting through the lines are very great, and will become greater every day. The Post-office says that it tries to send letters through, but I understand that the authorities have little hope of succeeding. Just now I saw drawn up in the courtyard of the Grand Hotel a travelling carriage, with hampers of provisions, luggage, and an English flag flying. Into it stepped four Britons. Their passports were viséd, they said, by their Embassy, and they were starting for England *viâ* Rouen. Neither French nor Prussians would, they were convinced, stop them. I did not even confide a letter to their hands, as they are certain, even if they get through the French outposts, to be arrested by the Prussians and turned back. Yesterday on the return of Jules Favre he announced that the King of Prussia required as a condition of Peace the cession of Alsace and Lorraine, and as the condition of an armistice immediate possession of Metz, Strasburg, and Mont Valérien. The Government immediately met, and a proclamation was at once posted on the walls signed by all the members. After stating it had been reported that the Government was inclined to abandon the policy to which it owed its existence, it goes on in the following words :—" Our policy is this. Neither an inch of our territory nor a stone of our fortresses. The Government will maintain this until the end."

Yesterday afternoon we "manifested" against peace. We "manifest" by going, if we are in the National Guard, with bouquets at the ends of our muskets to deposit a crown of *immortelles* before the statue of Strasburg. If we are unarmed, we walk behind a drum to the statue and sing the "Marseillaise." At the statue there is generally some orator on a stool holding forth. We occasionally applaud him, but we never listen to him. After this we go to the Place before the Hôtel de Ville, and we shout " Point de Paix." We then march down the Boulevards, and we go home satisfied that we have deserved well of our country. As yesterday was the anniversary of the proclamation of the First Republic, we were in a very manifesting mood. M. Gambetta issued proclamations every half hour, calling upon us, in more or less flowery language, to die for our country. M. Arago, the Mayor, followed suit, heading his manifestoes with the old rallying cry, "Liberté, Egalité, Fraternité." I suppose the French are so constituted that they really cannot exist without processions, bouquets to statues, and grand phrases. Notwithstanding all this humbug, a large portion of them mean, I am sure, to fight it out. They have taken it into their heads that Paris can be successfully defended, and if it is not, they are determined that it shall not be their fault. It is intended, I understand, to keep well beneath the cover of the forts, not to risk engagements more than is necessary—gradually to convert the splendid raw material of the Mobiles into good soldiers, by accustoming them to be under fire, and then, if things go well, to fall on one or other of the Prussian armies. It is hoped, too, that the Prussian communications will be menaced. Such is the plan, and every one pretends to believe that it will succeed; whether they are right or wrong time will show.

The Government, an ex-diplomatist, who has been talking to several of its members this morning, tells me, is a "unit." There was a party ready to accept the dismantling of Metz and Strasburg, but as this concession will not disarm the Prussians, they have rallied to the "not a stone of one fortress" declaration.

Of course I cannot be expected to give aid and comfort to our besiegers by telling them, if they seize this letter, what is being done inside to keep them out. But this I think it will do them no harm to know. The National Guard man the ramparts. In the angles of the bastions there are Mobiles. At points close by the ramparts there are reserves of Mobiles and National Guards, ready at a moment's notice both by day and night to reinforce them. In the centre of the town there are reserves under arms. Outside the gates, between the forts and the ramparts, troops are massed with artillery, and the forts are well garrisoned. A gentleman who has lately been under a cloud, as he was the inventor of the Orsini bombs, has several thousand men at work on infernal machines. This magician assures me that within a week he will destroy the German armies as completely as were the Assyrians who besieged Jerusalem under Sennacherib. He is an enthusiast, but an excellent chemist, and I really have hopes that he will before long astonish our friends outside. He promises me that I shall witness his experiments in German corpore vili; and though I have in mind a quotation about being hoisted with one's own petard, I shall certainly keep him to his word. On the whole the King of Prussia, to use Mr. Lincoln's phrase, will find it a big job to take Paris if the Parisians keep to their present mood. Mr. Washburne told me yesterday that he does not think he shall leave. There is to be a consultation of the Corps Diplomatique to-morrow, under the presidency of the Nuncio, to settle joint action. I admire the common sense of Mr. Washburne. He called two days ago upon the Government to express his sympathy with them. Not being a man of forms and red tape, instead of going to the Foreign-office, he went to the Hôtel de Ville, found a Council sitting, shook hands all round, and then withdrew. I have serious thoughts of taking up my quarters at the English Embassy. It belongs to me as one of the nation, and I see no reason why I should not turn my property to some account.

Yesterday's papers contained an official announcement that a company of mutual assurance against the consequences of the bombardment has been formed. Paris is divided into three zones, and according to the danger proprietors of houses situated in each of them are to be admitted into the company on payment of one, two, or three per cent. It comforts me, comparatively, to find that I am in the one per cent. zone, and, unless my funds give way, I shall remain there.

Spies are being arrested every half hour. Many mistakes are made from over zeal, but there is no doubt that a good many Germans are in the town disguised in French uniforms. The newspapers ask what becomes of them all, and suggest that they should be publicly shot. It is beautiful weather, and as I sit writing this at my open window I have great difficulty in believing that we are cut off from the rest of the world by a number of victorious armies, who mean to burn or starve us out. M. John Lemoinne in the *Journal des Débats* this morning has a very sensible article upon the position of the Government. He says that between the first and the second of these two ultimatums there is a vast difference, and he exhorts the Government to stand by the first, but not to refuse peace if it can be obtained by the dismantling of Metz and Strasburg. The *Temps* of this evening takes the same view of the proclamation. The ultra Republican journals, on the other hand, support the policy of the Government. M. Felix Pyat, in his organ, *Le Combat*, urges war to the death, and proposes that we should at once have Spartan banquets, at which rich and poor should fare alike. A proposal has been made to start a national subscription for a musket of honour to be given to the man who shoots the King of Prussia. There are already 2,000 subscribers of one sou each to the testimonial. The latest proclamation I have seen on the walls is one from the Mayor of Paris, informing the public that the coachmen of Paris are not to be ill-treated by their fares because they are not on the ramparts. As the coachmen of Paris are usually excessively insolent, I shall not be sorry to hear that they have at length met with their deserts. A coachman who was driving me yesterday told me in the strictest confidence that he was a man who never meddled in politics, and, consequently, it was a matter of absolute indifference to him whether Napoleon or a "Général Prussien" lived in the Tuileries; and this, I suspect, is the view that many here take, if they only dared say it.

It is amusing to observe how every one has entered into the conspiracy to persuade the world that the French nation never desired war—to hear them, one would suppose that the Rhine had never been called the national frontier of France, and that the war had been entered into by Badinguet, as they style the late Emperor, against the wishes of the army, the peasantry, and the bourgeoisie. Poor old Badinguet has enough to answer for already, but even sensible Frenchmen have persuaded themselves that he, and he alone, is responsible for the war. He is absolutely loathed here. I sometimes suggest to some Gaul that he may possibly be back again some day; the Gaul immediately rolls his eyes, clenches his fists, and swears that if ever Badinguet returns to Paris he (the Gaul) will himself shoot him.

An American, who took an active part in the Confederate defence of Richmond, has just been in to see me. He does not believe that the town will hold out long, and scoffs at the mode in which it is being defended. I reserve my opinion until I have seen it under fire. Certainly they " do protest too much." The papers contain lists of citizens who have sworn to die rather than surrender. The bourgeois, when he goes off to the ramparts, embraces his wife in public, and assumes a martial strut as though he were a very Curtius on the way to the pit. Jules is perpetually hugging Jacques, and talking about the altar of his country on which he means to mount. I verily believe that the people walking on the Boulevards, and the assistants of the shops who deal out their wares, in uniform, are under the impression that they are heroes already, perilling life and limb for their country. Every girl who trips along thinks that she is a Maid of Saragossa. It is almost impossible for an Englishman to realise the intense delight which a Frenchman has in donning a uniform, strutting about with a martial swagger, and listening to a distant cannonade. As yet the only real hardships we have suffered have been that our fish is a little stale, and that we are put on short allowance of milk. The National Guards on the ramparts, I hear, grumble very much at having to spend the night in the open air. The only men I think I can answer for are the working men of the outer faubourgs and a portion of the Provincial Gardes Mobiles. They do mean to fight. Some of the battalions of the National Guards will fight too, but I should be afraid to trust the greater portion of them, even behind earthworks. "Remember," says the *Figaro* to them to-day, "that you have wives and children; do not be too venturesome." This advice, I think, was hardly needed. As for the regular troops, they are not to be trusted, and I am not sorry to think that there are 10,000 sailors in the forts to man the guns.

We have been manifesting again to-day. I was in hopes that this nonsense was over. On the Place de la Concorde there was a crowd all the afternoon, applauding orators, and companies of National Guards were bringing bouquets to the statue of Strasburg. At the Hôtel de Ville a deputation of officers of the National Guards came to urge the Government to put off the elections. After a short parley this was promised. Another demonstration took place to urge the Government not to make peace, to accept as their colleagues some "friends of the people," and to promise not to re-establish in any form a police force. An evasive answer was given to these demonstrators. It seems to me that the Government, in its endeavours to prevent a collision between the moderates and the ultras, yield invariably to the latter. What is really wanted is a man of energy and determined will. I doubt if Trochu has either.

The bold Britons who tried to run the blockade have returned. They managed to get over the bridge of Neuilly, but were arrested a few yards beyond it and brought back to General Ducrot. One of them was taken in with the passports of the five. "I cannot understand you English," the General said; "if you want to get shot we will shoot you ourselves to save you trouble." After some parley, General Ducrot gave them a pass to go through the French lines, but then he withdrew it, and said he must consult General Trochu. When the spokesman emerged, he found his friends being led off by a fresh batch of patriots for having no passports, but they at length got safely back to the Grand Hotel. Their leader, who is an intelligent man in his way, gives a very discouraging account of what he saw outside. The Mobiles were lying about on the roads, and everyone appeared to be doing much what he pleased. This afternoon I went up to the Trocadero to look at the heights on which they say that there are already Prussian guns. They appear most uncomfortably near.

Those who had telescopes declared that they could see both guns and Prussians. We were always told until within a few days that Mont Valérien would protect all that side of Paris. How can the engineers have made such a mistake?

This evening I went to call upon one of the chiefs of '48, and had an interesting conversation with him. He says that many think that he and his friends ought to be in the Government, and that eventually they all will be; he added "the Reds are determined to fight, and so long as the Government does not make a humiliating peace they will support it." I tried to get out what he considered a humiliating peace, but he rather fenced with the question. He tells me that at the Folies Bergères, the head-quarters of the ultras, great dissatisfaction is felt with the Committees of the "Clubs" for having gone yesterday to the Hôtel de Ville, and endeavoured to force the Government to declare that it would not treat with the Prussians whilst they were on French soil, and to allow them to establish a "Commune" as an *imperium in imperio*. "The army of the Loire," said my friend, "will soon fall on the rear of the Prussians; we have only to hold out for a few weeks, and this, depend upon it, we shall do." Now, to the best of my belief, the army of the Loire only exists on paper, but here was a sensible man talking of it as though it consisted of some 200,000 seasoned troops; and what is more strange, he is by no means singular in his belief. A fortnight ago it was the army of Lyons, now it is the army of the Loire. How reasonable men can allow themselves to put their faith in these men of buckram, I cannot imagine.

September 23rd.

Firing has been going on since three o'clock this morning. The newspapers contain accounts more or less veracious respecting fights outside the forts, in which great numbers of Prussians have been killed. M. Jules Favre publishes an account of his interview with Count Bismarck in the

Journal Officiel. M. Villemessant in the *Figaro* informs the world that he has left his wife outside," and would willingly allow one of his veins to be opened in exchange for a letter from her. We are still engaged in our old occupation—willing to die for our country. I hear that there has been serious fighting in the neighbourhood of St. Denis. This morning I saw another of the '48 Republicans—he seemed inclined to upset the Government more on the ground that they are incapable than because he differs with them in politics. I give this letter to a friend who will get it into the balloon, and go off to the Trocadero, to see how things are getting on.

The Solferino Tower on the Buttes Montmartre has been pulled down. No one is to be allowed to hoist the Geneva flag unless the house contains at least six beds for wounded. We have now a bread as well as a meat maximum.

September 24th.

We are as despondent to-day as we were jubilant yesterday. The success at the front seems to have dwindled down to an insignificant artillery combat. The *Electeur Libre* gives the following account of it. On the previous evening 8,000 Prussians had taken the redoubt of Villejuif. At one in the morning some regiments advanced from there towards Vitry, and occupied the mill of Sagui, while on the left about 5,000 established themselves on the plateau of Hautes-Bruyères. The division of General Maud'huy re-took these positions. At five o'clock in the morning the Prussians tried to occupy them a second time, but failed, and at half-past seven o'clock they fell back. At nine they attacked again, when a column of our troops, issuing from the Porte d'Italie, arrived. The fray went on until ten o'clock, when the Prussians retreated towards Sceaux. This tallies to a great extent with what I was told by an officer this morning who had taken part in the engagement.

The *Gazette Officielle* contains a decree cashiering M. Devienne, President of the Cour de Cassation, and sending him to be judged by his own court, for having been the intermediary between Badinguet and his mistress, Marguerite Bellanger. Two letters are published which seem to leave no doubt that this worthy judge acted as the go-between of the two lovers.

Mr. George Sanders, whilom United States Consul in London, and one of the leaders of the ex-Confederacy, is here; he is preparing plans for a system of rifle pits and zigzags outside the fortifications, at the request of General Trochu. Mr. Sanders, who took an active part in the defence of Richmond, declares that Paris is impregnable, if it be only well defended. He complains, however, that the French will not use the spade.

4 o'clock P.M.

We have been in a state of wild enthusiasm all this afternoon. At about 1 o'clock it was rumoured that 20,000 Prussians and 40 cannon had been taken. There had been a heavy firing, it was said, this morning, and a Prussian force had approached near the forts of Ivry and Bicêtre. General Vinoy had issued forth from Vincennes, and, getting behind them, had forced them under the guns of the forts, where they were taken prisoners. The Boulevards immediately were crowded; here a person announcing that he had a despatch from the front, here another vowing he had been there himself. Wherever a drum was heard there was a cry of "Here come the prisoners!" Tired of this, at about 4 o'clock I drove to Montrouge. It is a sort of Parisian Southwark. I found all the inhabitants lining the streets, waiting, too, for news. A regiment marched in, and there was a cry that it had come from the front; then artillery filed by out of the city gate. I tried myself to pass, and had got half-way through before I was stopped, then I was turned back. The prisoners here, close by the scene of action, had dwindled down to 5,000. Imagine Southwark, with every man armed in it, and a battle going on at Greenwich, and you will have an idea of the excitement of Montrouge.

6 *o'clock* P.M.

The Boulevards almost impassable ; the streets before the Mairies absolutely impassable ; no official confirmation of the victory. Everyone who is not inventing news is waiting for it. A proclamation has been issued by General Trochu conceived in a very sensible spirit, telling the National Guard that the moment is ill chosen for pacific demonstrations, with crowns and bouquets. I hear that some of the soldiers who ran away at Clamart have been shot.

Some of the papers discovered in the Tuileries are published. There is a letter from Jecker to Conti, in which he says that De Morny had promised him to get the Mexican Government to pay his claims on condition of receiving 30 per cent. of profits. A letter signed Persigny complains that an *employé* in the Cabinet Noir is in want, and ought to be given money to prevent his letting out secrets. A letter from the Queen of Holland tells Napoleon that if he does not interfere in Germany his own dynasty will suffer. A note of the Emperor, without date, says, " If France boldly places itself on the terrain of the nationalities, it is necessary to prove that the Belgian nationality does not exist. The Cabinet of Berlin seeming ready to enter into negotiations, it would be well to negotiate a secret *acte*, which would pledge both parties. This act would have the double advantage of compromising Prussia and of being for her a pledge of the sincerity of the Emperor." The note then goes on to say that it is necessary to dissipate the apprehensions of Prussia. " An *acte* is wanted," it continues ; " and one which would consist of a regulation of the ulterior fate of Belgium in concert with

Prussia would, by proving at Berlin that the Emperor desires the extension which is necessary to France since the events which have taken place in Germany, be at least a relative certainty that the Prussian Government would not object to our aggrandisement towards the North."

I drove this morning through the fighting faubourgs with a member of the Barricade Committee. Barricades are being erected everywhere, and they are even stronger than the outer fortifications. There are, too, some agreeable little chemical surprises for the Prussians if ever they get into the town. In reply to some suggestions which I made, my friend said, "Leave these people to form their own plans. They understand street fighting better than any one in the world." At La Villette, Grenelle, and other faubourgs inhabited by the blouses, there is no lack of patriotism, and they will blow themselves and their homes up rather than yield.

The bold Britons started again in their Derby turn-out yesterday. Nothing has been heard of them since. We do not know whether they have been imprisoned or what has become of them. I have already entrusted my letters to balloons, boatmen, peasants, and Americans, but I do not know whether they have reached you or not. The last balloon was pursued by a Prussian one, the newspapers say!

Yesterday the Nuncio called together all the diplomatists still here, and they determined to try to communicate with Bismarck. They seem to imagine that a twenty-four hours' notice will be given before a bombardment commences, when they will have time to get out. I send this letter by a Government balloon. I shall send a copy to-morrow by a private balloon, if it really does start as announced.

The *Gazette Officielle* "unites with many citizens in asking Louis Blanc to go to England, to obtain the sympathies of the English nation for the Republic." This is all very well, but how is he to get there?

September 25th.

No news of any importance from the front. It is a fête day, but there are few holiday makers. The presence of the Prussians at the gates, and the sound of the cannon, have at last sobered this frivolous people. Frenchmen, indeed, cannot live without exaggeration, and for the last twenty-four hours they have taken to walking about as if they were guests at their own funerals. It is hardly in their line to play the *justum et tenacem* of Horace. Always acting, they are now acting the part of Spartans. It is somewhat amusing to see the stern gloom on the face of patriots one meets, who were singing and shouting a few days ago—more particularly as it is by no means difficult to distinguish beneath this outward gloom a certain keen relish, founded upon the feeling that the part is well played. One thing, however, is certain, order has at length been evolved from disorder. Except in the morning, hardly any armed men are to be seen in the streets, and even in the central Boulevards, except when there is a report of some success or during an hour in the evening, there are no crowds. In the fighting faubourgs there is a real genuine determination to fight it out to the last. The men there have arms, and they have not cared to put on uniforms. Men, women, and children are all of one mind in the quarters of the working men. I have been much struck with the difference between one of these poor fellows who is prepared to die for the honour of his country, between his quiet, calm demeanour, and the absurd airs, and noisy brawls, and the dapper uniforms of the young fellows one meets with in the fashionable quarters. It is the difference between reality and sham, bravery and bombast.

The newspapers are beginning to complain of the number of Chevaliers of the Red Cross, who are daily becoming more numerous. Lazy men, they say, should not enrol themselves in a corps of non-combatants. It is said, also, that at Clamart these chevaliers declined to go under fire and pick up the wounded, and that the ambulances themselves made a strategic movement to the rear at the commencement of the combat. The flag of the Convention of Geneva is on far too many houses. From my window I can count fifteen houses with this flag floating over them.

We have most wonderful stories about the Prussians, which, although they are generally credited, I take leave to doubt. Villagers who have slipped through the lines, and who play the part of the intelligent contraband of the American Civil War, are our informants. They represent the Prussian army without food, almost without clothing, bitterly repenting their advance into France, demoralised by the conviction that few of their number will be again in their homes. We are treated every day, too, to the details of deeds of heroism on the part of Mobiles and Nationaux, which would make Achilles himself jealous. There is, we are told, a wonderful artilleryman in the fort before St. Denis, the perfection of whose aim carries death and destruction into the Prussian ranks.

I am not sorry to learn that the sale of the ultra papers is not large. M. Blanqui's office was yesterday broken into by some National Guards, who made it clear to this worthy that he had ill chosen his moment to attack the Government. I have not myself the slightest dread of a general pillage. The majority of the working men no doubt entertain extreme Socialist ideas, but any one of them who declined to make any distinction between his property and that of his richer neighbours would be very roughly handled. So long as the Government sticks to its policy of no surrender, it will be supported by the faubourgs; if, however, it attempts to capitulate upon humiliating terms, it will be ejected from the Hôtel de Ville. A sharp bombardment may, perhaps, make a change in public opinion, but I can only speak of the opinion of to-day. The Government declares that it can never be run short of ammunition; but it seems to me that we cannot fire off powder and projectiles always, and that one of these mornings we shall be told that we must capitulate, as there is no more ammunition. Americans who are here, complain very much of the Parisians in not using the spade more than they do. Earthworks, which played so large a part in the defence both of Sebastopol and Richmond, are unknown at Paris. Barricades made of paving stones in the streets, and forts of solid masonry outside, are considered the *ne plus ultra* of defensive works. For one man who will go to work to shovel earth, you may find a thousand who will shoulder a musket. "Paris may be able to defend itself," the Americans say, "but it is not defending itself after what our generals would consider the most approved method." We have no intelligence of what is passing in France beyond our lines. We presume that a great army is forming beyond the Loire; but yesterday a friend of mine, who received this assurance from M. Gambetta, could not discover that he had any reason to believe it, except the hope that it was true.

It is a somewhat singular thing that Rochefort, who was regarded even by his friends as a vain, mad-brained demagogue, has proved himself one of the most sensible and practical members of the Government. He has entirely subordinated his own particular views to the exigencies of the defence of the capital; and it is owing to his good sense that the ultras have not indulged in any revolutionary excesses.

I have already endeavoured to forward to you, by land, water, and air, copies of the Tuileries papers which have been published. That poor old pantaloon, Villemessant, the proprietor and editor of the *Figaro*, who is somewhat roughly handled by them, attempts to defend himself in his paper this morning, but utterly fails to do so. His interested connection with the Imperial Government is proved without the shadow of a doubt, and I trust that it will also prove the death of his newspaper, which has long been a disgrace to the press of France. I went to look after the proprietor of another paper yesterday, as he had promised me that, come what may, he would get his own and my letters through the Prussian lines. My friend, I found, had taken himself off to safe quarters before the last road was closed. For my part I despise any Parisian who has not remained here to defend his native city, whether he be Imperialist or Republican, noble or merchant.

Evening (Sunday).

They could stand it no longer; the afternoon was too fine. Stern patriotism unbent, and tragic severity of demeanour was forgotten. The Champs Elysées and the Avenue de la Grande Armée were full of people. Monsieur shone by his absence; he was at the ramparts, or was supposed to be there; but his wife, his children, his *bonne*, and his kitchen wench issued forth, oblivious alike of dull care and of bombarding Prussians, to enjoy themselves after their wont by gossiping and lolling in the sun. The Strasburg fetish had its usual crowd of admirers. Every bench in the Champs Elysées was occupied. Guitars twanged, organs were ground, merry-go-rounds were in full swing, and had it not been that here and there some regiment was drilling, one would have supposed oneself in some country fair. There were but few men; no fine toilets, no private carriages. It was a sort of Greenwich-park. At the Arc de Triomphe was a crowd trying to discover what was going on upon the heights above Argenteuil. Some declared they saw Prussians, while others with opera glasses declared that the supposed Prussians were only trees. In the Avenue de l'Impératrice was a large crowd gazing upon the Fort of Mont Valérien. This fort, because I presume it is the strongest for defence, is the favourite of the Parisians. They love it as a sailor loves his ship. "If I were near enough," said a girl near me, "I would kiss it." "Let me carry your kiss to it," replied a Mobile, and the pair embraced, amid the cheers of the people round them. At Auteuil there were *fiacres* full of sightseers, come to watch the Prussian batteries at Meudon, which could be distinctly seen. Occasionally, too, there came a puff of smoke from one of the gunboats.

September 26*th*.

Do the Prussians really mean to starve us out? The Government gave out a fortnight ago that there was food then within the city for two months' consumption for a population of two millions. It is calculated that, including the Mobile, there are not above 1,500,000 mouths at present to feed, so that with proper care the supplies may be made to last for three months. Prices are, however, already rising. We have a bread and a meat maximum, but to force a butcher to sell you a cutlet at the tariff price, one has to go with a corporal's guard, which cannot always be procured. The *Gazette Officielle* contains a decree regulating the sale of horseflesh. I presume if the siege lasts long enough, dogs, rats, and cats will be tariffed. I have got 1000 francs with me. It is impossible to draw upon England; consequently, I see a moment coming when, unless rats are reasonable, I shall not be able to afford myself the luxury of one oftener than once a week. When I am at the end of my 1000 francs, I shall become an advocate for Felix Pyat's public tables, at which, as far as I understand his plan, those who have money pay, and those who have not eat.

Yesterday was a quiet day. The forts occasionally fired to "sound the enemy's lines," but that was all. But how is it all to end? In a given time the Parisians will eat themselves out and fire themselves out. The credulity of the public is as great as ever. We are told that "France is rising, and that in a few weeks three armies will throw themselves on the Prussians, who are already utterly disorganised." In vain I ask, "But what if these three armies do not make their appearance?" I am regarded as an idiot for venturing to discredit a notorious fact. If I dared, I would venture to suggest to some of my warlike friends that a town which simply defends itself by shutting its gates, firing into space, and waiting for apocryphal armies, is not acting a very heroic part.

M. F. Pyat announces in the *Combat* that the musket of honour which is to be given to the man who shoots the King of Prussia is to have inscribed upon it the word "Peacemaker." We have taken it into our heads that the German army, Count Bismarck, the Crown Prince, and all the Generals of the Corps d'Armée are in favour of peace, and the only obstacle to its being at once concluded lies in the obstinacy of the Monarch, whom we usually term "that mystic drunkard."

The *Rappel* contains the report of a meeting which was held last night of all the Republican Committees. Resolutions were adopted blaming the Government for putting off the municipal elections. The adjournment, however, of these elections is, I am convinced, regarded as a salutary measure by a majority even of the ultras.

I dropped into the English Embassy this morning to see what was doing there. Mr. Wodehouse, I understand, intends to leave before the bombardment commences. He is a civilian, and cannot be blamed for this precautionary measure. I cannot, however, suppose that the military attaché, who is a colonel in the army, will remain. There is a notion among the members of the Corps Diplomatique that the Prussians before they bombard the town will summon it to surrender. But it seems to me very doubtful whether they will do so. Indeed, I for one shall not believe in a general bombardment before I see it. To starve us out seems to me their safest game. Were they to fire on the town, the public opinion of the civilised world would pronounce against them.

The Mobiles, who receive 1 franc 50 centimes a day, complain that they are unable to support themselves on this pittance. The conduct of these peasants is above all praise. Physically and morally they are greatly the superiors of the ordinary run of Parisians. They are quiet, orderly, and, as a rule, even devout. Yesterday I went into the Madeleine, where some service was going on. It was full of Mobiles listening to the prayers of the priest. The Breton regiments are accompanied by their priests, who bless them before they go on duty. If the Parisians were not so thoroughly conceited, one might hope that the presence of these villagers would have a beneficial effect upon them, and show them that the Frenchmen out of Paris are worth more than those within it. The generation of Parisians which has arrived at manhood during the existence of the Empire is, perhaps, the most contemptible that the world has ever seen. If one of these worthies is rich enough, his dream has been to keep a mistress in splendour; if this has been above his means, he attempts to hang on to some wealthy *vaurien*. The number of persons without available means who somehow managed to live on the fat of the land without ever doing a single day's honest work had become enormous. Most of them have, on some pretext or other, sneaked out of Paris. One sees now very few ribbons of the Legion of Honour, notwithstanding the reckless profusion with which this order was lavished: the Emperor's flock, marked with the red streak, have disappeared.

We have received news through a carrier pigeon that one

of the postal balloons has reached Tours. I trust that it will have carried my letter to you. I intend henceforward to confide my letter to the post every second day, and as I have got a copying machine, to send copy by any messenger who is attempting to run the blockade. We are told that balloons are to leave every evening; but as the same announcement informs us that they will not only take letters but officials appointed to functions in the provinces, I am afraid that there is almost too much promised to render it likely that the programme will be carried out.

Afternoon.

I have just made an attempt to see what is going on between the forts and the ramparts, which has been a failure. I had obtained an order to circulate for the necessities of the defence from a member of the Government, and with this in my pocket I presented myself at several of the gates. In vain I showed my pass, in vain I insisted upon the serious consequences to Paris in general, and to the officer whom I was addressing in particular, if I were not allowed to fulfil my circulating mission. I had to give it up at last, and to content myself with circulating inside the ramparts. On them, however, I managed to get, thanks to a tradesman with whom I had often dealt, who was in command. I was told that a member of the Government, his name no one seemed to know, had addressed the "poste" yesterday, and urged the men to resist until one or other of the armies which were forming in the provinces could arrive and crush the enemy. Everything appeared where I was ready for an attack. The sentinels were posted at short intervals, the artillerymen were lying about near their guns, and in the Rue des Remparts there were several hundred National Guards. They appeared to be taking things easily, complained that the nights were a little chilly and that business at home was at a standstill. In the course of my walk I saw a great many barricades in process of formation. Eventually, I presume, we shall have a second line of defences within the outer walls. This second line has already been divided, like the ramparts, into nine sections, each with a separate commander. I met at least a dozen *soi-disant* Prussian spies being conducted to prison. Each of them was surrounded by twelve men, with bayonets fixed. Coming home I saw nine French soldiers with placards bearing the inscription, "Miserable cowards." Of course, the usual crowd accompanied them. I heard that they were on their way to be shot.

The newspapers of this afternoon make a good deal of noise about the exploits of the gunboat in the bend of the Seine between Point du Jour and Boulogne. They claim that its gun has dismounted the Prussian batteries on the terrace of Meudon, and that it successfully engaged several field batteries which fired upon it from the Park of St. Cloud. This may or may not be true. We are also called upon to believe that five shots from Fort Ivry destroyed the Prussian batteries at Choisy le Roi.

The latest proclamation issued is one from General Trochu, in which he says that it was the fault of no one that the redoubts which were in course of construction when the Prussians arrived before the town were not finished, and that they were abandoned for strategical reasons.

The latest Ultra paper publishes the account of a meeting which was remarkable, it observes, for the "excellent spirit which animated it, and the serious character of the speeches which were delivered at it." This is one of these serious orations—"The Citizen Arthur de Fonvielle recommends all citizens to exercise the greatest vigilance as regards the manœuvres of the police, and more especially those of the Préfet of the Police. This Ministry has passed from the hands of a Corsican into those of one of the assassins of the

Mexican Republic." I derive considerable amusement from the perusal of the articles which are daily published reviling the world in general for not coming to the aid of Paris. I translate the opening paragraphs of one of them which I have just read:—"In the midst of events which are overwhelming us, there is something still more melancholy than our defeat: it is our isolation. For a month the world looks on with an impassibility, mingled with shame and cynicism, at the ruin of a nation which possesses the most exquisite gifts of sociability, the principal jewel of Europe, and the eternal ornament of civilisation." Nothing like having a good opinion of oneself.

Evening.

I hear of some one going to try to-morrow to get through the lines, so I give him a copy of this letter. My last letter went off—or rather did not go off—by a private balloon. The speculator rushed in, just as I expected him to be off, and said, "Celestine has burst." To my horror I discovered that he was speaking of the balloon. He then added, "Ernestine remains to us," and to Ernestine I confided my letter. I have not seen the speculator since; it may be that Ernestine has burst too.

The latest *canard* is that 10,000 Prussians are in a wood near Villejuif, where they have been driven by the French. As they in the most cowardly manner decline to come out of it, the wily Parisian braves are rubbing the outer circle of trees over with petroleum, as a preparatory step to burn them out. This veracious tale is believed by two-thirds of Paris.

CHAPTER III.

September 27th, 8 A.M.

I HAVE sent you numerous letters, but I am not aware whether you have received them. As very probably they are now either in the clouds or in the moon, I write a short *résumé* of what has passed since we have been cut off from the outer world, as I believe that I have a very good chance this morning to communicate with you.

When the town was first invested the greatest disorder existed. For a few days officers, even generals, were shot at by regiments outside the fortifications; the National Guards performed their service on the ramparts very reluctantly, and, when possible, shirked it. The Mobiles were little better than an armed mob of peasants. The troops of the line were utterly demoralised. The streets were filled with troopers staggering about half drunk, and by groups of armed Mobiles wandering in ignorance of the whereabouts of their quarters and of their regiments. The Government was divided into two parties—one supported by the Moderates, and anxious to make peace on reasonable terms; the other supported by the Ultras, and determined to continue the contest at all hazards. The Ministers were almost in despair at finding the utter disorder in which everything had been left by their predecessors. Little by little this condition of things has mended for the better. Since the failure of the mission of M. Jules Favre, and the exorbitant demands which were then put forward by Count Bismarck, both Moderates and Ultras have supported the men who are in power. It is felt by all that if Paris is to be defended with any prospect of success, there must be absolute union among its defenders. The Deputies of Paris are not thought perhaps to be endowed with any very great administrative ability, but Mr. Lincoln's proverb respecting the difficulty of a person changing his horse whilst he is crossing a stream is acted on, and so long as they neither commit any signal act of folly, nor attempt to treat with Prussia either for peace or a capitulation, I think that no effort will be made to oust them. They are, I believe, doing their best to organise the defence of this city, and if they waste a little time in altering the names of the streets, and publishing manifestoes couched in grand and bombastic phrases, it must be remembered that they have to govern Frenchmen who are fond of this species of nonsense. With respect to the military situation, the soldiers of all sorts are kept well together, and appear to be under the command of their officers. The National Guard, although it still grumbles a little, does its duty on the ramparts. The soldiers of the line are kept outside the town. The Mobiles have passed many hours in drill during the last ten days; they are orderly and well conducted, and if not soldiers already, are a far more formidable force than they were at the commencement of the siege. Whether they will ever become available for operations in the open field is, perhaps, questionable, for their regiments would probably be thrown into confusion if called upon to act together. Within the line of the forts, however, there is no reason to suppose that they will not fight well. The forts are manned by sailors, who are excellent artillerists, and the guns are formidable ones. On the Seine there is a flotilla of gun-boats. The city has food and ammunition for two months.

Paris, therefore, ought to be able to hold out for these two months. She has her own population, a large portion of which consists of the working men, who have never been backward in fighting. The provinces have been drained of their best blood, which has been brought up to the capital. All that remains of the French army is here. At the lowest average the armed force in Paris amounts to 450,000 men, and there are about 500,000 more from which this force can recruit itself. If, then, the capital does not hold out for two months, she will deserve the contempt of the world—if she does hold out for this period, she will at least have saved her honour, and, to a certain extent, the military reputation of France.

The newspapers are still pursuing the very questionable policy of exaggerating every little affair of the outposts into a victory, and assuring those who read their lucubrations that powerful armies are on the march to raise the siege. The only real military event of any consequence which has taken place has resulted in a Prussian success. The French were driven back from some half-finished redoubts at Chatillon, and the Prussians now occupy the heights between Sèvres and Meudon, from whence, if they establish batteries, they will be able to shell a portion of the town. In the second affair which took place, absurd stories have been repeated respecting the advantages gained by the French; but they are, to say the least, extremely apocryphal, and even were they true they are of small importance. For the last few days the forts have fired upon any Prussian troops that either were or were supposed to be within shot; and the gunboats have attempted to prevent the erection of batteries on the Sèvres-Meudon plateau. In point of fact, the siege has not really commenced; and until it is seen how this vast population bears its hardships, how the forts resist the guns which may be brought to bear upon them, and how the armed force conducts itself under fire, it is impossible to speculate upon results.

Considering the utter stagnation in trade, the number of working men out of employment, and the irritation caused by defeat, it must be admitted that the Parisians of all classes are behaving themselves well. The rich residents have fled, and left to their poorer neighbours the task of defending their native city. There have been no tumults or disorders, except those caused by the foolish mania of supposing every one who is not known must necessarily be a spy. Political manifestations have taken place before the Hôtel de Ville, but the conciliatory policy adopted by the Government has prevented their degenerating into excesses. Public opinion, too, has pronounced against them. ✗From what I have heard and observed, I am inclined to think that the majority of the bourgeoisie are in favour of a capitulation, but that they do not venture to say so ; and that the majority of the working men are opposed to peace on any terms. They do not precisely know themselves what would be the result of holding out, but they vaguely trust to time, and to the chapter of accidents. In the middle and upper classes there are also many who take the same view of the situation. "Let us," they say, " hold out for two months, and the condition of things will in all probability be altered, and if so, as we cannot be worse off, any change must be to our advantage."

Shut up with the Parisians in Paris, I cannot help feeling a good deal of sympathy for them, notwithstanding their childish vanity, their mendacity, and their frivolity. I sincerely trust, therefore, if they do seriously resist their besiegers, that the assurances of the Government that there are ample supplies of food and of ammunition, are not part of the system of official lying which was pursued by their predecessors; and I hope that the grandiloquent boasts and brave words that one hears from morning to night will be followed by brave deeds.

This morning Messenger Johnson was sent off with despatches to England from the British Embassy. He was provided with a safe-conduct, signed by General Trochu, and a letter to the Commandant of the Fort of Vanves, enjoining him to forward Mr. Johnson under a flag of truce to the Prussian lines. At half-past nine Messenger Johnson, arrayed in a pair of high boots with clanking spurs, the belongings, I presume, of a Queen's messenger, stepped into his carriage, with that " I should like to see any one touch me" air which is the badge of his tribe. His coachman being already drunk, he was accompanied by a second man, who undertook to drive until Jehu had got over the effect of his potations. I myself have always regarded Queen's messengers as superior beings, to be addressed with awe, and whose progress no one would venture to arrest. Such, however, was not the opinion of the National Guards who were on duty at the gate through which Messenger Johnson sought to leave this beleagured town. In vain Messenger Johnson showed his pass; in vain he stated that he was a free-born Briton and a Queen's messenger. These suspicious patriots ignored the pass, and scoffed at the *Civis Romanus*. In fact, I tremble as I write it, several of them said they felt somewhat inclined to shoot any Briton, and more particularly a Queen's Messenger, whilst others proposed to prod Messenger Johnson with their bayonets in his tenderest parts. Exit under these circumstances was impossible. For some time Messenger Johnson sat calm, dignified, and imperturbable in the midst of this uproar, and then made a strategical retreat to the Ministry of War. He was there given an officer to accompany him; he again set forth, and this time he was more fortunate, for he got through the gate, and vanished from our horizon. I called at the Embassy this afternoon, and found our representative, Mr. Wodehouse, confident that Messenger Johnson would arrive at his destination. Mr. Wodehouse when I left him was engaged in pacifying a lunatic, who had forced his way into the Embassy, and who insisted that he was the British Ambassador. I was surprised to learn that there are still at least 300 of our countrymen and women in Paris. Most of them are in a state of absolute destitution, some because they have no means, others because they are unable to draw upon the funds in England. Mr. Herbert has established a species of soup kitchen, so they will not starve until we all do. Mr. Wallace, the heir of Lord Hertford, who had already given the munificent donation of 12,000*l.* to the Ambulance fund, has also provided funds for their most pressing wants.

In to-day's *Journal des Débats* M. John Lemoinne points out to his readers that M. Bismarck, in his remarks to M. Jules Favre, expressed the opinion of Germany, and that the expression of his views respecting the necessity of Germany annexing Alsace and Lorraine is not necessarily an insult to France. The war, says M. Lemoinne, never was a war of monarchs, but a war of nations. France as well as the Emperor is responsible for it. It must continue to be, he continues, a war *à outrance* between two races. The terms of peace proposed by M. Bismarck cannot be accepted by France. The moderate tone and dignified melancholy of this article contrast favourably with that of almost all the leaders in the other papers, and more particularly in those of the ultra-Republican press. In *La France*, a moderate and well-conducted journal, I find the following remarks:—" Paris is the capital of France and of the world. Paris besieged is a beautiful, a surprising spectacle. The sky is blue, the atmosphere is pure, this is a happy augury, fifteen days of patience on the part of the Parisians, fifteen days to arm in the provinces, and the German army will be irreparably compromised. It will then be unable to cut its way out of the circle of fire which will surround it." When journals of the standing of *La France* deal in this sort of nonsense it is not surprising that the ex-Imperialist organs, which are endeavouring to curry favour with the mob, are still more absurd. The *Figaro* concludes two columns of bombast with the following flight:—"But thou, O country, never diest. Bled in all thy veins by the butchers of the North, thy divine head mutilated by the heels of brutes, the Christ of nations, for two months nailed on the cross, never hast thou appeared so great and so beautiful. Thou needest this martyrdom, O our mother, to know how we love thee. In order that Paris, in which there is a genius which has given her the empire of the world, should fall into the hands of the barbarians, there must cease to be a God in heaven. As God she exists, and as God she is immortal. Paris will never surrender." When it is remembered that this ignorant, vain, foolish population has for nearly twenty years been fed with this sort of stuff, it is not surprising that even to this hour it cannot realise the fact that Paris is in any danger of being captured. The ultra-Republican press is becoming every day more virulent. M. Blanqui, in his organ, *La Patrie en Danger*, after praising the act of a person of the name of Malet, who last February shot an officer who refused to shout "Vive la République," thus continues:—"I was reminded of this when the other day I saw defile on the boulevards a regiment of rustic peasants. I raised my hat to salute these soldiers of liberty, but there was no response from them. Malet would have raised the kepi of one of the captains with a bullet, and he would have done well. Let us be without pity. Vive Marat! We will do justice ourselves. . . ." The ultra-Republicans, of the stamp of M. Blanqui and M. Felix Pyat, seem to be under the impression that it is far more important to establish a

Republican form of Government in France than to resist the Prussians. In the meetings which they hold every evening they clamour for the election at once of a municipality, because they hope to become themselves members of it, and then to absorb all the power which is now wielded by the Provisional Government. ✶Beyond discrediting themselves by these attempts to disturb the harmony within the walls, which is of such vital importance at the present moment, I do not think that they will do much. I have talked to many working men, and whatever may be their political opinions, they are far too sensible to play the game of the Prussians by weakening the existing Government. After the Prussians perhaps the deluge; but as long as they are before Paris, and the Provisional Government does not capitulate, I do not dread any political disorders. What we may come to, are bread riots. There is already an immense deal of misery, and, as the siege continues and provisions rise in price, it will of course increase.

I was talking this morning to a gentleman who used at one time to play a very important part in public life, who is well acquainted with most of the members of the Government, and who is a man of calm judgment. I was anxious to obtain his opinion upon the situation, and this is a *résumé* of what he told me. "When Jules Favre," he said, "went to Bismarck, he was prepared to agree to the dismantlement of the fortresses of Alsace and Lorraine, the cession of half the fleet, the payment of an indemnity of eighty millions of pounds, and an agreement for a term of years not to have a standing army of more than 200,000 men. A Constituent Assembly would have ratified these terms. The cession of a portion of the fleet is but tantamount to the payment of money. The conscription is so unpopular that a majority of the nation would have been glad to know that the standing army would henceforward be a small one. As for the fortresses, they have not been taken, and yet they have not arrested the Prussian advance on Paris; consequently their destruction would not seriously weaken the defences of the country." I asked whether Paris would now consent to these terms. "No," he said, "if the Government offered them there would be a revolution. Paris, rightly or wrongly, believes that she will be able to hold out for two months, and that during this time there will be a *levée en masse.*" "And do you share this opinion?" I asked. "I am not of a very sanguine character," he replied; "but I really am now inclined to believe that the Prussians will never enter Paris unless they starve us into a surrender." "Then," I said, "I suppose they will starve us out." "I am an old man," he said, "and I always remember Philip's saying, 'Time and I are two.' In two months many things may happen. Winter is coming on. The Prussian army is composed of men engaged in business at home and anxious to return; the North does not love the South, and divisions may arise. The King of Prussia is an old man, and he may die. Without absolutely counting upon a French army raising the siege, there are *levées* forming in Lyons and elsewhere, and the Germans will find their communications seriously menaced. Russia, too, and Austria may interfere, so I think that we are wise to resist as long as we can." "But if you have to capitulate, what will happen?" I asked. "If we do capitulate, our disaster will be complete," he answered. "I do not anticipate disorders; the population of Paris is an intelligent one, it wishes the Government to resist as long as it can, but not to prolong an impossible situation. Paris must do her part in defending the country, she can do no more." "Well," I said, "supposing that the Prussians were to withdraw, and peace were to be concluded on reasonable terms, what do you think would take place?" "Gambetta, Jules Favre, and the majority of the

Parisian Deputies would call a Constituent Assembly as soon as possible, and resign power into its hands. They are moderate Republicans, but between a Red Republic and a Constitutional Monarchy they would prefer the latter. As practical men, from what I know of them, I am inclined to think that they would be in favour of the Orleanist family—either the Comte de Paris or the Duc d'Aumale."
"And would the majority of the Constituent Assembly go with them?" I asked. "I think it would," he replied. "The Orleanist family would mean peace. Of late years Frenchmen have cared very little for military glory; their dream has been to save money. One advantage of our disasters is that it has limited the number of pretenders to the Throne, for after the capitulation of Sedan, neither the army nor the peasants will support a Bonaparte. There will be two parties—the ultra-Republicans, and the advocates of a Constitutional Monarchy under a Prince of the House of Orleans. Unless the friends of the Orleans Princes commit some great fault, they are masters of the situation."

I went down this morning to the Halles Centrales. There was very little going on. *Bonnes* were coming to market, but most of the booths were untenanted, and the price of vegetables, eggs, and butter was exorbitant. "Why do you complain of me?" said a dealer to a customer—"is it my fault? Curse Badinguet and that wretch of a Bismarck; they choose to fight, so you must pay double for these carrots." The butchers yesterday published an appeal against the maximum; they said that the cost of animals was so great that they positively were losing upon every joint which they sold. A new proclamation of the Mayor has just been issued, announcing that 500 oxen and 4,000 sheep will daily be slaughtered and sold to the butchers at a price to enable them to gain 20 per cent. by retailing meat at the official tariff. I find that, come what may, we have coffee and sugar enough to last many months, so that provided the bread does not fail, we shall take some time to starve out.

This afternoon a dense column of smoke was seen rising in the air in the direction of La Villette, and it gradually covered the town with a dark cloud. The pessimists among the Boulevard gendarmes insisted that the town had been set on fire by the Prussians; the optimists were convinced that the 10,000, who for some reason or other are supposed to be in a wood, patiently waiting to be roasted, were being burnt. It turns out that some petroleum in the Buttes de Chaumont caught fire. After burning about two hours, the fire was put out by heaping dirt on it.

The Prussians still occupy the plateau of Meudon, and despatches from the forts say that troops are supposed to be concentrating between Meudon and Sèvres. We have come to the conclusion that as the Prussians do not fire upon Grenelle and Auteuil, they have neither Krupp nor siege guns. I trust this may prove true. News has been received from Tours; it was brought by an officer who ran the blockade. We are much elated to learn that the result of M. Jules Favre's interview has been posted up throughout France. We believe that the effect of this measure "will be equal to an army." The Post Office informs the public that a regular system of balloons has been organised, and that letters will be received and forwarded to the provinces and abroad, provided they do not weigh above four grammes. A deputation of English and American correspondents waited to-day on M. Jules Favre, to ask him to give them facilities to send their letters by the balloons. This he promised to do. He also half promised to let all correspondents have a pass, on stating who they are. The worst of a pass is, that it is no protection against arrest, for, say your captors, "Prussian spies are so cunning that they would be precisely the persons to have papers, either forged or stolen." Another trouble is, that if you are arrested, you are generally shut up, with half-a-dozen thieves and drunkards, for about twenty-four hours, before a Commissary condescends to inquire into your case. No one as yet has ever troubled me; but the spy mania certainly does not add to the charm of the residence of a stranger in Paris just now. I would rather run the chance of being hit during a bombardment, than affront the certainty of twenty-four hours in a filthy police cell. Suspicion is, no doubt, carried to a ridiculous excess; but it is equally true that unquestionable spies are arrested every day under every sort of disguise. Mr. Washburne told me yesterday that he saw a *soi-disant* "Invalide" arrested, who turned out to be a regular spectacled Dutchman.

September 28th.

Nothing new at the front. We suppose that the enemy are concentrating troops on the Sèvres-Meudon plateau, and that they intend to attack on that side. We are confident that the guns of Mont Valérien will prevent the success of this attack. On the opposite side of Paris they are endeavouring to erect batteries; but they are unable to do so on account of the fire of Fort Nogent. It seems to me that we are shouting before we are quite out of the wood; but we are already congratulating ourselves upon having sustained a siege which throws those of Saragossa and Richmond into the shade. If we have not yet been bombarded, we have assumed "an heroic attitude of expectation;" and if the Prussians have not yet stormed the walls, we have shown that we were ready to repel them if they had. Deprived of our shepherd and our sheep-dogs, we civic sheep have set up so loud a ba-ba, that we have terrified the wolves who wished to devour us. In the impossible event of an ultimate capitulation we shall hang our swords and our muskets over our fire-places, and say to our grandchildren, "I, too, was one of the defenders of Paris." In the meantime, soldiers who have run away when attacked are paraded through the streets with a placard on their breasts, requesting all good citizens to spit upon them. Two courts-martial have been established to judge spies and marauders, and in each of the nine sections there is a court-martial to sit upon peccant National Guards. "The sentence," says the decree, "will at once be executed by the detachment on duty." We are preparing for the worst; in the Place of the Pantheon, and other squares, it is proposed to take up the paving stones, because they will, if left, explode shells which may strike them. The windows of the Louvre and other public edifices are being filled with sand bags. This morning I was walking along the Rue Lafayette, when I heard a cry "A bas les cigares!" and I found that if I continued to smoke, it was thought that I should set light to some ammunition waggons which were passing.

Yesterday evening there was a report, which was almost universally credited, that a revolution had broken out in London, because the English Government had refused to aid Paris in driving back the Prussians. The Parisians find it impossible to understand that the world at large can see little distinction between a French army entering Berlin and a Prussian army entering Paris. Their capital is to them a holy city, and they imagine that the Christian world regards the Prussian attack upon it much as the Mahometan world would regard a bombardment of Mecca. No doubt it will be a shocking thing to bombard a city such as this, filled with women and children; still, being an Englishman, I cannot see that it would be worse than to bombard London. The newspapers of this morning contain a *précis* of a letter from "our Fritz" to William "the mystic drunkard." Our Fritz writes to his papa to say that he ought to have accepted peace when it was proffered by Jules Favre. How the contents of the letter are known in Paris is not stated. But here we know everything. We know that at a council of war held two days ago at Versailles a majority declared that it was impossible to take Paris. We know that the German soldiers are dying of starvation and clothed in rags. We know that they are forced by their officers, against their will, to attack their French brothers. Did not yesterday a National Guard himself take five Prussian prisoners? They were starving, and thankfully accepted a piece of bread. They had a wounded companion in a wheelbarrow, who continually shook his fist in the direction of the "mystic drunkard," and plaintively moaned forth the only French word he knew, " Misérable, misérable !" Did not another National Guard go into a house recently occupied by " Bavarians," and find the following words written on a shutter—" Poor Frenchmen, we love you : they force us to fight against you?" I believe all this, and many other strange facts, because I see them in print in the newspapers. Can it possibly be that I am over-credulous? Am I wrong, too, in believing that France is rising *en masse*, that Moltke did not understand his business in advancing on Paris, and that he will be crushed by the armies of the Loire and a dozen other places—if, indeed, our gallant heroes congregated in Paris give their brethren outside time to share in the triumph of defeating him? *En attendant*, we eat, drink, and are reasonably merry ; our defenders mount guard, and drill when they are off guard. Our wary Mobiles outside not only refuse to allow Prussians to pass, but such is their vigilance, they generally arrest officers of any regiment except their own who come within their ken. These worthy fellows will, I believe, fight with bravery. The working men, too, are engaged in heaping up barricades, and are ready to allow themselves to be killed and their landlords' houses to be blown up rather than surrender.

The sailors in the forts are prepared to hold them like ships against all comers. The "infantry of the marine" is commanded by an old tar who stands no nonsense. A few days ago he published an order complaining that the marines "undulated under fire." Some of his officers went to him as a deputation to protest against this slur on them and their men; but he cut their remonstrances short by immediately cashiering the spokesman. To-day he announces that if his men are supplied with drink within the limits of his command he will burn down all the pot-houses. It is greatly to be deplored that the determined spirit of this Admiral does not animate all his brother commanders; they are perpetually engaged in discussing with those who are under their orders, and appear to be afraid to put down insubordination with a high hand. If ever they venture upon any act of rigour, they are called upon by the Ultra press to justify it, and they generally do so in a lengthy letter.

I have been, as the Americans say, much exercised of late respecting certain persons whom I have seen strolling about the streets, avoiding as much as possible their species. Whenever anyone looked at them they sneaked away with deprecating glances. They are dressed in a sort of pea-jacket, with hoods, black trousers, and black caps, and their general appearance was a cross between a sailor and a monk. I have at length discovered with surprise that these retiring innocents are the new sergents-de-ville of M. Keratry, who are daily denounced by the Ultras as ferocious wolves eager to rend and devour all honest citizens. If this be true, I can only say that they are well disguised in sheep's clothing.

Letters from Paris, if ever they do get to London, must necessarily be so dull, that they can hardly repay the trouble of reading them. Life here is about as lively as life on board a ship. The two main subjects of conversation, the military preparations within the town, and the amount of food, are in honour tabooed to correspondents. With respect to the former I will only say, that if the Prussians do carry the forts and the enceinte, they will not have taken Paris; with regard to the latter, I can state that we shall not be starved out for some time. Besides the cattle which have been accumulated, we have 90,000 horses; and although a cab horse may not taste as good as Southdown mutton, I have no doubt that Parisian cooking will make it a very palatable dish for hungry men; there are, too, a great many dogs, and the rats have not yet left the sinking ship. As for coffee and sugar we have enough to last for six months; and, unless the statistics of the Government are utterly worthless, come what may we shall not lack bread for many a day.

The Rump of the Corps Diplomatique has held a second meeting, and a messenger has been sent to Bismarck to know—1st, whether he means to bombard the city; 2nd, whether, if he does, he intends to give the usual twenty-four hours' notice. Diplomates are little better than old women when they have to act on an emergency. Were it not for Mr. Washburne, who was brought up in the rough-and-ready life of the Far West, instead of serving an apprenticeship in Courts and Government offices, those who are still here would be perfectly helpless. They come to him at all moments, and although he cannot speak French, for all practical purposes he is worth more than all his colleagues put together. Lord Lyons would, I believe, have remained, had he not been over persuaded by timid colleagues, who were ordered to do as he did. It is a great pity that he did not act according to his own judgment; but Republics, we know, are not in good odour with courtiers. As for that poor creature Metternich, he was utterly demoralized. He was more of a Chamberlain of Badinguet than an Ambassador, and, of course, when his friend disappeared, he took the earliest opportunity to follow his example.

September 29th.

We still are cut off from the outer world, but neither "the world forgetting," nor, we imagine, "by the world forgot." The inhabitants of the "Mecca of civilization" are still, like Sister Anne, looking out for some one to come to their assistance. I am utterly sick and tired of the eternal brag and bombast around me. Let the Parisians gain some success, and then celebrate it as loudly as they please: but why, in the name of common sense, will they rejoice over victories yet to come? "We are preserving," they say, "a dignified expectative attitude." Mr. Micawber put the thing in more simple vernacular when he said that he was waiting for something to turn up. "First catch your hare" is a piece of advice which our patriots here would scoff at. They have not yet caught the Prussians, but they have already, by a flight of imagination, cooked and eaten them. Count Moltke may as well—if I am to believe one quarter of what I hear—like the American coon, come down. In a question of military strategy between the grocers of Paris and the Prussian generals I should have thought that the odds were considerably in favour of the latter, but I am told that this is not so, and that in laying siege to Paris they are committing a mistake for which a schoolboy would be deservedly whipped. If you eliminate the working-class element, which has not been corrupted by the Imperial system, the population of this town is much what I imagine that of Constantinople to have been when it was taken by the Turks. They are Greeks of the lower empire. Monsieur sticks his kepi on one side of his head, and struts and swaggers along the Boulevard as though he were a bantam cock. We have lost the *petits crevés* who formed so agreeable an element in society, but they have been replaced by the military dandy, a being, if possible, still more offensive. This creature mounts some sorry screw and parades the Boulevard and the Champs Elysées, frowning dismally upon the world in general, and twirling his moustache with the one hand, whilst he holds on to the saddle with the other. His sword is of the longest, his waist is of the tightest, and his boots are of the brightest. His like is only to be seen in England when the *Battle of Waterloo* is played at Astley's, but his seat is not as good as that of the equestrian warriors of that establishment. As he slowly paces along he gazes slyly to see how many people are looking at him, and it must be owned that those who do see him, vastly admire him. What manner of beings these admirers are may be imagined from their idol. No contrast can be greater than that which exists between the Parisian Bobadils and the Provincial Mobiles. The latter are quiet and orderly, eager to drill and without a vestige of bluster—these poor peasants are of a very different stuff from the emasculated, conceited scum which has palmed itself off on Europe as representative Frenchmen. The families with whom they lodge speak with wonder of their sobriety, their decency, and their simple ways, and in their hearts almost despise them because they do not ravish their daughters or pillage their cellars ; and neither swear every half-hour to die for their country, nor yell the "Marseillaise." If Paris be saved, it will be thanks to them and to the working men of the capital. But it will be the old *sic vos non vobis* story ; their brave deeds and undemonstrative heroism will be forgotten, and Jules and Alphonse, the dandies and braggarts of the Boulevard, will swear to their own heroism. I trust that the Prussians will fail to take Paris, because I think that the French are right to fight on rather than submit to the dismemberment of their country ; and because I prefer a Republic to a Monarchy where a King reigns by right divine. But when I read the bombastic articles in the newspapers—when I see the insane conceit and the utter ignorance of those with whom I am thrown—when I find them really believing that they are heroes because they are going, they say, to win battles, it is difficult to entertain any great sympathy for them. How utterly must poor old Badinguet, before whom they cringed for years—who used them, bought them, and made his market out of their vanity, their ignorance, and their love of theatrical claptrap, despise them, as he dreams again through life's dream in the gardens of his German prison. They call him now a "sinister scoundrel" and a "lugubrious stage player." But he was their master for many a long year, and they owe their emancipation from his yoke to Prussian arms and not to themselves.

A committee of "subsistence" has been established. The feud between the butchers and the public still continues, and most of the meat stalls are closed. The grocers, too, are charging absurd prices for their goods. *La Liberté* suggests that their clients should do themselves justice, and one of these mornings, unless these gentry abate their prices, some grocer will be found hanging before his door. Although provisions are plentiful, the misery is very great. Beggars increase in number every day—they are like one of the plagues of Egypt. I was taking a cup of coffee this morning before a café, and I counted twenty-three beggars who asked me for money whilst I was sitting there. We still derive much comfort from caricaturing Badinguet, William, and Bismarck. The latest effort represents Badinguet and William as Robert Macaire and Bertrand. Another represents Badinguet eating an eagle. "Coquin," says William, "what are you doing with your eagle?" "Eating it," replies Badinguet; "what else can I do with it?" Little statuettes, too, of the "two friends," Badinguet and William, are in great request. William, with an immense moustache, scowls at Badinguet, who humbly kneels before him.

M. Jules Favre, in reply to the English press deputation, sent last night to say that each correspondent must make a personal application to General Trochu. I know what that means already. All I ask is that my letters should be put up in a balloon. As for passes, I have one already, and it has not been of the slightest service to me. *Les Nouvelles* heads an article "English Spies," and proposes that to simplify the question of whether they are spies or not, all English in Paris should at once be shot. I cannot say that I personally have found any ill-feeling to exist against me because I am an Englishman. Yesterday afternoon I was in a crowd, and some one suggested that I was a spy; I immediately mounted on a chair and explained that I was a "journalist Anglais," and pointed out to my friends that they ought to be obliged to me for remaining here. "If any one doubts me," I added, "let us go to the nearest commissary." No one did doubt me, and fifty patriots immediately shook hands with me. The French people are apt to form hasty judgments sometimes, and to act on them still more hastily, but if one can get them to listen for a moment, they are reasonable, and soon their natural good nature asserts itself. The zealous but well-intended Mobiles are the most dangerous, for they shoot you first and then apologise to your corpse. An order is placarded to-day of Governor Trochu's, announcing that anyone trying to pass the lines will be sent before the Courts Martial, or if he or she runs away when ordered to stop, will be shot on the spot. This latter clause allows a very great latitude for zeal, more particularly as the "lines" just now are little more than a geographical expression. Their Emperor is a prisoner, the enemy is thundering at their gates, they are shut up here like rats in a hole; they have been vanquished in the only engagement they have had with their besiegers, and yet they still believe that, compared with them, the Germans are an inferior race, and, like the slave before Marius, will shrink abashed before the majesty of Paris. "If we," say their newspapers, "the wisest, the best, the noblest of human beings, have to succumb to this horde of barbarians that environ us, we shall cease to believe in the existence of a Providence."

The movement on the part of the "Ultras" to elect at once a municipality is gaining strength. Yesterday several chiefs of the faubourg battalions of the National Guard interviewed Jules Ferry on the subject. Ledru Rollin has declared himself in favour of it, and this morning there are evidences that the Government is inclined to give way to the pressure, for a decree is published in the *Journal Officiel* ordering a registration of voters. The worst of Frenchmen is that, no matter how patriotic each one may be, he is convinced that the interests of his country require that he should be one of its rulers. The men of '48 who have returned from exile are surprised that they are almost forgotten by the present generation, who regard them as interesting historical relics, and put their faith in new gods. At the clubs every evening the Government is denounced for refusing to admit into its ranks this or that patriot, or adjourning the municipal elections, and for not sending revolutionary agents into the provinces. A newspaper this morning makes the excellent suggestion that M. Blanqui, M. F. Pyat, and their principal adherents should be invited to proceed at once to the provinces in a balloon, invested with the rank of Government agents. "They cannot," it adds, "do so much harm there as they are doing here; and then, too, the balloon may burst." Personally, I should be glad to see a moderate Republic established here, for I regard a Court as a waste of public money; but it seems to me that Republicans should remember that it is for the nation, and not for them, to decide what shall henceforward be the form of government.

CHAPTER IV.

September 30*th.*

WE are still beating our tom-toms like the Chinese, to frighten away the enemy, and our braves still fire off powder at invisible Uhlans. The Prussians, to our intense disgust, will not condescend even to notice us. We jeer at them, we revile them, and yet they will not attack us. What they are doing we cannot understand. They appear to have withdrawn from the advanced positions which they held. We know that they are in the habit of making war in a thoroughly ungentlemanly manner, and we cannot make up our minds whether our "attitude" is causing them to hesitate, or whether they are not devising some new trick to take us by surprise. That they are starving, that their communications with Germany are cut off, that their leaders are at loggerheads, that the Army of the Loire will soon be here to help us to demolish them, we have not the slightest doubt. The question is no longer whether Paris will be taken—that we have solved already; it is whether the Prussians will be able to get back to the Rhine. We are thankful that Bismarck did not accept Jules Favre's offer of a money indemnity. We would not give a hundred francs now to ensure peace or an armistice. I went this morning into a shop, the proprietor of which, a bootmaker, I have long known, and I listened with interest to the conversation of this worthy man with some of his neighbours who had dropped in to have a gossip, and to congratulate him on his martial achievements, as he had been on guard in a bastion. We first discussed why the Army of the Loire had not arrived, and we came to the conclusion that it was engaged in rallying Bazaine. "I should like to read your English newspapers now," said one; "your *Tims* told us we ought to cede Alsace and Lorraine, but its editor must now acknowledge that Paris is invincible." I told him that I felt convinced that he did so regularly every morning. "No peace," shouted a little tailor, who had been prancing about on an imaginary steed, killing imaginary Prussians, "we have made a pact with death; the world knows now what are the consequences of attacking us." The all-absorbing question of subsistence then came up, and some one remarked that beef would give out sooner than mutton. "We must learn," observed a jolly-looking grocer, "to vanquish the prejudices of our stomach. Even those who do not like mutton must make the sacrifice of their taste to their country." I mildly suggested that perhaps in a few weeks the stomachs which had a prejudice against rats would have to overcome it. At this the countenance of the gossips fell considerably, when the bootmaker, after mysteriously closing the door, whispered, "A secret was confided to me this morning by an intimate friend of General Trochu. There is a tunnel which connects Paris with the provinces, and through it flocks and herds are entering the town." This news cheered us up amazingly. My bootmaker's wife came in to help him off with his military accoutrements; so, with a compliment about Venus disarming Mars, I withdrew in company with an American, who had gone into the shop with me. This American is a sort of transatlantic Bunsly. He talks little, but thinks much. His sole observation to me as we walked away was this, "They will squat, sir, mark my words, they will squat." I received this oracular utterance with respect, and I leave it to others to solve its meaning. I am myself a person of singular credulity, but even I sometimes ask myself whether all I hear and read can be true. Was there really, as all the newspapers this morning inform me, a meeting last Sunday at London of 400,000 persons, who were addressed by eminent M.P.'s, and by the principal merchants and owners of manufactories in England, at which resolutions were adopted denouncing the Queen, and calling upon Mr. Gladstone either to retire from office, or to declare war against Prussia?

The Tuileries correspondence, of which I gave a short summary yesterday, reveals the fact that both M. de Cassagnac and Baron Jerome David were regular pensioners on the Civil List. The cost of the Prince Imperial's baptism amounted to 898,000fr. The cousins, male and female, of the Emperor, received 1,310,975fr. per annum; the Duc de Persigny received in two months, 60,000fr.; Prince Jablonowyski, Countess Gajan, Madame Claude Vignon, Le Général Morris, and many other ladies and gentlemen who never did the State any service, are down for various sums. Among other items is one of 1,200fr. to General de Failly for sugar plums. The Duchess of Mouchy, whose name continually appears, received 2,000,000fr. as a marriage portion. The son of the American Bonaparte had a pension of 30,000fr.; Madame Ratazzi of 24,000fr.; her sister, Madame Turr, the same; Marquis Pepoli, 25,000fr. But the poor relations do not appear to have been contented with their pensions, for on some pretext or other they were always getting extra allowances out of their rich cousin. As for Prince Achille Murat, the Emperor paid his debts a dozen times. Whatever he may have been to the outer world, poor old Badinguet seems to have been a Providence to his forty-two cousins and to his personal friends. He carried out Sidney Smith's notion of charity—put his hand into someone else's pocket, and gave away what he stole liberally.

Figaro, with its usual good taste, recommends the battalions of the National Guard to choose celebrities of the *demi-monde* for their vivandières. From what I hear every day, I imagine that the battalions will be far more likely to hang the editor of this facetious paper than to take his advice. I hear from the kiosque women that its sale is falling off daily.

The clubs and their organs have announced that the municipal elections are to take place, with or without the consent of the Government, on October 2, and that not only the inhabitants of Paris, but the Gardes Mobiles and the peasants who have taken refuge within the walls of the city are to vote. In the working men's quarters there is undoubtedly a strong feeling in favour of these elections being held at once. But the working men do not attend the clubs. I have dropped into several of them, and the audience appeared to me principally to be composed of strong-minded women and demagogues, who never did an honest day's work in their lives. The Government has, however, been "interviewed" on the subject of the municipal elections by the chiefs of the battalions of the National Guards of the Faubourgs, and, if only some men of position can be found to put themselves at the head of the movement, it will cause trouble. As yet, Ledru-Rollin is the only known politician who avowedly favours it. The Government is, I believe, divided upon the expediency of holding the elections at once, or rather I should say, upon the possibility of putting them off without provoking disturbances. I am inclined to think that, as is usually the case, the Moderates will yield on this point to their Ultra colleagues. Very possibly they may think that if ever a capitulation becomes necessary, it will be as well to make the nominees of the Faubourgs share in the responsibility. As Jules

Favre said of Rochefort, they are perhaps safer in the Government than outside of it.

The column of the Place Vendôme is daily bombarded by indignant patriots, who demand that it should be razed to the ground, and the metal of which it is composed be melted down into cannon. The statue of Napoleon I., in the cocked hat and great-coat, which used to be on its summit, was removed a few years ago to a pedestal at the end of the Avenue de la Grande Armée. It has been concealed to preserve it from the iconoclasts. There has been a lull of late in M. Gambetta's proclamations. Within the last twenty-four hours, not above two fresh ones have appeared. The newspapers are beginning to clamour for a sortie. Why, they ask, are we to allow ourselves to be besieged by an army which does not equal in numbers our own? Why are we to allow them quietly to establish their batteries? There is a certain amount of sense in these complaints, though the vital question of how regiments which have never had an opportunity of being brigaded together, will be able to vanquish in the open field the disciplined troops of Germany, is the unknown x in the problem which has yet to be solved. It is evident, however, that the question must be tested, unless we are to remain within the fortifications until we have digested our last omnibus horse. If the enemy attacks, there is fair ground to suppose that he will be repelled; but then, perhaps he will leave us to make the first move. Without entering into details, I may say that considerable engineering skill has been shown of late in strengthening the defences, that the Mobiles and the National Guard, if their words mean anything, which has yet to be proved, are full of fighting, and that the armed force at our disposal has at length been knocked into some sort of shape. Every day that the Prussian attack is delayed diminishes its chance of success. "If they do carry the town by assault," said a general to me yesterday, "it will be our fault, for, from a military point of view, it is now impregnable." What the effect of a bombardment may be upon the morale of the inhabitants we have yet to see. In any case, however, until several of those hard nuts, the forts, have been cracked, a bombardment can only be partial.

There was heavy firing last night, and it increased in intensity this morning. At about one o'clock I saw above 100 wounded being brought to the Palais de l'Industrie, and on going to Montrouge I found the church near the fortifications full of them. The following is the official account of what has happened:

Our troops in a vigorous sortie, successively occupied Chevilly and l'Hay, and advanced as far as Thiais and Choisy-le-Roi. All these positions were solidly occupied, the latter with cannon. After a sharp artillery and musketry engagement our troops fell back on their positions with a remarkable order and *aplomb*. The Garde Mobile were very firm. *En somme, journée très honorable.* Our losses have been considerable. Those of the enemy probably as considerable. TROCHU.

I need not add that as usual we have had rumours all day of a great victory and a junction with the Army of the Loire. General Trochu's despatch, dated 10·30, Bicêtre, reduces matters to their real dimensions.

October 1st.

Although the Government statistics respecting the amount of food in Paris have been published, and are consequently, in all probability, in the hands of the Prussians, I do not like to give them myself. It can, however, do no harm to explain the system which is being adopted by the authorities to make our stores hold out as long as possible. Every butcher receives each morning a certain amount of meat, calculated upon his average sales. Against this meat he issues tickets in the evening to his customers, who, upon presentation of the ticket the next morning, receive the amount for which they have inscribed themselves at the price fixed by the tariff of the week. When tickets have been issued by the butcher equivalent to the meat which he is to receive, he issues no more. Yesterday a decree was promulgated, ordering all persons having flour on sale to give it up to the Government at the current price. It will, I presume, be distributed to the bakers, like the meat to the butchers. As regards meat, the supply does not equal the demand —many persons are unable to obtain tickets, and consequently have to go without it. Restaurants cannot get enough for their customers. This evening, for instance, at seven o'clock, on going into a restaurant, I found almost everything already eaten up. I was obliged to "vanquish the prejudices of my stomach," and make a dinner on sheeps' trotters, pickled cauliflower, and peaches. My stomach is still engaged in "vanquishing its prejudice" to this repast, and I am yet in the agonies of indigestion. In connection, however, with this question of food, there is another important consideration. Work is at a stand-still. Mobiles and Nationaux who apply *formâ pauperis* receive one franc and a half per diem. Now, at present prices, it is materially impossible for a single man to buy sufficient food to stave off hunger for this sum, how then those who depend upon it for their sustenance, and have wives and families to support out of it, are able to live, it is difficult to understand. Sooner or later the population will have to be rationed like soldiers, and if the siege goes on, useless mouths will have to be turned out. It was supposed that the peasants in the neighbourhood of Paris, who were invited to take refuge within its walls, would bring more than enough food with them for themselves and their families, but they preferred to bring their old beds and their furniture. Besides our stores of flour, of sheep, and of oxen, we have twenty-two million pounds of horse-flesh to fall back upon, so that I do not think that we shall be starved out for some time; still the misery among those who have no money to buy food will, unless Government boldly faces the question, be very great. Everything, except beef, mutton, and bread, is already at a fancy price. Ham costs 7fr. the kilo.; cauliflowers, 1.50fr. a head; salt butter 9fr. the kilo. (a kilo. is about two pounds); a fat chicken 10fr.; a thin one, 5fr.; a rabbit, 11fr.; a duck, 9fr.; a fat goose, 20fr.

Rents, too, are as vexed a question as they are in Ireland. In a few days the October term comes due. Few can pay it; it is proposed, therefore, to allow no landlord to levy it either before the close of the siege or before December.

General Trochu, in his Rapport Militaire of yesterday's proceedings, expands his despatch of yesterday evening. The object, he says, was, by a combined action on both banks of the Seine, to discover precisely in what force the enemy was in the villages of Choisy-le-Roi and Chevilly. Whilst the brigade of General Giulham drove the enemy out of Chevilly, the head of the column of General Blaize entered the village of Thiais, and seized a battery of cannon, which, however, could not be moved for want of horses. At this moment the Prussians were reinforced, and a retreat took place in good order. General Giulham was killed. General d'Exea, while this combat was going on, marched with a brigade on Creteil, and inflicted a severe loss with his mitrailleuse on the enemy. This report contrasts favourably with the florid, exaggerated accounts of the engagement which are published in this morning's papers. I am glad to find that France possesses at least one man who tells the truth, and who can address his fellow-citizens in plain language. The credulity of the Parisians, and their love of high-flown bombast, amount to a disease, which, if this city is not to sink into a species of Baden

Baden, must be stamped out. Mr. O'Sullivan recently published an account of his expedition to the Prussian headquarters in the *Electeur Libre*. Because he said that the Prussians were conducting themselves well in the villages they occupied, the editor of the paper has been overwhelmed with letters reviling him for publishing such audacious lies. Most Frenchmen consider anyone who differs from them to be either a knave or a fool, and they fabricate facts to prove their theories. An "intelligent young man" published a letter this morning saying that he had escaped from Versailles, and that already 700 girls have been ravished there by the Prussians. This intelligent young man's tale will be credited, and Mr. O'Sullivan will be disbelieved by nine-tenths of this population. They believe only what they wish to believe.

M. Rochefort has issued a "poster" begging citizens not to construct private barricades. There must, he justly observes, be "unity in the system of interior defences." The *Reveil* announces that the Ultras do not intend to proceed to revolutionary elections of a municipality to-morrow, because they have hopes that the Government intend to yield on this question. The Prefect of the Police is actively engaged in an attempt to throw light upon Pietri's connection with the plots which periodically came to a head against the Empire. Documents have been discovered which will show that most of these plots were got up by the Imperial police. Pietri, Lagrange, and Barnier, a *juge d'instruction*, were the prime movers. A certain Bablot received 20,000fr. for his services as a conspirator.

The complaints of the newspapers against the number of young men who avoid military duty by hooking themselves on in some capacity or other to an ambulance are becoming louder every day. For my part I confess that I look with contempt upon any young Frenchman I meet with the red cross on his arm, unless he be a surgeon. I had some thoughts of making myself useful as a neutral in joining one of these ambulances, but I was deterred by what happened to a fellow-countryman of mine who offered his services. He was told that thousands of applicants were turned away every day, and that there already were far more persons attached to every ambulance than were necessary.

Dr. Evans, the leading spirit of the American ambulance, the man whose speciality it was to have drawn more royal teeth, and to have received more royal decorations than any other human being, has left Paris. Mr. Washburne informs me that there are still about 250 Americans here, of whom about forty are women. Some of them remain to look after their homes, others out of curiosity. "I regard," said an American lady to me to-day, who had been in a southern city (Vicksburg, if I remember rightly), when it was under fire, "a bombardment as the finest and most interesting effort of pyrotechnical skill, and I want to see if you Europeans have developed this art as fully as we have, which I doubt."

October 2nd.

I wrote to General Trochu yesterday to ask him to allow me to accompany him outside the walls to witness military operations. His secretary has sent me a reply to-day regretting that the General cannot comply with my request. The correspondent of the *Morning Post* interviewed the secretary yesterday on the same subject, but was informed that as no *laissez passer* was recognised by the Mobiles, and as General Trochu had himself been arrested, the Government would not take upon itself the responsibility of granting them. This is absurd, for I hear that neither the General nor any of his staff have been fired upon or arrested during the last week. The French military mind is unable to understand that the world will rather credit the testimony of impartial neutrals than official bulletins. As far as correspondents are concerned, they are worse off under the Republic than even under the Empire.

M. Louis Blanc's appeal to the people of England is declamatory and rhetorical in tone, and I am inclined to think that the people of England are but a Richard Doe, and that in reality it is addressed to the Parisians. M. Blanc asks the English in Paris to bear witness that the windows of the Louvre are being stuffed with sandbags to preserve the treasures within from the risks of a bombardment. I do so with pleasure. I cannot, however, bear him out in his assertions respecting the menacing calm of Paris, and the indomitable attitude of its National Guards. M. Blanc, like most of his countrymen, mistakes the wish for the will, words for deeds, promises for performance. What has happened here, and what is happening? The forts are manned with sailors, who conscientiously fire off their cannon. A position has been lost. Two sorties consisting of troops and armed peasants have been driven back. The National Guard does duty on the ramparts, drills in the streets, offers crowns to the statue of Strasburg, wears a uniform, and announces that it has made a pact with death. I sincerely trust that they may distinguish themselves, but they have not had an opportunity to do so. Not one of them has as yet honoured his draft on death. Behind their forts, their troops, their crowd of peasants, and their ramparts, they boast of what they will do. If they do really bury themselves beneath the ruins of their capital they will be entitled to the admiration of history, but as yet they are civilians of the present and heroes of the future. Noisy blusterers may be brave men. I have no doubt there are many in Paris ready to die for their country. I can, however, only deal with facts, and I find that the Parisians appear to rely for safety upon everything except their own valour. One day it is the Army of the Loire; another day it is some mechanical machine; another day dissensions among the Prussian generals; another day the intervention of Russia or Austria. In the meantime, clubs denounce the Government; club orators make absurd and impracticable speeches, the Mayor changes the names of streets, and inscribes Liberté, Egalité, and Fraternité on the public buildings. The journals of all colours, with only one or two exceptions, are filled with lies and bombast, and the people believe the one and admire the other. The Minister of the Interior placards the walls with idle proclamations, and arrests Bonapartists. Innocent neutrals are mobbed as Prussian spies, and the only prisoners that we see are French soldiers on their way to be shot for cowardice. Nothing is really done to force the Prussians to raise the siege, although the defenders exceed in number the besiegers. How can all this end? In a given time provisions and ammunition will be exhausted, and a capitulation must ensue. I wish with all my heart that the hosts of Germany may meet with the same fate as befell the army of Sennacherib; but they are not likely to be killed or forced to retreat by speeches, pacts with death, sentimental appeals, and exaggerated abuse.

The *Temps* calculates that our loss on Friday amounted to about 500 wounded and 400 killed. The object of the sortie was to blow up a bridge over the Seine, and to rouse the courage of the Parisians by obtaining a marked success at a point where the Prussians were not supposed to be in force. Neither end was attained, and consequently we are greatly depressed. Count Bismarck has not condescended to send a reply to the Corps Diplomatique, requesting to be allowed to establish postal communication with their Governments, much to the disgust of that estimable body.

The result of the pryings of the Government into the papers of their predecessors has as yet only disclosed the facts, that most of the conspiracies against the Empire were got up by the police, and that the Emperor bribed porters and postmen to open letters. His main object seems to have been to get hold of the letters of his Ministers to their mistresses. The fourth livraison of the Tuileries papers contains the report of a spy on the doings of the Russian Military Attaché. This gentleman lost some document, and observes that it can only be his Prussian colleague who took it from him. Such is diplomacy. The weather is beautiful. Women and children are making holiday in the streets. The inner line of barricades is nearly finished.

Evening.

The news of the fall of Strasburg and Toul was received by the Government here this morning, and has just been made public. "In falling," says M. Gambetta, "they cast a glance towards Paris to affirm once more the unity and indivisibility of the Republic; and they leave us as a legacy the duty to deliver them, the honour to revenge them." The Boulevards were crowded, and everyone seemed as much astonished as if they had never believed this double disaster to be possible. Many refused to credit the news. *L'Electeur Libre* proposes to meet the emergency by sending "virile missionaries into the provinces to organise a *levée en masse,* to drive from our territory the impious hordes which are overrunning it." These missionaries would, I presume, go to their posts in balloons. It never seems to occur to anyone here that the authority of a Parisian dropping down from the clouds in a parachute in any province would be contested. The right of Paris to rule France is a dictum so unquestioned in the minds of the Parisians, that their newspapers are now urging the Government to send new men to Tours to oust those who were sent there before the commencement of the siege. It occurs to no one that the thirty-eight million of Frenchmen outside Paris may be of opinion that the centralization of all power in the hands of the most corrupt and frivolous capital in the universe has had its share in reducing France to her present desperate condition, and may be resolved to assert their claim to have a voice in the conduct of public affairs. The Parisians regard all provincials as helots, whose sole business it is to hear and to obey. If the result to France of her disasters could be to free her at once from the domination of the Emperor and of Paris, she would in the end be the gainer by them.

I hear that General Vinoy expresses himself very satisfied with the soldierly bearing of the Mobiles who were under fire on Friday. It was far better, he says, than he expected. He ascribes the failure of his sortie to the forts having forewarned the Prussians by their heavy firing between three and four o'clock in the morning. M. de Rohan, " delegate of the democracy of England," has written a long letter to M. Jules Favre informing him that a friend who has arrived from London (!) has brought news of an immense meeting which has been held in favour of France, and that this meeting represents the opinion of the whole of England. M. Jules Favre, in his reply, expresses his sincere thanks "for the sentiments which have been so nobly expressed in the name of the English nation." The correspondence occupies two columns in the *Journal Officiel*. M. de Rohan's residence in England is, I should imagine, in the vicinity of Tooley-street.

October 3rd.

The *Journal Officiel* contains a decree ordering the statue of Strasburg, on the Place de la Concorde, to be replaced by one in bronze. No war news.

CHAPTER V.

October 6th.

FROM a military, or rather an engineering point of view, Paris is stronger to-day than it was two weeks ago. The defences have been strengthened. With respect, however, to its defenders, they are much what they were. The soldiers of the line and the marines are soldiers; the Mobiles and the Nationaux, with some few exceptions, remain armed citizens. Each battalion is an *imperium in imperio*. The men ignore every one except their own officers, and these officers exercise but little influence except when they consent to act in strict accordance with the feelings of those whom they are supposed to command. Some of the battalions appear to be anxious to fight, but it unfortunately happens that these are the very ones which are most undisciplined. The battalions of the *bourgeois* quarters obey orders, but there is no go in them. The battalions of some Faubourgs have plenty of go, but they do not obey orders. General Trochu either cannot, or does not, desire to enforce military discipline. Outside the enceinte, the hands of the Mobiles are against every man, but no notice is taken when they fire at or arrest officers of other corps. The Courts-martial which sit are a mere farce. I see that yesterday a Franc-tireur was tried for breaking his musket when ordered to march. He was acquitted because the court came to the conclusion that he was "un brave garçon." The application of military law to the Nationaux is regarded by these citizens as an act of arbitrary power. Yesterday several battalions passed the following resolution :—" In order to preserve at once necessary discipline and the rights of citizens, no man shall henceforward be brought before a council of war, or be awarded a punishment, except with the consent of the family council of his company."

I am not a military man, but it certainly does appear to me strange that the Prussians are allowed quietly to entrench themselves round the city, and that they are not disturbed by feints and real sorties. We can act on the inner lines, we have got a circular railroad, and we have armed men in numbers. General Trochu has announced that he has a plan, the success of which he guarantees; he declines to confide to a soul any of its details, but he announces that he has deposited it with his notary, Maître Duclos, in order that it may not be lost to the world in the event of his being killed. As yet none has fathomed this mysterious plan; it appears to contemplate defensive rather than offensive operations.

Mont Valérien now fires daily. Its commander has been changed; its former one has been removed because the protests against the silence of this fort were so loud and strong. His successor, with the fate of his predecessor before him, bangs away at every Uhlan within sight. For the commanders of forts to be forced to keep up a continual fire in order to satisfy public opinion, is not an encouraging state of things. The assertion of the Government that no reports of what is going on in France have been received from Tours is discredited. They have got themselves in a mess by their former declarations that communications with the exterior were kept up; for if they know nothing, it is asked what can these communications have been worth. Our last news from outside is derived from a Rouen newspaper of the 29th ult., which is published to-day.

A few days ago it was announced that all pledges below the value of 20fr. would be returned by the Mont-de-Piété without payment. Since then everyone has been pledging articles for sums below this amount, as a second decree of the same nature is expected. It is not a bad plan to give relief in this manner to those in want. As yet, however, there is no absolute want, and as long as the provisions last I do not think that there will be. As long as flour and meat last, everyone with more or less trouble will get his share. As the amount of both these articles is, however, finite, one of these days we shall hear that they are exhausted. The proprietors have been deprived of their power to sue for rents, consequently a family requires but little ready money to rub on from hand to mouth. My landlord every week presents me with my bill. The ceremony seems to please him, and does me no harm. I have pasted upon my mantlepiece the decree of the Government adjourning payment of rent, and the right to read and re-read this document is all that he will get from me until the end of the siege. Yesterday I ordered myself a warm suit of clothes; I chose a tailor with a German name, and I feel convinced that he will not venture to ask for payment under the present circumstances, and if he does he will not get it. If my funds run out before the siege is over I shall have at least the pleasure to think that it has not been caused by improvidence.

Some acquaintances of mine managed in the course of yesterday to get out to Villejuif without being arrested. I have not been so fortunate. I have charged the *barrières* three times, and each time have had to retire discomfited. They describe the soldiers of the line in the front as utterly despising their allies the Mobiles. They camp out without tents, in order to be ready at any moment to resist an attack.

October 7th.

Paris would hardly be recognised under its present aspect by those citizens of the Far West who are in the habit of regarding it as a place where good Americans go when they die. In the garden of the Tuileries, where *bonnes* used to flirt with guardsmen, there is an artillery camp. The guns, the pickets of horses, the tents, the camp-fires, and the soldiers in their shirt-sleeves, have a picturesque effect under the great trees. On the Place de la Concorde from morning to evening there is a mob discussing things in general, and watching the regiments as they defile with their crowns before the statue of Strasburg. In the morning the guns of the forts can be heard heavily booming; but the sound has now lost its novelty, and no one pays more attention to it than the miller to the wheel of his mill. In the Champs Elysées there are no private carriages, and few persons sitting on the chairs. The Palais de l'Industrie is the central ambulance; the Cirque de l'Impératrice a barrack. All the cafés chantants are closed. Some few youthful votaries of pleasure still patronise the merry-go-rounds; but their business is not a lucrative one. Along the quays by the river side there are cavalry and infantry regiments with the tentes d'abri. The Champ de Mars is a camp. In most of the squares there are sheep and oxen. On the outer Boulevards lines of huts have been built for the Mobiles, and similar huts are being erected along the Rue des Remparts for the Nationaux on duty. Everywhere there are squads of Nationaux, some learning the goose-step, others practising skirmishing between the carts and fiacres, others levelling their guns and snapping them off at imaginary Prussians. The omnibuses are crowded; but I fear greatly that their horses will be far from tender when we eat them. The cabbies, once so haughty and insolent, are humble and conciliatory, for Brutus and Scævola have taught them manners, and usually pay their fares in patriotic speeches. At the Arc de Triomphe, at the Trocadero, and at Passy, near the Point du Jour, there are always crowds trying to see the Prussians on the distant hills, and in the Avenue de l'Impératrice (now the Avenue Uhrich), there are always numerous admirers of Mont Valérien gazing silently upon the object of their worship. In the Faubourg St. Antoine workmen are lounging about doing nothing, and watching others drilling. In the outer faubourgs much the same thing goes on, except where barricades are being built. Round each of these there is always a crowd of men and women, apparently expecting the enemy to assault them every moment. At the different gates of the town there are companies of Mobiles and National Guards, who sternly repel every civilian who seeks to get through them. On an average of every ten minutes, no matter where one is, one meets either a battalion of Nationaux or Mobiles, marching somewhere. The asphalt of the boulevards, that sacred ground of dandies and smart dresses, is deserted during the daytime. In the evening for about two hours it is thronged by Nationaux with their wives; Mobiles who ramble along, grinning vaguely, hand in hand, as though they were in their native villages; and loafers. There, and in the principal streets, speculators have taken advantage of the rights of man to stop up the side walks with tables on which their wares are displayed. On some of them there are kepis, on others ointment for corns, on others statuettes of the two inseparables of Berlin, William and his little Bismarck, on others General Trochu and the members of the Government in gilt gingerbread. The street-hawkers are enjoying a perfect carnival—the last editions of the papers—the Tuileries' papers—the caricatures of Badinguet—portraits of the heroic Uhrich, and infallible cures for the small-pox or for worms, are offered for sale by stentorian lungs. Citizens, too, equally bankrupt alike in voice and in purse, place four lighted candles on the pavement, and from the midst of this circle of light dismally croak the "Marseillaise" and other patriotic songs. As for beggars, their name is legion; but as every one who wants food can get it at the public cantines, their piteous whines are disregarded. Lodgings are to be hired in the best streets for about one-tenth part of what was asked for them two months ago, and even that need not be paid. Few shops are shut; but their proprietors sit hoping against hope for some customer to appear. The grocers, the butchers, and the bakers, and the military tailors, still make money; but they are denounced for doing so at the clubs as bad patriots. As for the hotels, almost all of them are closed. At the Grand Hotel there are not twenty persons. Business of every kind is at a standstill. Those who have money live on it; those who have not, live on the State: the former shrug their shoulders and say, "Provided it does not last;" the latter do not mind how long it lasts. All are comparatively happy in the thought that the eyes of Europe are on them, and that they have already thrown Leonidas and his Spartans into the shade.

The Government has placarded to-day a despatch from Tours. Two armies are already formed, we are told—one at Lyons, and the other at ——. The situation of Bazaine is excellent. The provinces are ready. The departments are organising to the cry of "Guerre à outrance, ni un pouce de terrain, ni une pierre de nos forteresses!" I trust that the news is true; but I have an ineradicable distrust of all French official utterances. A partial attempt is being made to relieve the population. At the Mairies of the arrondissements, tickets are delivered to heads of families, giving them the right to a certain portion of meat per diem until January. The restaurants are still fairly supplied;

so that the system of rationing is not yet carried out in its integrity.

I am not entirely without hopes that the trial through which France is passing will in the end benefit it. Although we still brag a good deal, there is within the last few days a slight diminution of bluster. Cooped up here, week after week, the population must in the end realise the fact that the world can move on without them, and that twenty years of despotism has enervated them and made other nations their equals, if not their superiors. As Sydney Smith said of Macaulay, they have occasional flashes of silence. They sit, now and then, silent and gloomy, and mourn for the "Pauvre France." "Nous sommes bien tombés." This is a good sign, but will it outlive a single gleam of success? Shall we not in that case have the Gallic cock crowing as lustily as ever? The French have many amiable and engaging qualities, and if adversity would only teach them wisdom, the country is rich enough to rise from the ruin which has overtaken it. M. Jules Simon has published a plan of education which he says in twenty years will produce a race of virile citizens; but this is a little long to wait for a social regeneration. At present they are schoolboys, accustomed to depend on their masters for everything, and the defence of Paris is little more than the "barring out" of a girls' school. They cannot, like Anglo-Saxons, organise themselves, and they have no man at their head of sufficient force of character to impose his will upon them. The existing Government has, it is true, to a certain extent produced administrative order, but they have not succeeded in inspiring confidence in themselves, or in raising the spirit of the Parisians to the level of the situation. The Ultras say justly, that this negative system cannot last, and that prompt action is as much a political as it is a military necessity.

The sixth livraison of the Tuileries papers has just appeared. Its contents are unimportant. There is a receipt from Miss Howard, the Emperor's former mistress, showing that between 1850 and 1855 she received above five million francs. This sum was not, however, a sufficient remuneration in her opinion, for her services, as in July, 1855, she writes for more, and says "the Emperor is too good to leave a woman whom he has tenderly loved in a false position." This and several other of her letters are addressed to the Emperor's Secretary, whose functions seem to have been of a peculiarly domestic character. Indeed, the person who fulfilled them would everywhere, except at a Court, have been called something less euphonious than "secretary." A long report from M. Duvergier, ex-Secretary-General of the Police, is published respecting the *Cabinet Noir*. It is addressed to the then Minister of the Interior. It is long, and very detailed. It appears that occasionally the Emperor's own letters were opened.

I went to the Hôtel de Ville this afternoon, to see whether anything was going on there. Several battalions passed by, but they did not demonstrate *en passant*. The place was full of groups of what in England would be called the "dangerous classes." They were patiently listening to various orators who were denouncing everything in general, and the Government in particular. The principal question seemed to be the question of arms. Frenchmen are so accustomed to expect their Governments to do everything for them, that they cannot understand why, although there were but few Chassepots in the city, every citizen should not be given one. It is indeed necessary to live here and to mix with all classes to realise the fact that the Parisians have until now lived in an ideal world of their own creation. Their orators, their statesmen, and their journalists, have traded upon the traditions of the First Empire, and persuaded them that they are a superior race, and that their superiority is universally recognised. Utterly ignorant of foreign languages and of foreign countries, they believe that their literature is the only one in the world, and that a Frenchman abroad is regarded as little less than a divinity. They regard the Prussians round their city much as the citizens of Sparta would have regarded Helots, and they are so astonished at their reverses, that they are utterly unable to realise what is going on. As for trying to make them comprehend that Paris ought to enjoy no immunity from attack which Berlin or London might not equally claim, it is labour lost. "The neutrals," I heard a member of the late Assembly shouting in a café, "are traitors to civilisation in not coming to the aid of the Queen of Europe." They did their very best, they declare, to prevent Napoleon from making war. Yet one has only to talk with one of them for half an hour to find that he still hankers after the Rhine, and thinks that France wishes to be supreme in Europe.

October 8th.

Yesterday I happened to be calling at the Embassy, when a young English gentleman made his appearance, and quietly asked whether he could take any letters to England. He is to start to-day in a balloon, and has paid 5,000f. for his place. I gave him a letter, and a copy of one which I had confided on Wednesday to an Irishman who is trying to get through the lines. I hear that to-morrow the Columbian Minister is going to the Prussian Headquarters, and a friend of mine assures me that he thinks if I give him a letter by one o'clock to-day this diplomatist will take it. The Corps Diplomatique are excessively indignant with the reply they have received from Count Bismarck, declining to allow any but open despatches through the Prussian lines. They have held an indignation meeting. M. Kern, the Swiss Minister, has drawn up a protest, which has been signed by himself and all his colleagues. The Columbian

Minister is to be the bearer of it. It bombards Bismarck with copious extracts from Puffendorf and Grotius, and cites a case in point from the siege of Vienna in the 15th century. It will be remembered that Messenger Johnson, at the risk of his life and at a very great expense to the country, brought despatches to the Parisian Embassy on the second day of the siege. I recommend Mr. Rylands, or some other M.P. of independent character, to insist upon Parliament being informed what these important despatches were. The revelation will be a curious one.

Yesterday afternoon I made an excursion into the Bois de Boulogne under the convoy of a friend in power. We went out by the Porte de Neuilly. Anything like the scene of artificial desolation and ruin outside this gate it is impossible to imagine. The houses are blown up—in some places the bare walls are still standing, in others even these have been thrown down. The Bois itself, from being the most beautiful park in the world, has become a jungle of underwood. In the roads there are large barricades formed of the trees which used to line them, which have been cut down. Between the ramparts and the lake the wood is swept clean away, and the stumps of the trees have been sharpened to a point. About 8,000 soldiers are encamped in the open air on the race-course and in the Bois. Near Suresnes there is a redoubt which throws shell and shot into St. Cloud. We are under the impression that the firing from this redoubt, from Valérien, Issy, and the gunboat Farcy, which took place on Thursday morning, between 2 a.m. and 8 am., has destroyed the batteries and earthworks which the Prussians were erecting on the heights of St. Cloud and Meudon-Clamart. You, however, are better informed respecting the damage which was done than we are. When I was in the Bois the redoubt was not firing, and the sailors who man it were lounging about, exactly as though they had been on board ship. Occasionally Mont-Valérien fired a shot, but it was only a sort of visiting card to the Prussians, for with the best glasses we could see nothing of them. Indeed, the way they keep under cover is something wonderful. "I have been for three weeks in a fort," said the aide-de-camp of one of the commanders of a southern fort, "every day we have made reconnaissances, and I have not seen one single Prussian."

From what I learn, on good authority, the political situation is this. The Government consists mainly of Orleanists. When they assumed the direction of public affairs, they hoped to interest either Austria or Russia in the cause of France. They were, therefore, very careful to avoid as much as possible any Republican propagandism either at home or abroad. Little by little they have discovered that if France is to be saved it must be by herself. Some of them, however, still hanker after a Russian intervention, and do not wish to weaken M. Thiers' prospects of success at St. Petersburg. They have, however, been obliged to yield to the Republicanism of the Parisian "men of action," and they have gradually drifted into a Government charged not only with the defence of the country, but also with the establishment of a Republic. As is usual in all councils, the extreme party has gained the ascendancy. But the programme of the Ultras of the "ins" falls far short of that of the Ultras of the "outs." The latter are continually referring to '93, and as the Committee of Public Safety then saved France, they are unable to understand why the same organisation should not save it now. Their leaders demand a Commune, because they hope to be among its members. The masses support them, because they sincerely believe that in the election of a Commune Paris will find her safety. The Government is accused of a want of energy. "Are we to remain cooped up here until we are starved out?" ask the Ultras. "As a military man, I decline to make a sortie," replies General Trochu. "We are not in

'93. War is waged in a more scientific manner," whispers Ernest Picard. The plan of the Government, if plan it has, appears to be to wear out the endurance of the besiegers by a defensive attitude, until either an army from the provinces cuts off their communications, or the public opinion of Europe forces them to raise the siege. The plan of the Ultras is to save Paris by Paris; to make continual sorties, and every now and then one in such force that it will be a battle. I am inclined to think that theoretically the Government plan is the best, but it ignores the material it has to do with, and it will find itself obliged either to adopt the policy of the Ultras, or to allow them to elect a "Commune," which would soon absorb all power. The position appears to me to be a false one, owing to the attempt to rule France from Paris through an occasional despatch by balloon. What ought to have been done was to remove the seat of Government to another town before the siege commenced, and to have left either Trochu or some other military man here to defend Paris as Uhrich defended Strasburg. But the Government consisted of the deputies of Paris; and had they moved the seat of Government, they would have lost their *locus standi*. Everyone here sees the absurdity of Palikao's declaration, that Bazaine was commander-in-chief when he was invested in Metz, but no one seems to see the still greater absurdity of the supreme civil and military Government of the whole country remaining in Paris whilst it is invested by the German armies. Yesterday, for instance, a decree was issued allowing the town of Roubaix to borrow, I forget how much. Can anything be more absurd than for a provincial town to be forced to wait for such an authorisation until it receives it from Paris? It is true that there is a delegation at Tours, but so long as it is nothing but a delegation it will be hindered in its operations by the dread of doing anything which may conflict with the views of its superiors here. Paris at present is as great an incubus to France as the Emperor was. Yesterday M. Gambetta started in a balloon for Tours, and in the interests of France I shall be glad to see his colleagues one and all follow him. The day before a balloon had been prepared for him, but his nerves failed him at the last moment, and he deferred his departure for twenty-four hours.

M. Rochefort was "interviewed" yesterday by a deputation of women, who asked to be employed in the hospitals instead of the men who are now there. He promised to take their request into consideration. I was down yesterday at the headquarters of the Ambulance Internationale, and I cannot say that I think that the accusations of the Ultra-press respecting the number of young Frenchmen there is borne out by facts. There have been, however, a vast number of *petits crevés* and others who have shirked military service by forming themselves into amateur ambulances. The "sergents de ville" have received orders to arrest anyone wearing the Red Cross who is unable to produce his certificate as an *infirmier*. This has thrown the *petits crevés*—the pets of priests and old ladies—those youths who are best described by the English expression, "nice young men for a small tea-party"—into consternation. I saw yesterday one of these emasculated specimens of humanity arrayed in a suit of velvet knickerbockers, with a red cross on his arm, borne off to prison, notwithstanding his whining protests.

Another abuse which has been put an end to is that of ladies going about begging for money for the " wounded." They are no longer allowed to do so unless they have an authorisation. I have a lively recollection of an old grandaunt of mine, who used to dun every one she met for a shilling for the benefit of the souls of the natives of Southern Africa, and as I know that the shillings never went beyond ministering to the wants of this aged relative, warned by a precious experience, I have not allowed myself to be caught by the "ladies."

A singular remonstrance has been received at the British Embassy. In the Rue de Chaillot resides a celebrated English courtezan, called Cora Pearl, and above her house floats the English flag. The inhabitants of the street request the "Ambassador of England, a country the purity and the decency of whose manners is well known," to cause this bit of bunting, which is a scandal in their eyes, to be hauled down. I left Mr. Wodehouse consulting the text writers upon international law, in order to discover a precedent for the case. Colonel Claremont is doing his best to look after the interests of his fellow-countrymen. I had a prejudice against this gentleman, because I was unable to believe that any one hailing from the Horse Guards could under any circumstances make himself a useful member of society. I find, however, that he is a man of energy and good common sense, with very little of the pipeclay about him.

From Monday next a new system of the distribution of meat is to come into force. Between 450 and 500 oxen and 3,500 sheep are to be daily slaughtered. This meat is to be divided into twenty lots, one for each arrondissement, the size of each lot to be determined by the number of the inhabitants of the particular arrondissement. The lot will then be divided between the butchers in the arrondissement, at twenty centimes per kilogramme below the retail price. Each arrondissement may, however, adopt a system of rations. I suspect most of the beef I have eaten of late is horse; anyhow, it does not taste like ordinary beef. To obtain a joint at home is almost impossible. In the first place, it is difficult to purchase it; in the second place, if, when bought, it is spotted by patriots going through the street, it is seized upon on the ground that any one who can obtain a joint for love or money must be an aristocrat who is getting more than his share. I met a lady early this morning, who used to be most fashionable. She was walking along with a parcel under her shawl, and six dogs were following her. She asked me to drive them away, but they declined to go. I could not understand their sudden affection for my fair friend, until she confided to me that she had two pounds of mutton in her parcel. A tariff for horse-flesh is published to-day; it costs—the choice parts, whichever they may be—1f. 40c. the kilo.; the rest, 80c. the kilo.

Figaro yesterday published a "correspondence from Orleans." The *Official Gazette* of this morning publishes an official note from the Prefect of Police stating that this correspondence is "a lie, such as those which the *Figaro* invents every day."

Afternoon.

I have just returned from the Place de l'Hôtel de Ville. When I got there at about two o'clock six or seven thousand manifesters had already congregated there. They were all, as is the nature of Frenchmen in a crowd, shouting their political opinions into their neighbours' ears. Almost all of them were Nationaux from the Faubourgs, and although they were not armed, they wore a kepi, or some other distinctive military badge. As well as I could judge, nine out of ten were working men. Their object, as a sharp, wiry artizan bellowed into my ear, was to force the Government to consent to the election of a Commune, in order that the Chassepots may be more fairly distributed between the bourgeois and the ouvriers, and that Paris shall no longer render itself ridiculous by waiting within its walls until its provisions are exhausted and it is forced to capitulate. There appeared to be no disposition to pillage; rightly or wrongly, these men consider that the Government is wanting in energy, and that it is the representative of the bourgeoisie and not of the entire population. Every now and then some one shouted out " Vive la Commune!" and all waved their caps and took up the cry. After these somewhat monotonous proceedings had continued about half an hour, several bourgeois battalions of National Guards came along the quay, and drew up in line, four deep, before the Hôtel de Ville. They were not molested except with words. The leading ranks of the manifesters endeavoured by their eloquence to convince them that they ought not to prevent citizens peacefully expressing their opinions; but the grocers stood stolidly to their arms, and vouchsafed no reply. At three o'clock General Trochu with his staff rode along inside the line, and then withdrew. General Tamisier then made a speech, which of course no one could hear. Shortly afterwards there was a cry of " Voilà Flourens—Voilà nos amis," and an ouvrier battalion with its band playing the Marseillaise marched by. They did not halt, notwithstanding the entreaties of the manifesters, for they were bound, their officers explained, on a sacred mission, to deposit a crown before the statue of Strasburg. When I left the Place the crowd was, I think, increasing, and as I drove along the Rue Rivoli I met several bourgeois battalions marching towards the Hôtel de Ville. I presume, therefore, that General Trochu had thought it expedient to send reinforcements. "We will come back again with arms," was the general cry among the ouvriers, and unless things mend for the better I imagine that they will keep their word. The line of demarcation between the bourgeois and the ouvrier battalions is clearly marked, and they differ as much in their opinions as in their appearance. The sleek, well-fed shopkeeper of the Rue Vivienne, although patriotic, dreads disorder, and does not absolutely contemplate with pleasure an encounter with the Prussians. The wild, impulsive working man from Belleville or La Villette dreads neither Prussians without, nor anarchy within. If he could only find a leader he would blow up himself and half Paris rather than submit to the humiliation of a capitulation. Anything he thinks is better than this "masterly inactivity." Above the din of the crowd the cannon could be heard sullenly firing from the forts; but even this warning of how near the foe is, seemed to convey no lesson to avoid civil strife. Unless General Trochu is a man of more energy than I take him to be, if ever the Prussians do get into the town they will find us in the condition of the Kilkenny cats.

October 9th.

The representative of the Republic of Columbia, to whom I had given my letter of yesterday, has returned it to me, as he was afraid to cross the lines with it. The Briton who has paid for a place in a balloon is still here, and he imagines that he will start to-morrow, so I shall give him my Columbian letter and this one. I understand that any one who is ready to give assurances that he will praise everything and every one belonging to the Government, is afforded facilities for sending out letters by the Post-office balloons, but I am not prepared to give any other pledge except that I shall tell the truth without fear or favour.

The *Journal Officiel* of this morning, and the Moderate papers, boast that the Ultra manifestation of yesterday was a complete failure. As usual, they cry before they are out of the wood. After I left the Place it appears that there was a counter manifestation of bourgeois National Guards, who arrived in military order with their arms. Jules Favre addressed them. Now as far as I can make out, these battalions went to the Hôtel de Ville on their own initiative. No one, however, seems to see any incongruity in the friends of the Government making an armed demonstration as a protest against armed and unarmed demonstrations in general. The question of the municipal elections will lie dormant for a few days, but I see no evidence that those who were in favour of it have altered their minds. As far as yesterday's proceedings were concerned, they only go to prove the fact, which no one ever doubted, that the bourgeoisie and their adherents are ready to support the Government, but they have also proved to my mind conclusively that the working men as a body have entirely lost all confidence in the men at the head of affairs.

On the pure merits of the question, I think that the working men have reason on their side. They know clearly what they want—to make sorties and to endeavour to destroy the enemy's works; if this fails—to make provisions last as long as possible by a system of rationing—and then to destroy Paris rather than surrender it. The Government and their adherents are waiters on Providence, and except that they have some vague idea that the Army of the Loire will perform impossibilities, they are contented to live on from day to day, and to hope that something will happen to avert the inevitable catastrophe. I can understand a military dictatorship in a besieged capital, and I can understand a small elected council acting with revolutionary energy; but what I cannot understand is a military governor who fears to enforce military discipline, and a dozen respectable lawyers and orators, whose sole idea of Government is, as Blanqui truly says, to issue decrees and proclamations, and to make speeches. The only practical man among them is M. Dorian, the Minister of Public Works. M. Dorian is a hard-headed manufacturer, and utterly ignoring red tape, clerks, and routine; he has set all the private ateliers to work, to make cannon and muskets. I have not yet heard of his making a single speech, or issuing a single proclamation since the commencement of the siege, and he alone of his colleagues appears to me to be the right man in the right place. I do not take my views of the working men from the nonsense which is printed about them in official and semi-official organs. They are the only class here which, to use an Americanism, is not " played out." The Government dreads them as much as the Empire did; but although they are too much carried away by their enthusiasm and their impulsiveness, they are the only persons in Paris who appear to have a grain of common sense. "As for the Army of the Loire," said one of them to me this morning, "no one, except a fool or a Government employé, can believe that it will ever be able to raise the siege, and as for all these bourgeois, they consider that they are heroes because once or twice a week they pass the night at the ramparts; they think first of their shops, then of their country." "But how can you imagine that you and your friends would be able to defeat the Prussians, who are disciplined soldiers?" I asked. "We can at least try," he replied. I ventured to point out to my friend that perhaps a little discipline in the ouvrier battalions might not be a bad thing; but he insisted that the indiscipline was caused by their distrust of their rulers, and that they were ready to obey their officers. "Take," he said "Flourens' battalions. They do not, it is true, march as regularly as the bourgeois, and they have nothing but képis and old muskets; but, as far as fighting goes, they are worth all the bourgeois put together." I do not say that Trochu is not wise to depend upon the bourgeois; all I say is, that as the Empire fell because it did not venture to arm any except the regular soldiers, so will Paris render itself the laughing stock of Europe, if its defence is to depend upon an apocryphal Army of the Loire, marines from the Navy, peasants from the provinces, and the National Guards of the wealthy quarters. To talk of the heroic attitude of Paris, when the Parisians have not been under fire, is simply absurd. As long as the outer forts hold out, it is no more dangerous to "man the ramparts" than to mount guard at the Tuileries. I saw to-day a company of mounted National Guards exercising. Their uniforms were exquisitely clean, but I asked myself of what earthly use they were. Their commander ordered them to charge, when every horse butted against the one next to him. I believe a heavy gale of wind would have disconnected all these warriors from their chargers. I fully recognise the fact that the leaders of the ouvriers talk a great deal of nonsense, and that they are actuated as much by personal ambition as by patriotism; but it is certain that the individual working man is the only reality in this population of corrupt and emasculated humbugs; everyone else is a windbag and a sham.

A decree has been issued, informing all who have no means of subsistence that they will receive a certain amount of bread per diem upon application at their respective mairies. We are also told that if we wish to make puddings of the blood of oxen, we must mix pigs' blood with it, otherwise it will be unwholesome.

It has been showery to-day, and I never have witnessed a more dismal Sunday in Paris. A pigeon from Gambetta's balloon has returned, but this foolish bird lost *en route* the message which was attached to its neck.

CHAPTER VI.

October 10*th.*

IT is very curious how close, under certain conditions of wind and temperature, the cannonade appears to be, even in the centre of the town. This morning I was returning home at about two o'clock, when I heard a succession of detonations so distinctly, that I literally went into the next street, as I imagined that a house must be falling down there. It is said that the palace of St. Cloud has been destroyed.

As well as I can learn, General Burnside came into Paris mainly to discuss with Mr. Washburne the possibility of the American families who are still here being allowed to pass the Prussian lines. He saw Jules Favre, but, if he attempted any species of negotiation, it could have led to nothing, as we are so absolutely confident that the Army of the Loire will in a few days cut off the Prussian supplies, and we are so proud of our attitude, that I really believe if Jules Favre were to consent to pay a war indemnity as a condition of peace, he and his friends would be driven from power the next day.

Having nothing particularly to boast of to-day, the newspapers request the world to be good enough to turn its eyes upon Gambetta traversing space in a balloon. A nation whose Minister is capable of this heroic feat must eventually drive the enemy from its soil. The *Figaro*, in fact, hints that in all probability peace will be signed at Berlin at no very distant date. The *Gaulois*, a comparatively sensible newspaper, thus deals with this aërial voyage:—"As the balloon passed above the Prussian armies, amid the clouds and the birds, the old William probably turned to Bismarck and asked, 'What is that black point in the sky?' 'It is a Minister,' replied Bismarck; 'it is the heroic Gambetta, on his way to the Loire. In Paris he named prefects; on the Loire he will assemble battalions.' Favourable winds wafted the balloon on her course; perhaps Gambetta landed at Cahors, his natal town, perhaps somewhere else—perhaps in the arms of Crémieux, that aged lion. To-morrow the provinces will resound with his voice, which will mingle with the rattling of arms and the sound of drums. Like a trumpet, it will peal along the Loire, inflaming hearts, forming battalions, and causing the manes of St. Just and Desmoulins to rise from their graves."

Yesterday a battalion of the National Guard was drawn up before the Hôtel de Ville, but there was no demonstration of the Ultras. M. Arago, the Mayor of Paris, made a few speeches from a window, which are described as inflaming the hearts of these heroic soldiers of the country. The rain, however, in the end, sent the heroic soldiers home, and obliged M. Arago to shut his window. A day never passes without one or more of our rulers putting his head out of some window or other, and what is called "delivering himself up to a fervid improvisation." The Ultra newspapers are never tired of abusing the priests, who are courageously and honestly performing their duty. Yesterday I read a letter from a patriot, in which he complains that this caste of crows are allowed upon the field of battle, and asks the Government to decree that the last moments of virtuous citizens, dying for their country, are not to be troubled by this new horror. To-day a citizen writes as follows:—
"Why are not the National Guards installed in the

churches? Not only might they find in these edifices dedicated to an extinct superstition, shelter from the weather, but orators might from time to time from the pulpits deliver speeches. Those churches which are not required by the National Guard might serve as excellent stables for the oxen, the sheep, and the hogs, which are now parked out in the open air."

Next to the priests and the churches, the streets named after members and friends of the late Imperial family excite the ire of patriots. The inhabitants of the quartier Prince Eugène, have, I read to-day, decided that the Boulevard Prince Eugène shall henceforward be called the Boulevard Dussault, " the noble child of the Haute Vienne, who was murdered by the aides of the infamous Bonaparte."

We are not, as you might perhaps suppose, wanting in news. The French journalists, even when communications with the rest of the world were open, preferred to evolve their facts from their moral consciousness—their hand has not lost its cunning. Peasants, who play the part here of the intelligent contraband of the American civil war, bring in daily the most wonderful stories of the misery which the Prussians are suffering, and the damage which our artillery is causing them—and these tales are duly published. Then, at least three times a week we kill a Prussian Prince, and " an army " relieves Bazaine. A few days ago a troop of 1500 oxen marched into our lines, " they were French oxen, and they were impelled by their patriotism." This beats the ducks who asked the old woman to come and kill them.

The clubs appear to be divided upon the question of the " commune." In most of them, however, resolutions have been passed reaffirming their determination to hold the elections with or without the consent of the Government. Rochefort to-day publishes a sensible reply to Flourens, who called upon him to explain why he does not resign. " I have," he says, " descended into the most impenetrable recesses of my conscience, and I have emerged with the conviction that my withdrawal would cause a conflict, and this would open a breach to the Prussians. You will say that I am capitulating with my convictions; if it be so, I do not necessarily capitulate with the Prussians. I silence my political instincts; let our brave friends in Belleville allow theirs to sleep for a time." I understand that in the council which was held to decide upon the advisability of adjourning these elections, Rochefort, Simon, Ferry, and Arago voted against the adjournment, and Pelletan, Garnier Pagés, Picard, and Favre in favour of it. Trochu then decided the question in the affirmative by a threat that, if the elections were allowed to take place, he would resign.

October 11th.

The notions of a Pall Mall dandy respecting Southwark or the Tower Hamlets are not more vague than those of the Parisian bourgeois or the Professional French journalist respecting the vast Faubourgs peopled by the working men which encircle this city. From actual observation they know nothing of them. They believe them to be the homes of a dangerous class—communistic and anarchical in its tendencies, the sworn foes alike of law, order, and property. The following are the articles of faith of the journalist:— France is the world. Paris is France. The boulevards, the theatres, some fifty writers on the press, and the bourgeoisie of the fashionable quarters of the city are Paris. Within this narrow circle he may reason justly, but he never emerges from it, and consequently cannot instruct others about what he does not know himself. Since the fall of the Emperor, the Parisian bourgeois has vaguely felt that he has been surrounded by two hostile armies—the Prussian without the walls, and the working men within. He has placed his trust in Trochu, as twenty years ago he did in Cavaignac. The siege had not lasted a week before he became convinced that the Prussians were afraid of him, because they had not attacked the town; and within the last few days he has acquired the conviction, upon equally excellent grounds, that the working men also tremble before his martial attitude. On Friday last he achieved what he considers a crowning triumph, and he is now under the impression that he has struck terror into the breasts of the advocates of the Commune by marching with his battalion to the Hôtel de Ville. "We"—and by "we" he means General Trochu and himself—"we have shown them that we are not to be trifled with," is his boast from morning to night. Now, if instead of reading newspapers which only reflect his own views, and passing his time, whether on the ramparts or in a café, surrounded by men who share his prejudices, the worthy bourgeois would be good enough to accompany me to Belleville or La Villette, he would perhaps realise the fact that, as usual, he is making himself comfortable in a fool's paradise. He would have an opportunity to learn that, while the working men have not the remotest intention to pillage his shop, they are equally determined not to allow him and his friends to make Paris the laughing-stock of Europe. With them the "Commune" is but a means to an end. What they want is a Government which will carry out in sober earnest M. Jules Favre's rhetorical figure that "the Parisians will bury themselves beneath the ruins of their town rather than surrender." The lull in the "demonstrations" to urge the Government either to carry out this programme, or to associate with themselves men of energy who are ready to do so, will not last long; and when next Belleville comes to the Hôtel de Ville, it will not be unarmed. The bourgeois and the working man worship different gods, and have hardly two ideas in common. The bourgeois believes in the Army of the Loire; believes that in sacrificing the trade profits of a few months, and in catching a cold by keeping guard occasionally for a night on the ramparts, he has done his duty towards his country, and deserves the admiration of all future ages. As for burying himself beneath the ruins of his shop, it is his shop as much as his country that he is defending. He is gradually wearying of the siege; the pleasure of strutting about in a uniform and marching behind a drum hardly compensates for the pecuniary losses which he is incurring. He feels that he is already a hero, and he longs to repose upon his laurels. When Bazaine has capitulated, and when the bubble of the Army of the Loire has burst, he will, if left to himself, declare and actually believe that Paris has surpassed in heroism and endurance Troy and Saragossa; and he will accept what is inevitable —a capitulation. The working man, on the other hand, believes in no Army of the Loire, troubles himself little about Bazaine, and has confidence in himself alone. Far from disliking the siege, he delights in it. He lives at free quarters, and he walks about with a gun, that occupation of all others which is most pleasing to him. He at least is no humbug; he has no desire to avoid danger, but rather courts it. He longs to form one in a sortie, and he builds barricades, and looks forward with grim satisfaction to the moment when he will risk his own life in defending them, and blow up his landlord's house to arrest the advance of the Prussians. What will be the upshot of this radical divergence of opinion between the two principal classes which are cooped up together within the walls of Paris, it is impossible to say. The working men have, as yet, no leaders in whom they place confidence, and under whose guidance they would consent to act collectively. It may be that this will prevent them from giving effect to their views before the curtain drops; they are strongly patriotic, and they are disinclined to compromise the success of the defence by internal quarrels. Very possibly, therefore, they will be deceived by promises on the part of the Government, and assurances that Paris will fight it out to the last ditch, until the moment to act has passed. As for the bourgeois and the Government, their most powerful ally is the cry, "No division; let us all be united." They are both, however, in a radically false position. They have called upon the world to witness how a great capital can die rather than surrender; and yet, if no external agency prevents the surrender, they have no intention to fulfil their boast of dying. Any loophole for escape from the alternative in which they have thrust themselves they would welcome. "Our provisions will last three months," they say; "during this time something must happen to our advantage." "What?" I inquire. "The Army of the Loire will advance, or Bazaine will get out of Metz, or the Prussians will despair of success, or we shall be able to introduce convoys of provisions." "But if none of these prophecies are realised—what then?" I have asked a hundred times, without ever getting a clear answer to my question. By some strange process of reasoning in what, as Lord Westbury would say, they are pleased to call their minds, they appear to have arrived at the conviction that Paris never will be taken, because they are unable to realise the possibility of an event which they seem to consider is contrary to that law of nature, which has made her the capital and the mistress of the world. A victorious army is at their gates; they do not dare even to make a formidable sortie; there is no regular army in the field outside; their provisions have a limit; they can only communicate with the rest of the world by an occasional balloon; and yet they regard the idea of a foreign occupation of Paris much as we do a French invasion of England—a thing so improbable as to be barely possible.

Yesterday there were a few groups on the Place de l'Hôtel de Ville, but they were rather curious spectators than "manifesters." At about two o'clock the rappel was beaten in the Place Vendôme, and several battalions of the National Guard of the quartier marched there and broke up these groups. M. Jules Ferry's head then appeared from the window, and he aired his eloquence in a speech congratulating the friends of order on having rallied to the defence of the Government. It is a very strange thing that no Frenchman, when in power, can understand equal justice between his opponents and his supporters. The present Government is made up of men who clamoured for a Municipal Council during the Empire, and whose first step upon taking possession of the Hôtel de Ville was to decree the immediate election of a "Commune." Since then, yielding to the demands of their own supporters, they have withdrawn this decree, and now, if I go unarmed upon the Place de l'Hôtel de Ville and cry "Vive la Commune," I am arrested; whereas if any battalion of the National Guard chooses, without orders, to go there in arms and cry, "à bas la Commune," immediately it is congratulated for its patriotism by some member of the Government.

Nothing new has passed at the front since yesterday. I learn from this morning's papers, however, that Moltke is dead, that the Crown Prince is dying of a fever, that Bismarck is anxious to negotiate, but is prevented by the obstinacy of the King, that 300 Prussians from the Polish provinces have come over to our side, and that the Bavarian and Wurtemberg troops are in a state of incipient rebellion. "From the fact that the Prussian outposts have withdrawn to a greater distance from the forts," the *Electeur Libre* tells me, "it is probable that the Prussians despair of success, and in a few days will raise the siege." Most of the newspapers make merry over the faults in grammar in a letter which has been discovered and published from the Empress to the Emperor, although I doubt if there is one Frenchman in the world who could write Spanish as well as the Empress does French.

Evening.

It appears that yesterday the cheques signed by M. Flourens were not recognised by the Etat Major of his " secteur." On this he declared that he would beat the " generale " in Belleville and march on the Hôtel de Ville. The quarrel was, however, patched up—no disturbance occurred. For some reason or other M. Flourens, until he gave in his resignation, commanded five battalions of the National Guard; he has been told that he can be reelected to the command of any one of them, but that he cannot be allowed to be at the head of more than one. This man is an enthusiast, and, I am told, not quite right in his head. In personal appearance he is a good-looking gentlemanly fellow. As long as Belleville acts under his leadership there is no great fear that any danger will arise, because his own men distrust, not his good faith, but his sense.

Gambetta has sent a despatch from Montdidier, by a pigeon. He says, " Everywhere the people are rising; the Government of the National Defence is universally acclaimed."

The Papal Nuncio is going to try to get through on Thursday. He says he is anxious about the Pope—no wonder.

October 12*th.*

" What is truth ?" said jesting Pilate, and would not wait for an answer; the Parisians of 1870 are as indifferent about truth as this unjust Roman judge was. It is strange that their own want of veracity does not lead them to doubt that of others; they are alike credulous and mendacious. A man comes into a café, he relates every detail of an action in which he says he was engaged the day before; the action has never taken place, but every one believes him; one of the auditors then perhaps says that he has passed the night in a fort, and that its guns destroyed a battery which the enemy was erecting; the fort has never fired a shot, but the first speaker goes off convinced that a battery has been dismounted. For my part I have given up placing the least faith in anything I hear or read. As for the newspapers they give currency to the most incredible stories, and they affect not only to relate every shot that has been fired, but the precise damage which it has done to the enemy, and the number of men which it has killed and wounded. They have already slain and taken prisoner a far greater number of Prussians than, on any fair calculation, there could have been in the besieging army at the commencement of the siege. Since the commencement of the war the Government, the journalists, the generals, and the gossips have been engaged apparently in a contest to test the limits of human credulity. Under the Republic the game is still merrily kept up, and although the German armies are but a few miles off, we are daily treated to as many falsehoods respecting what goes on at the front as when they were at Sedan, or huddled together in those apocryphal quarries of Jaucourt. "I saw it in a newspaper," or "I was told it by an eye-witness," is still considered conclusive evidence of the truth of no matter what fact. To-day, I nearly had a dispute with a stout party, who sat near me as I was breakfasting in a café, because I ventured, in the mildest and most hesitating manner, to question the fact that an army of 250,000 men was at Rouen, and would in the course of this week attack the Prussians at Versailles. "It is here, sir," he said indignantly pointing to his newspaper; "a peasant worthy of belief has brought the news to the Editor; are we to believe no one?" There were a dozen persons breakfasting at the same time, and I was the only one who did not implicitly believe in the existence of this army. This diseased state of mind arises mainly, I presume, from excessive vanity. No Parisian is able to believe anything which displeases him, and he is unable not to believe anything which flatters his *amour propre*. He starts in life with a series of delusions, which all he has read and heard until now have confirmed. No journal dares to tell the truth, for if it did its circulation would fall to nothing. No Parisian, even if by an effort he could realise to himself the actual condition of his country, would dare to communicate his opinion to his neighbour, for he would be regarded as a traitor and a liar. The Bostonians believe that Boston is the "hub of the universe," and the Parisian is under the impression that his city is a species of sacred Ark, which it is sacrilege to touch. To bombard London or Berlin would be an unfortunate necessity of war, but to fire a shot into Paris is desecration. For a French army to live at the expense of Germany is in the nature of things; for a German army to live at the expense of Frenchmen is a barbarity which the civilised world ought to resent. If the result of the present campaign is to convince Frenchmen that, as a nation, they are neither better nor worse than other nations, and to convince Parisians that Paris enjoys no special immunity from the hardships of war, and that if it sustains a siege it must accept the natural consequences, it will not have been waged in vain, but will materially conduce to the future peace of the world. As yet—I say it with regret—for I abominate war and Prussians, and there is much which I like in the French—this lesson has not been learnt. Day by day I am becoming more convinced that a lasting peace can only be signed in Paris, and that the Parisians must be brought to understand by hard experience that, if victory means an accession of military glory, defeat means humiliation, and that the one is just as possible as the other. If the siege were raised to-morrow, the occupation of Alsace and Lorraine by an enemy would be disbelieved within six months by this vain, frivolous populace; and even if the German army does ever defile along the Boulevards, I shall not be surprised if we are told, as soon as they have withdrawn, that they never were here. Shut up in this town with its inhabitants, my sympathies are entirely on their side, but my reason tells me that Bismarck is right in insisting upon treating in Paris. Let him, if he can, come in here; let him impose upon France such a war indemnity, that every man, woman, and child in the country will curse the folly of this war for the next fifty years; and let him give up his scheme of annexation, and he will then have acted in the interests of Europe, and ultimately in those of France herself. Prussia, after the battle of Jena, was as low as France is now. Napoleon stripped her of her provinces, and she acceded to the treaty of her spoliation, but at the first favourable opportunity she protested her signature, and the world has never blamed her for so doing. France, if she is deprived of Alsace, will do the same. If she signs the treaty, it will only be binding on her until she is strong enough to repudiate it. A treaty of territorial spoliation imposed by force never has and never will bind a nation. The peace of Europe will not be lasting if France hawks about her alliance, and is ready to tender it to any Power who wishes to carry out some scheme of aggrandisement, and who will aid her to reconquer the provinces which she has lost. I have always regarded the Prussians as a disagreeable but a sensible nation, but if they insist upon the annexation of Alsace, and consider that the dismemberment of France will conduce to the unity of Germany, I shall cease to consider them as more sensible than the Gauls, with whom my lot is now cast. The Austrians used to say that their defensive system rendered it necessary that they should possess the Milanese and Venetia; but the possession of these two Italian provinces was a continual source of weakness to them, and in the end dragged them into a disastrous war. The Prussians should meditate over this, and over the hundred other instances in history of territorial greed overreaching itself, and they will then perhaps be more inclined to take a fair and impartial view of the terms on which peace ought to be made. "Moderation in success is often more difficult to practise than fortitude in disaster," says the copy-book. My lecture upon European politics is, I am afraid, somewhat lengthy, but it must be remembered that I am a prisoner, and that Silvio Pellico, under similar circumstances, wrote one of the most dreary books that it ever was my misfortune to read and to be required to admire. I return to the recital of what is passing in my prison house.

Last night and early this morning I had an opportunity to inspect the bars of the cage in which I am confined. I happened to say before a superior officer that I was very desirous to see what was going on on the ramparts and in the forts at night, but that I had as yet been foiled in my endeavours to do so, when he told me that he would take me to both, provided in any account that I might give of them I would not mention localities, which might get him into trouble, or in general anything which might afford aid and comfort to the enemy. Of course I accepted his offer, and at eleven o'clock P.M. we started on horseback. We soon struck the Rue des Remparts, and dismounted. Along the top of the ramparts there was a line of sentinels. They were so numerous in some places that they almost touched each other. Every few minutes the cry, " Sentinelles, prenez garde à vous," went along. Behind them grandes gardes and other patrols were continually passing, and we could hardly move a step without being obliged to give the password, with a bayonet in close proximity to our chests. The National Guards were sleeping, in some places in tents, in others in huts, and I found many more in the neighbouring houses. Here and there there was a canteen, where warm coffee and other such refreshments were sold, and in some places casemates were already built. In the bastions there were camps of Artillerymen, Mobiles, and Nationaux. All was very quiet, and I was agreeably surprised to find with what order and method everything was conducted. At about four o'clock this morning we passed through one of the gates, outside there were patrols coming and going, and I could see numerous regiments on each side of the road, some in tents, others sleeping in the open air, or trying to do so, for the nights are already very chilly. We were stopped almost every two minutes, and my friend had to explain who and what he was. At last we reached a fort. Here we had a long parley before we were admitted. When we got in, the day was breaking. We were taken into the room of the Commandant, with whom my friend had some business to transact. He was a sailor, and from his cool and calm demeanour, I am convinced that he will give a good account of himself if he is attacked. In the fort there were Mobiles and soldiers, and by the guns stood the sailors. I talked to several of them as they leant against their guns, or walked up and down as though they were keeping watch on deck. None of them had left the fort for the last three weeks, and they seemed to have no particular desire to go "on shore," as they called Paris. Their fire, they said, had, they believed, done considerable damage to the works which the Prussians had tried to erect, within their range. The Commandant now came out with some of his officers, and we tried to search with telescopes the distant woods which were supposed to conceal the enemy. I confess that I saw absolutely nothing except trees and some houses, which were in ruins. "Throw a shell into those houses," cried the Commandant, and off went one of the great guns. It fell wide. "Try again," he said. This time we could see through the glasses that the house had been hit, for a portion of one of the walls toppled over, and a column of dust arose. No Prussians, however, emerged. A few shots were then fired promiscuously into the woods, in order to sound the lines; and then Commandant, officers, friend and I, withdrew to breakfast. I was, of course, cautious in my conversation, and all that was said I do not care to repeat—the general feeling, however, seemed to be that the prospects of Paris defending itself successfully were considerably weakened by the " lot of lawyers " who interfered with matters about which they knew nothing. The National Guards, who I hear are to occupy the forts, were laughed at by these warriors; as for the Mobiles, it was thought that in two months they might become good soldiers, but that their discipline was most defective. " When we get them in here," said a gruff old Captain, " we do not stand their nonsense; but outside, when they are alone with their officers, they do very much what they please." The soldiers of the regular army, I was told, had recovered their *morale*, and if well led, might be depended upon. As was natural, the sailors were greatly extolled, and I think they deserved it; the best came from Brittany; and like Joe Bagstock, they are tough, sir, very tough—what are called in French, " wolves of the sea." Breakfast over, we returned to Paris in company with two or three officers, who had been given leave of absence for the day. This afternoon, hearing that egress was allowed at the Barrière de Neuilly, I started out in a fiacre, to see what was to be seen in that direction. Along the Avenue de Neuilly there were encampments of soldiers of the line and Mobiles. At the bridge of Neuilly my fiacre was stopped, but having explained to the commander of the picket that I wanted to take a walk, and shown my papers, for some reason best known to himself, he allowed me to go forward on foot. In Courbevoie all the houses were shut up, except those occupied by troops, and the windows of these were filled with sandbags. Right and left trees were being cut down, and every moment some old poplar was brought to the ground. I passed through Courbevoie, as no one seemed to notice me, and held on to the right until I struck Asnières. It is a species of French Greenwich, full of hotels, tea-gardens, and restaurants. The last time I had been there was on a Sunday, when it was crowded with Parisian bourgeois, and they were eating, drinking, dancing, and making merry. The houses had not been destroyed, but there was not a living soul in the place. On the promenade by the river the leaves were falling from the trees under which were the benches as of old. The gay signs still hung above the restaurants, and here and there was an advertisement informing the world that M. Pitou offered his hosts beer at so much the glass, or that the more ambitious Monsieur Some One Else was prepared to serve an excellent dinner of eels for 2fr., but I might as well have expected to get beer or eels in Palmyra as in this village where a few short weeks ago fish, flesh, and fowl, wine and beer were as plentiful as at Greenwich and Richmond during the season.. Goldsmith's "Deserted Village," I said to myself, and I should have repeated some lines from this admirable poem had I remembered any; as I did not, I walked on in the direction of Colombes, vaguely ruminating upon Pompeii, Palmyra, fish dinners at Greenwich, and the mutability of human things. I had hardly left Asnières, however, and was plodding along a path, when I was recalled to the realities of life by half-a-dozen Mobiles springing up from behind a low wall, and calling upon me to stop, while they enforced their order by pointing their muskets at my head. I stood still, and they surrounded me. I explained that I was an Englishman inhabiting Paris, and that I had come out to take a walk. My papers were brought out and narrowly inspected. My passport, that charter of the Civis Romanus, was put aside as though it had been a document of no value. A letter from one of the authorities, which was a species of unofficial *laissez passer*, was read, and then a sort of council of war was held about what ought to be done with me. They seemed to be innocent and well meaning peasants; they said that they had orders to let no one pass, and they were surprised that I had got so far without being stopped. I told them that they were quite right to obey their *consigne*, and that I would go back the way I had come. One of them suggested that I might be a spy, but he accepted my assurance that I was not. Another proposed to keep me as a captive until some officer passed; but I told them that this was contrary to all law, human and divine, civil and military. "Well, gentlemen," I at last said, "I will now wish you good day, my mother will be anxious about me if I do not return, otherwise I should have been happy to remain in such good society;" and with this speech I turned back and went towards Asnières; they did not follow me, but remained with their mouths open, utterly unable to grasp the idea why an Englishman should be taking a walk in the neighbourhood of Paris, and why he should have an aged mother anxiously awaiting his return in the city. N.B.—If you want to inspire a Frenchman with a sort of sentimental respect, always talk of your mother; the same effect is produced on a German by an allusion to your bride. At the bridge of Neuilly the guard had been changed, and I had a lengthy discussion whether I ought to be imprisoned or allowed to pass. I was inclined to think that I owe the latter motion being carried, to a very eloquent speech which I threw off, but this may perhaps be vanity on my part, as Mont Valérien was also discoursing at the same time, and dividing with me the attention of my auditors.

M. de Kératry has resigned his post of Prefect of the Police, and has been succeeded by M. Edmond Adam, who is said to be a man of energy. Yesterday M. Jules Ferry went down to Belleville, and delivered several speeches, which he informs us to-day in a letter were greatly applauded. The *Official Gazette* contains an intimation that M. Flourens is to be prosecuted, but I greatly question whether it is more than *brutum fulmen*. The Council of War has condemned five of the soldiers who ran away at the fight of Chatillon. Several others who were tried for the same offence have been acquitted. It is reported that an engagement took place this afternoon at Villejuif, but no details are yet known. There is no doubt that the Prussians have enlarged their circle round Paris, and that they have massed troops near Choisy-le-Roi. What these two manœuvres portend, we are all anxiously discussing.

Several balloons went off this morning. I have deluged the Post-office with letters, but I doubt if they ever get any farther. Mr. Hoar, the naval attaché of the British Embassy, also left this morning for Tours. As the Parisian fleet consists of one gun-boat, I presume that he considers that his valuable services may be utilised elsewhere.

October 13th.

Frenchmen have none of that rough and tumble energy which enables Anglo-Saxons to shake themselves, no matter under what circumstances, into some sort of shape. Left to themselves they are as helpless as children, it takes a certain time to organize them, and to evolve order from chaos, but when once the process is effected, they surpass us in administrative mechanism, and in readiness to fall into new ways. The organization of Paris, as a besieged city, is now in good working trim, and it must be admitted that its results are more satisfactory than a few weeks ago could have been anticipated. Except when some important event is taking place at the front, there are no crowds in the streets, and even the groups which used to impede circulation are now rare. The National Guards go in turn to the ramparts, like clerks to their office. In the morning the battalions are changed, and those who come off duty march to their respective "quartiers" and quietly disband. Unless there is some extraordinary movement, during the rest of the day and night there is little marching of troops. In the evening the Boulevards are moderately full from eight to ten o'clock, but now that only half the number of street lamps are lit—they look gloomy even then—at half-past ten every *café* and shop is closed, and half-an-hour later every one has gone home. There are no quarrels and no drunkards. Robberies occasionally occur, but they are rare. "Social evils" have again made their appearance, but they are not so insolently conspicuous as they were under the paternal rule of the Empire. Paris, once so gay, has become as dull as a small German capital. Its inhabitants are not in the depths of despair, but they are thoroughly bored. They are in the position of a company of actors shut up in a theatre night and day, and left to their own devices, without an audience to applaud or to hiss them. "What do you think they are saying of us in England?" is a question which I am asked not less than a hundred times every day. My interrogator usually goes on to say, that it is impossible that the heroism of the population has not elicited the admiration of the world. It seems to me that if Paris submits to a blockade for another month, she will have done her duty by France; but I cannot for the life of me see that as yet she has done anything to entitle her to boast of having set the world an example of valour.

Yesterday, it appears by the official report, there was a reconnaissance in force under General Ducrot in the direction of Bougival and Rueil. The Mobiles, we are told, behaved well, but the loss on either side was insignificant. Our amateur strategists are divided as to the expediency of taking Versailles, with the whole Prussian quartier-général, or reopening communications with the provinces by the way of Orleans. The relative advantage of these two schemes is hotly debated in the newspapers and the pothouses. A more practical suggestion to form mobilised regiments of National Guards by taking the most active men from the existing battalions is being seriously considered by the Government. This is all the news, except that a battalion of Amazons is in course of formation. They are to wear trousers, kepis, and blouses, and to be armed like the National Guard. The walls are covered with large placards inviting enlistments. It is reported that the Government are in possession of evidence to show that many of those female ornaments of the Imperial Court who were called cocodettes, and who spent in dress every year three times the annual income of their husbands, were in the pay of Bismarck. This intelligent and unscrupulous gentleman also, it is said, has a corps of spies recruited from all nations, consisting of good-looking men of pleasant address and of a certain social standing, whose business it was to insinuate themselves into the good graces of the beauties of Parisian society, and then endeavour to pick up the secrets of their husbands and friends. I am inclined to think that there is a good deal of truth in this latter allegation, because for several years I have known fascinating foreigners who used to frequent the clubs, the Bois, and the salons of the great world, and lead a joyous life without having any recognised means of existence. I have been struck more than once with the anxiety of these gentry to hook themselves on to the train of any lady who was either the relative of a man in power or who was supposed to be on intimate terms with a minister or a courtier. Every man, said Sir Robert Walpole, has his price, and Bismarck might be justified in making the same reflection as far as regards what is called European good society.

The eighth *livraison* of the Tuileries papers has appeared; it contains two letters from General Ducrot to General Frossard, a despatch from the French Foreign-office to Benedetti, a report on France by Magne, and a letter from a prefect to Pietri. From the few papers of any importance which have been discovered in the Imperial palaces, our friend Badinguet must have had an inkling when he last left Paris that he might not return, and must have put his papers in order, *i.e.*, in the fire-place.

CHAPTER VII.

Evening.

I AM very much afraid that it will be some time before my letters reach you, if indeed they ever do. I had entrusted one to Lord Lyons' butler, a very intelligent man, who was to accompany Mr. Hoar, our naval attaché, to Tours; but, alas, they did not get further than the Prussian lines at Epinay, and they are back again at the Embassy. Mr. Hoar had with him a letter from the Nuncio to the Crown Prince, but the officer in command of the outpost declined to take charge of it. The Columbian Minister, too, who was charged with the protest of the Corps Diplomatique to Bismarck on account of his refusal to allow their despatches to go out, has also returned, to re-peruse Grotius and Puffendorf, in order to find more precedents with which to overwhelm Bismarck. The Greek Minister has managed to run the blockade. A son of Commodore Lynch made an attempt to get out, but after being kept twelve hours at the Prussian outposts, and fired on by the French, he has returned to share our imprisonment. This morning I read in one of the papers a wonderful account of what Mr. Lynch had seen when with the Prussians. Meeting him this evening, I asked him whether it was true. He told me that he had already been to the newspaper to protest against its appearance, as every statement in it was destitute of foundation. He could, however, get no redress; the editor or his *locum tenens* told him that one of their reporters had given it him, and that he knew nothing more about it. This is an instance of the reckless mode in which the business of journalism is conducted here.

I made two visits this afternoon, one to a pothouse in Belleville, the other to a countess in the Faubourg St. Germain. I went to the former in order to find out what the Bellevillites thought of things in general. I found them very discontented with the Government, and divided in opinion as to whether it would be more in the interests of the country to turn it out at present, or to wait until the Prussians were defeated, and then do so. They are all very angry at the counter-manifestation of the bourgeois against them in the Commune. "The Government," said one of them to me, "is weak and incapable, it means to deceive us, and is thinking more of bringing back the Comte de Paris than of defending the town. We do not wish it to be said that we compromise the success of the defence by agitation, but either it must show more energy, or we will drive it from the Hôtel de Ville." I quoted to my friend Mr. Lincoln's saying, about the mistake of changing a horse when halfway over a river. "That is all very well," replied a citizen, who was discussing some fiery compound at a table near me, "but we, unfortunately, have only an ass to carry us over, and he will be swept away down the stream with us on his back." Somebody now asked me what I was doing in Paris. I replied that I was the correspondent of an English newspaper. Several immediately shook me by the hand, and one of them said to me, "Pray tell your countrymen that we men of Belleville are not what the bourgeois and their organs pretend. We do not want to rob our neighbours; all we ask is, to keep the Prussians out of Paris." He said a good deal more which it is needless to repeat, but I willingly fulfil his request, to give my testimony that he, and thousands like him, who are the bugbear of the inhabitants of the richer districts of the city, are not by any means as black as they are painted. They are impulsive and somewhat inclined to exaggerate their own good qualities and the faults of others —they seem to think that anyone who differs from them must be a knave or a fool, and that the form of government which they prefer ought at once to be established, whether it obtains the suffrages of the majority or not; their knowledge, too, of the laws of political and social economy is, to say the least, vague; but they are honest and sincere, mean what they say, do not mistake words for deeds, and after the dreary inflated nonsense one is compelled to listen to from their better educated townsmen, it is refreshing to talk with them. From the Belleville pothouse I went to the Faubourg St. Germain. In this solemn abode of a fossil aristocracy I have a relative—a countess. She is, I believe, my cousin about sixteen times removed, but as she is the only person of rank with whom my family can claim the most distant relationship, we stick to the cousinship and send her every year cheap presents, which she reciprocates with still more meretricious *bonbons*. When I was ushered into her drawing-room, I found her taking afternoon tea with two old gentlemen, also a mild young man, and a priest. A "Lady of the Faubourg," who has any pretensions to beauty, but who is of Cornelia's mood, always has two or three old gentlemen, a mild young man, and a priest, who drop in to see her almost every afternoon. "Are you come to congratulate us?" said my cousin, as I entered. I kissed her hand. "What," she continued, "have you not heard of the victory?" I opened my eyes. "Madame," said one old gentleman, "alludes to the taking of Choisy le Roy." I mildly hinted that the news of this important event had not reached me. "Surprising!" said he, "I saw Vinoy myself yesterday." "It does not follow," I suggested, "that he has taken Choisy to-day." "Monsieur, perhaps, is not aware," jeered old gentleman No. 2, "that 60,000 men have broken through the Prussian lines, and have gone to the relief of Bazaine." "I have not the slightest doubt of the fact; it is precisely what I expected would occur," I humbly observed. "As for the victory," struck in the mild young man, "I can vouch for it; I myself have seen the prisoners." "Surely," added my cousin, "you must have heard the cannon; ah! you English are all the same; you are all Prussians, your Queen, your '*Tims*,' and all of you." I took refuge in a cup of tea. One old gentleman came and stood before me. I knew well what was coming—the old, old question. "Well, what does England think of our attitude now?" I said that only one word could properly qualify it— sublime. "We are sacrificing our lives," said the mild young man. I looked at him, and I greatly fear that I smiled— "that is to say," he continued, "we are prepared to sacrifice them." "Monsieur is in the Garde Nationale?" I asked. "Monsieur is the only son of a widow," put in my cousin. "But I mean to go to the ramparts for all that," added the orphan. "You owe yourself to your mother," said the priest—" and to your country," I suggested, but the observation fell very flat. "It is a grand sight," observed one old gentleman, as he put a third lump of sugar in his tea, and another into his pocket, " a glorious spectacle, to see a population that was supposed to be given up to luxury, subsisting cheerfully week after week upon the simplest necessaries of existence." "I have not tasted game once this year, and the beef is far from good," sighed old gentleman No. 2; "but we will continue to endure our hardships for months, or for years if need be, rather than allow the Prussians to enter Paris." This sort of Lacedemonian twaddle went on during the whole time of my visit, and my cousin evidently was proud of being surrounded by such Spartans. I give a specimen of it, as I think these worthies ought to be gratified by their heroic sacrifices being made public. "I'd rough it in a campaign as well as any linesman," said the cornet of her Majesty's Life Guards; "give me a pint of claret and a chicken every day, or a cut at a joint, and I would ask for nothing more;" and the Belgravian knight's idea of the discomforts of war is very like that of the beleaguered Gaul. Want may come, but as yet never has a large city enjoyed greater abundance of bread and meat. The poor are nourished by the State. The rich have, perhaps, some difficulty in getting their supply of meat, but this is the fault of a defective organization; in reality they are only deprived of those luxuries the habitual use of which has impaired the digestions of half of them. It is surely possible to exist for a few weeks on beef, mutton, flour, preserved vegetables, wine, milk, eggs, and every species of sauce that cook ever contrived. At about seven, provisions at the restaurants sometimes run short. I dined to-day at a bouillon at six o'clock for about half-a-crown. I had soup, salt cod, beef (tolerable, but perhaps a shade horsey), rabbit, French beans, apple fritters, grapes, and coffee. This bill of fare is a very long way from starvation.

October 14*th.*

According to the official account of yesterday's proceedings, General Trochu was anxious to discover whether the Prussians were in force upon the plateau of Chatillon, or had withdrawn from that position. The villages of Chatillon, Bagneux, and Clamart, were consequently attacked, and after an artillery and musketry engagement, the Prussian reserves were brought up, thus proving that the report that they had withdrawn was unfounded. The retreat then commenced under the fire of the forts. About 100 prisoners were taken; in the evening they were brought to the Place Vendôme. The newspapers are one and all singing peans over the valour of the Mobiles—those of the Côte d'Or most distinguished themselves. Although the whole thing was little more than a reconnaissance, its effect has been electrical. The battalions of the National Guard sing the Marseillaise as of old, and everyone is full of confidence. Some of the officers who were engaged tell me that the Mobiles really did show coolness under fire, and that they fought well with the bayonet in the village of Bagneux. Between carrying an advanced post and forcing the Prussian army to raise the siege, there is of course a slight difference, but I see no reason why these strong, healthy peasants should not become excellent troops. What they want are commanders who are old soldiers, and would force them to submit to regular discipline. The *Official Gazette* contains the following decree: "Every officer of the National Guard whose antecedents are of a nature to compromise the dignity of the epaulette, and the consideration of the corps in which he has been elected, can be revoked. The same punishment may be inflicted upon those officers who render themselves guilty of continuous bad conduct, or of acts wanting in delicacy. The revocation will be pronounced by the Government upon a report of the Minister of War." If the Government has enough determination to carry out this decree, the National Guard will greatly profit by it.

Yesterday evening at the Folies Bergères a demonstration was made against the Princes of the Orleans family, who are said to be in command of an army at Rouen. It was determined to send a deputation to the Government on the subject. This move is important, as the Folies Bergères is rather the rendezvous of the Moderate Republicans than of the Ultras.

A letter from Havre, dated October 4, has been received, in which it is stated that the ex-Emperor has issued an address to the nation. I do not know what his chances of restoration are in the provinces, but here they are absolutely hopeless. The Napoleonic legend was founded upon victories. Since the name of Napoleon has been coupled with the capitulation of Sedan, it is loathed as much as it once was adulated. Apart from his personal following, Napoleon III. has not 100 adherents in Paris.

October 15th.

Colonel Loyd Lindsay arrived here yesterday morning with £20,000 for the ambulances, and leaves to-morrow with the Comte de Flavigny, the President of the Ambulance Internationale. Mr. Herbert is getting anxious respecting the future of the destitute English still here; but with all due respect to our charitable friends at home, it appears to me that Paris is rich enough to look after its own wounded. The flag of the Cross of Geneva waves over several thousand houses, and such is the desire of brave patriots to become members of an ambulance corps, that the services of neutrals are declined.

October 16th.

We are told that the ex-Emperor has issued a proclamation, *urbi orbique*, and that his agents are engaged in London and elsewhere in intriguing in his behalf. I cannot believe that they have any chance of gaining adherents to their master's cause in England. That halo of success which blinded a portion of the English press to the iniquities which were concealed beneath the Imperial purple has now disappeared. The publication of the papers discovered in the Tuileries has stripped despotism of its tinsel, and has revealed the vile and contemptible arts by which a gallant nation has been enslaved. The Government of Napoleon, as Mr. Gladstone said of that of Bomba, "was a negation of God upon earth." His councillors were bold bad men, ever plotting against each other, and united alone in a common conspiracy to grow rich at the expense of their country, *creverunt in exitio patriæ*. His court was the

El Dorado of pimps and parasites, panders and wantons. For eighteen long years he retained the power, which he had acquired by perjury and violence, by pandering to the baser passions of his subjects, and by an organized system of fraud, mendacity, and espionnage. Beneath his blighting rule French women only sought to surpass each other in reckless extravagance, and Frenchmen lost the courage which had half redeemed their frivolity. Honest citizens there were, indeed, who protested against these Saturnalia of successful villany and rampant vice, but few listened to their warnings. They were jeered at by the vulgar, fined, imprisoned, or banished by Ministers and magistrates. All that was good, noble, and generous in the nation withered in the uncongenial atmosphere. The language of Pascal and of Corneille became the medium of corrupting the minds of millions. The events of the day were some actress who had discovered a new way to outrage decency, or some new play which deified a prostitute or an adulteress. Paris became the world's fair, to which flocked the vain, the idle, and the debauched from all corners of the globe. For a man to be rich, or for a woman to find favour in the eyes of some Imperial functionary, were ready passports to social recognition. The landmarks between virtue and vice were obliterated. The Court lady smiled in half-recognition on the courtezan, and paid her homage by endeavouring to imitate her dress and her manners. Cardsharpers and stockjobbers, disreputable adventurers and public functionaries were intimate friends. No one able to insult modest industry by lavish ostentation was asked how he had acquired his wealth. Honour and honesty were prejudices of the past. What has been the consequence? It is a comment upon despotism, which I hope will not be lost upon those who extol the advantages of personal government, and who would sacrifice the liberty of all to the concentrated energy of one. The armies of France have been scattered to the winds; the Emperor, who knew not even how a Cæsar should die, is a prisoner; his creatures are enjoying their booty in ignoble ease, not daring even to fight for the country which they have betrayed. The gay crowd has taken to itself wings; an emasculated bourgeoisie, grown rich upon fashionable follies, and a mob of working men, unused to arms, and distrustful even of their own leaders, are cowering beneath the ramparts of Paris, opposing frantic boasts, pitiful lamentations, unskilled valour, to the stern discipline of the legions of Germany, whose iron grasp is contracting closer and closer every day round the vaunted capital of modern civilization. You know better than we do what is passing in the provinces, but I can answer for it that the Parisians, low as they have fallen, are not so lost to every impulse of honour as to be ready to welcome back in triumph the prime cause of their degradation, the man of December and of Sedan. Titania, in the *Midsummer Night's Dream*, idealizes the weaver, and invests him with every noble attribute, and then as soon as she regains her senses, turns from him with disgust and exclaims, "Oh, how mine eyes do loathe thee now." So it was and so it is with Paris and Napoleon, "None so poor to do him honour now."

The Government is daily becoming more and more military, and the Parisian Deputies are becoming little more than lay figures. M. Gambetta, the most energetic of them, has left for the provinces. MM. Jules Favre, Picard, and Pelletan are almost forgotten. Rochefort devotes himself to the barricades, and M. Dorian, a hard-headed manufacturer, is occupying himself in stimulating the manufacture of cannon, muskets, and munitions of war. These gentlemen, with the exception of the latter, are rather men of words than of action. They do neither harm nor good. Of General Trochu, into whose hands, by the mere force of circumstances, all civil and military authority is concentrating, *Bonum virum, facile dixeris, magnum libenter.* He is, I believe, a good general and a good administrator. Although he awakens no enthusiasm, confidence is felt by the majority in his good sense. It is thought, however, that he is wanting in that energy and audacity which are requisite in a leader, if victory is to be wrested from the Germans. He forgets that time is not his ally, and that merely to hold Paris until that surely inevitable hour arrives when the provisions are exhausted will neither save France nor her capital. He is a man slow to form a plan, but obstinate in his adherence to it; unwilling to move until he has his forces perfectly under control, and until every administrative detail is perfected—better fitted to defend Troy for ten years than Paris for a few months—in fact, a species of French M'Clellan.

We are now in a position, according to our military authorities, to hold out as long as our provisions last. If Paris does this, without being so heroic as her citizens imagine that she already is, she will have done her duty by France. Nicholas said, when Sebastopol was besieged, that winter was his best ally; and winter will soon come to our aid. The Prussians are a long way from their homes; if the provinces rise it will be difficult for them to keep their lines of communication open, and to feed their troops. It may also be presumed that they will be harassed by the 300,000 armed men who are cooped up here, and who are acting on the inner circle. Cannon are being cast which, it is expected, will render the sorties far more effective. On the other hand, the question has not yet been solved whether the Parisians will really support the hardships of a siege when they commence, and whether there will not be internal dissensions. At present the greatest confidence is felt in ultimate success. The Parisians cannot realise to themselves the possibility of their city being taken; they are still, in their own estimation, the representative men of "la grande nation," and they still cite the saying of Frederick the Great that, were he King of France, not a sword should be drawn without his permission, as though this were a dictum that a sage had uttered yesterday. They feed every day on the vaunts and falsehoods which their newspapers offer them, and they digest them without a qualm. While they expect the provinces to come to their aid, they are almost angry that they should venture to act independently of their guidance. They are childishly anxious to send out commissaries to take the direction of affairs in Normandy and Touraine, for the provincials are in their eyes slaves, born to serve and to obey the capital. Indeed, they have not yet got over their surprise that the world should continue to move now that it is deprived of its pivot. All this folly may not prevent their fighting well. Fools and braggarts are often brave men. The Parisians have an indomitable pride, they have called upon the world to witness their achievements, and the thought of King William riding in triumph along the Boulevards is so bitter a one, that it may nerve them to the wildest desperation. If, however, Bazaine capitulates, and the armies of the Loire and of Lyons are only the figments of their own brains, it may be that they will bow to what they will call destiny. "Heaven has declared against us," is an expression that I already hear frequently uttered. It is indeed impossible to predicate here, as it is in London, what may be the mood of this fickle and impulsive population a week hence. All I can positively say is, that at the present moment they are in "King Cambyses' vein." We ought not to judge a foreign nation by our own standard, but it is impossible not to re-echo Lord Bolingbroke's "poor humanity" a hundred times a day, when one reads the inflated bombast of the newspapers, and hears the nonsense that is talked by almost everyone; when one sees the Gaul marching off to the ramparts convinced, because he wears a kepi and a sword, that he is a very Achilles; when regiments solemnly crown a statue with laurel crowns, and sign round robins to die for their country. All these antics ought not to make one forget that these men are fighting for the holiest of causes, the integrity of their country, and that the worst of Republics is better than the best of feudal monarchies; but I confess I frequently despair of their ever attaining to the dignity of free men, until they have been further tried in the school of adversity.

Yesterday M. Jules Favre, in reply to a deputation from the Club of the Folies Bergères, stated that he was not aware that the Orleans Princes were in France. "If the army of succour," he said, "comes to us, we will extend our hands to it; but if it marches under the Orleans banner, the Government will not recognise that banner. As a man, I deplore the law which proscribes this family; as a citizen and a politician, I maintain it. Even if these Princes were to abdicate their dynastic pretensions, the Government will remember Bonaparte, and how he destroyed the Republic in 1851, and energetically protest against their return." This reply when reported to the Club was greatly applauded. Probably none of its members had ever heard the proverb that beggars ought not to be choosers.

The event of the day has been the arrest of M. Portales, the editor of the *Vérité*. This newspaper, after asserting that the Government has received news from the provinces, asks a series of questions. In the afternoon the editor was arrested, and this morning the *Official Gazette* thus replies to the queries: No news has been concealed. The last official despatch received is one from Gambetta, announcing his safe arrival at Montdidier. The Government has received an old copy of the *Standard*, but this journal, "notoriously hostile to France," contained sensational intelligence, which appeared absolutely untrue. To-day it has received a journal of Rouen of the 12th, and it hastens to publish the news derived from this source. Bismarck never proposed an armistice through Burnside. The General only unofficially informed Trochu that Bismarck's views were not altered since he had met Favre at Ferrières, when he stated that "if he considered an armistice realizable for the convocation of an Assembly, he would only grant it for forty-eight hours; he would refuse to include Metz, or to permit provisions to enter Paris, and exclude from the Assembly our brave and unhappy compatriots of Alsace and Lorraine." The *Official Gazette* then gives extracts from the Rouen paper, which are very contradictory. Our newspapers, however, in commenting on them, come to the conclusion that there are two armies in the field well equipped, and that they have already achieved important successes. The situation also of Bazaine is proved to be excellent. *Quem Deus, &c.*

Two of the mayors have ordered all crucifixes to be removed from the ambulances in their arrondissements; their conduct is almost universally blamed. The enlistment of the Amazons, notwithstanding the efforts of the Government, still continues. The pretty women keep aloof from the movement; the recruits who have already joined are so old and ugly that possibly they may act upon an enemy like the head of Medusa.

October 17th.

The newspapers to-day almost universally blame the arrest of M. Portales. This gentleman, with M. E. Picard, started, just before the siege commenced, a paper called *L'Electeur Libre.* It was thought that M. Picard's position as a member of the Government rendered it impossible for him to remain the political director of a newspaper, so he withdrew, but appointed his brother as his successor. This did not please M. Portales, who with most of the staff left the *Electeur Libre*, and founded *La Vérité.* It is, therefore, somewhat suspicious that this new paper should be the

K

only one whose editor has been imprisoned for circulating "falsehoods." In the first place, almost every French newspaper of any circulation trades upon lies; in the second place, it appears that in this particular case the *Vérité* only put in the sensational form of questions a letter from the *Times*' correspondent at Tours. This letter it publishes to-day, and appeals to the public to judge between M. Portales and M. Picard. The fact is that this population can neither tell nor hear the truth. The English papers are one and all in bad odour because they declined to believe in the Emperor's victories, and if a *Daily News* comes in here with an account of some new French reverse, I shall probably be imprisoned. Government and people have laid down this axiom, "bad news false news." General Trochu again appears in print in a long circular letter to the commandants of the corps d'armée and the forts. He desires them each to send him in a list of forty men who have distinguished themselves, and their names and no others will appear in the order of the day. "We have," says the General, "to cause this grand thought, which monarchies decline to recognise but which the Republic should hold sacred, to penetrate into the minds of our officers and soldiers—opinion alone can worthily recompense the sacrifice of a life; remember that if you make a bad choice of the men you recommend, you will gravely compromise your responsibility towards me, and at the same time the great principle which I would have prevail." The General is a very copious writer, and it seems to me that he would do well to remember that if he can only drive away the Prussians, he will have time enough afterwards to introduce his "grand thoughts" into the army. Two things, says Thiers, impose upon Frenchmen—military glory and profound silence. Trochu has the first to win, and he apparently scorns the latter. He is a species of military doctrinaire, and he finds it difficult to avoid lecturing soldiers or civilians at least once a day. I was looking at him the other day, and I never saw calm, serene, self-complacency more clearly depicted upon the human countenance. Failure or success will find him the same—confident in himself, in his plans, and his grand thoughts. If he eventually has to surrender, he will console himself by coupling with the announcement of his intention many observations—very wise, very beautiful, very lengthy, and very stale.

Mr. Herbert tells me that there are more English here than he had imagined. He estimates their number at about 4000, about 800 of whom are destitute. The funds at his disposal for them would have already run short had not Mr. Wallace again largely contributed to them. They are fed with rice and Liebig, but the great difficulty has been to find fat to add to this mess. The beasts that are killed are so lean that it is almost impossible to obtain it except at an extravagant price. Tallow candles have been seriously suggested, but they too are scarce. The English, as foreigners, cannot claim rations, and were it not for the kindness of Mr. Herbert and Mr. Wallace, they would, I am afraid, really starve. All their rich fellow-countrymen, with the exception of Mr. Wallace, have left Paris, and even if they were here they would not be able to do anything unless they had money with them, as it is impossible to draw on London. Winter is coming on, and clothes and fuel as well as food will be wanted. I would suggest to the charitable in England to send contributions to Mr. Herbert. I can hardly suppose that Count Bismarck would decline to let the money pass through the Prussian lines. I hear that Mr. Washburne has obtained a half permission to send his countrymen out of the town, if so, I think it would be well if the poor English were also to leave; but this, of course, will require money.

The Nuncio has managed to get away; he declined to take letters with him. E. Washburne, United States

Minister, Lopez de Arosemana, Chargé d'Affaires of Honduras, Duke Aquaviva, Chargé d'Affaires of Monaco, and the other members of the Corps Diplomatique still here, have signed and published a protest against the refusal of Count Bismarck to let their despatches to their respective Governments leave Paris sealed. That Mr. Washburne should be indignant I can well understand; but although I do not personally know either Lopez de Arosemana, or Aquaviva, Chargé d'Affaires of Monaco, I can understand Count Bismarck not being absolutely satisfied with the assurance of these potent signors that nothing except official despatches should pass under their seal. That the Prince of Monaco should be debarred for a few months from receiving communications from his representative in Paris, may perhaps be unpleasant to him, but must be a matter of the most profound indifference to the rest of the world.

It is somewhat amusing to observe how justice is administered when any dispute arises in the streets. The sergents-de-ville immediately withdraw, in order not to prejudice the question by their presence. A sort of informal jury is impanelled, each disputant states his case, and the one who is thought by the tribunal to be in fault, is either taken off to prison, or cuffed on the spot. I have bought myself a sugar-loaf hat of the First Republic, and am consequently regarded with deference. To-day a man was bullying a child, and a crowd gathered round him; I happened just then to come up, room was immediately made for me and my hat, and I was asked to give my opinion as to what ought to be done with the culprit. I suggested kicking, and as I walked away, I saw him writhing under the boots of two sturdy executioners, amid the applause of the spectators. "The style is the man," said Buffon; had he lived here now he would rather have said "the hat is the man." An English doctor who goes about in a regulation chimney-pot has already been arrested twenty-seven times; I, thanks to my revolutionary hat, have not been arrested once. I have only to glance from under its brim at any one for him to quail.

October 18*th.*

A decree has been issued ordering a company of 150 men to be mobilised in each battalion of the National Guard. Three of these companies are together to form a mobilised battalion, and to elect their commander. The *Journal Officiel* contains two long reports upon the works of defence which have been executed since the commencement of the siege. They give the number of guns on each bastion, and the number of rounds to each gun, the number of cartridges, and the amount of powder in store. Unless these reports be patriotic fictions, it seems strange to publish them in the newspapers, as they must inevitably fall into the hands of the Prussians. Be this as it may, I do not feel at liberty to quote from them. General Ducrot publishes a letter protesting against a statement of the German journals that he escaped from Pont-à-Mousson when on parole. He asserts that his safe-conduct had been given up, and that he consequently was free to get away if he could. His evasion is very similar to that of F. Meagher from Australia. M. Jules Favre publishes a circular to the French Diplomatic Agents abroad, in reply to Count Bismarck's report of the meeting at Ferrières. You will probably have received it before you get this letter. It is more rhetorical than logical—goes over the old ground of the war having been declared against Napoleon rather than against the French nation, and complains that " the European Cabinets, instead of inaugurating the doctrine of mediation, recommended by justice and their own interests, by their inertness authorise the continuation of a barbarous struggle, which is a disaster for all and an outrage on civilization." M. Jules Favre cannot emancipate himself from the popular delusions of his country, that France can go to war without, if vanquished, submitting to the consequences, and that Paris can take refuge behind her ramparts without being treated as a fortified town; at the same time he very rightly protests against the Prussian theory of the right of conquest implying a moral right to annex provinces against the wishes of their inhabitants.

Few have been in Paris without having driven through the Avenue de l'Impératrice. What has been done there to render it impregnable to attack will consequently give an idea what has been done everywhere. At the Bois de Boulogne end of the avenue the gate has been closed up by a wall and a moat; behind them there is a redoubt. Between this and the Arc de Triomphe there are three barricades made of masonry and earth, and three ditches. Along the grass on each side of the roadway, the ground has been honey-combed, and in each hole there are pointed stakes. In every house Nationaux are billeted; in two of them there are artillerymen. In the Avenue de Neuilly, and in many other parts of the town, the preparations against an assault are still more formidable. Bagatelles, the villa of the late Lord Hertford, has been almost gutted by 2,000 Mobiles, who make it their headquarters. We are exceedingly proud of having burnt down St. Cloud, and we say that if this does not convince the Prussians that we are in earnest, we will burn down Versailles. I wonder whether the proverb about cutting off one's nose to spite one's face has an equivalent in French.

CHAPTER VIII.

October 19th.

A DESPATCH is published this morning from M. Gambetta, giving a very hopeful account of things in the provinces. As, however, this gentleman on his arrival at Tours issued a proclamation in which he announced that there were one-third more guns in Paris than it is even pretended by the Government that there are, I look with great suspicion upon his utterances. The latest declaration of the Government differs essentially from that which was made at the commencement of the siege. A friend of mine pointed out to one of its members this discrepancy, when he replied that the Government had purposely understated their resources at first. This may be all very fair in war, but it prevents a reasonable person placing the slightest confidence in anything official. Dr. Johnson did not believe in the earthquake at Lisbon for one year after the news reached London, and I shall not believe in the resources of the provinces until they prove their existence by raising the siege. I am very curious to discover what is thought of Paris by the world. There is but one step from the sublime to the ridiculous. If really by holding out for several months the situation can be altered for the better, the Parisians are right to do so, but if the Government is only humbugging them with false intelligence, if they are simply destroying their own villages in the neighbourhood, and exhausting their resources within the town, whilst a Prussian army is living at the cost of their country, it seems to me that they are acting like silly schoolboys rather than wise men, and that there really is something in the sneer of Bismarck that the Deputies of Paris are determined, *coûte qui coûte*, to preserve the power with which the hazards of a revolution invested them.

The newspapers this morning are full of articles lauding M. Jules Favre's circular, and reviling the proposals of Bismarck. The following extract from the *Liberté* will serve as an example of their usual tone :—" A word of gratitude to the great citizen, to Jules Favre. Let him know that his honest, eloquent, and brave words give us strength, dry our tears, and cure our wounds. Poor and dear France! Provinces crushed and towns blockaded, populations ruined, and thou, O Paris, once the city of the fairies, now become the city of the grave times of antiquity, raise thy head, be confident, be strong. It is thy heart that has spoken, it is thy soul unconquered, invincible, the soul of thy country that has appealed to the world and told it the truth." The *Liberté*, after this preliminary burst, goes on to say, that it knew before that Bismarck was everything that was bad, but that it has now discovered that, besides possessing every other vice, he is a liar, and if there is one thing that France and the *Liberté* cannot endure, it is a man who does not tell the truth. If the Prussians are not driven out of France by words, it certainly will be a proof that mere words have very little effect in shaping the destinies of nations.

Each person now receives 100 grammes of meat per diem, the system of distribution being that every one has to wait on an average two hours before he receives his meat at the door of a butcher's shop. I dine habitually at a bouillon; there horseflesh is eaten in the place of beef, and cat is called rabbit. Both, however, are excellent, and the former is a little sweeter than beef, but in other respects much like it; the latter something between rabbit and squirrel, with a flavour all its own. It is delicious. I recommend those who have cats with philoprogenitive proclivities, instead of drowning the kittens, to eat them. Either smothered in onions or in a ragout they are excellent. When I return to London I shall frequently treat myself to one of these domestic animals, and ever feel grateful to Bismarck for having taught me that cat served up for dinner is the right animal in the right place.

I went last night to the Theatre of the Porte St. Martin; it has become the clique of the optimists, and speeches were delivered to prove that everything was for the best in the best of worlds, and poetry was recited to prove that the Prussians must eventually be defeated. The chair was taken by M. Coquerel, who with great truth said that Paris had fallen so low that the siege might be considered almost a blessing, and that the longer it lasted, the more likely was it to aid in the work of regeneration, which alone can make this world a globe of honourable men and honest women. It will, indeed, do the Parisians all the good in the world to keep guard on the ramparts instead of doing nothing but gossip till one or two in the morning at cafés.

General Trochu, that complete letter-writer, to-day replies to General Ducrot, telling him that his proclamation respecting his evasion from Pont-à-Mousson is most satisfactory.

The military events of this week have been unimportant. The forts have continued silent, and reconnaissances have been made here and there. The faubourgs, too, have been quiet. Everything is being done to make the siege weigh as little upon the population as possible. Thus, for instance, few lamps are lit in the streets, but the shops and cafés are still a blaze of light; they close, however, early. Here is rather a good story; I can vouch for its truth. The Government recently visited the Tuileries. They were received by the governor, whom they found established in a suite of apartments. He showed them over the palace, and then offered them luncheon. They then incidentally asked him who had nominated him to the post he so ably filled. "Myself," he replied; "just by the same authority as you nominated yourselves, and no less." There was heavy firing all through the night in the direction of Vannes.

M. Mottu, the mayor of the 11th arrondissement, who had entered into a campaign against crucifixes, has been removed. The Government were "interviewed" last night by the chiefs of thirty battalions of Gardes Nationales of the 11th arrondissement on the subject. The deputation was assured that M. Mottu would be reinstated in his mairie if he would promise to moderate his zeal.

October 20th.

"The clients of M. Poiret are informed that they can only have one plate of meat," was the terrible writing which stared me on the wall, when I went to dine at my favourite bouillon—and, good heavens, what a portion it was! Not enough for the dinner of a fine lady who has previously gorged herself at a private luncheon. If meat is, as we are told, so plentiful that it will last for five weeks more, the mode in which it is distributed is radically bad. While at a large popular restaurant, where hundreds of the middle classes dine, each person only gets enough cat or horse to whet his appetite for more; in the expensive cafés on the Boulevards, feasts worthy of Lucullus are still served to those who are ready to part with their money with the proverbial readiness of fools. Far more practical, my worthy Republicans, would it be to establish "liberté, égalité, fraternité" in the cook shops, than to write the words in letters of gold over your churches. In every great city there always is much want and misery; here, although succour is supposed to be afforded to all who require it, many I fear are starving owing to that bureaucrat love of classification which is the curse of France. After my meagre dinner, I was strolling along the quays near the river, *l'estomac* as *leger* as M. Ollivier's heart, when I saw a woman leaning over the parapet. She turned as I was passing her, and the lamp from the opposite gate of the Tuileries shone on her face. It was honest and homely, but so careworn, so utterly hopeless, that I stopped to ask her if she was ill. "Only tired and hungry," she replied; "I have been walking all day, and I have not eaten since yesterday." I took her to a café and gave her some bread and coffee, and then she told me her story. She was a peasant girl from Franche Comté, and had come to Paris, where she had gone into service. But she had soon tired of domestic servitude, and for the last year she had supported herself by sewing waistcoats in a great wholesale establishment. At the commencement of the siege she had been discharged, and for some days she found employment in a Government workshop, but for the last three weeks she had wandered here and there, vainly asking for work. One by one she had sold every article of dress she possessed, except the scanty garments she wore, and she had lived upon bread and celery. The day before she had spent her last sou, and when I saw her she had come down to the river, starving and exhausted, to throw herself into it. "But the water looked so cold, I did not dare," she said. Thus spoke the grisette of Paris, very different from the gay, thoughtless being of French romance, who lives in a garret, her window shrouded with flowers, is adored by a student, and earns enough money in a few hours to pass the rest of the week dancing, gossiping, and amusing herself. As I listened to her, I felt ashamed of myself for repining because I had only had one plate of meat. The hopeless, desolate condition of this poor girl is that of many of her class to-day. But why should they complain?

Is not King William the instrument of Heaven, and is he not engaged in a holy cause? That Kings should fight and that seamstresses should weep is in the natural order of things. Frenchmen and Frenchwomen only deserve to be massacred or starved if they are so lost to all sense of what is just as to venture to struggle against the dismemberment of their country, and do not understand how meet and right it is that their fellow-countrymen in Alsace should be converted into German subjects.

General Vinoy, who was in the Crimea, and who takes a somewhat larger view of things than the sententious Trochu, has been good enough to furnish me with a pass, which allows me to wander unmolested anywhere within the French outposts. "If you attempt to pass them," observes the General, "you will be shot by the sentinels, in obedience to my orders." A general order also permits anyone to go as far as the line of the forts. Yesterday I chartered a cab and went to Boulogne, a village on the Seine, close by the wood of the same name. We drove through a portion of the Bois; it contained more soldiers than trees. Line and artillerymen were camped everywhere, and every fifty yards a group was engaged in skinning or cutting up a dead horse. The village of Boulogne had been deserted by almost all the inhabitants. Across some of the streets leading to the river there were barricades, others were open. In most of the houses there were soldiers, and others were in rifle-pits and trenches. A brisk exchange of shots was going on with the Prussians, who were concealed in the opposite houses of St. Cloud. I cannot congratulate the enemy upon the accuracy of their aim, for although several evilly disposed Prussians took a shot at my cab, their bullets whistled far above our heads, and after one preliminary kick, the old cab-horse did not even condescend to notice them. As for the cabman, he was slightly in liquor, and at one of the cross-streets leading to the river he got off his box, and performed a war-dance to show his contempt for the skill of the enemies of his nation. In the Grand Place there was a long barricade, and behind it men, women, and children were crouching watching the opposite houses, from which every now and then a puff of smoke issued, followed by a sharp report. The soldiers were very orderly and good-natured; as I had a glass, some of them took me up into the garrets of a deserted house, from the windows of which we tried in vain to espy our assailants. My friends fired into several of the houses from which smoke issued, but with what effect I do not know. The amusement of the place seemed to be to watch soldiers running along an open road which was exposed to fire for about thirty yards. Two had been killed in the morning, but this did not appear in any way to diminish the zest of the sport. At least twenty soldiers ran the gauntlet whilst I was there, but not one of them was wounded. As well as I could make out, the damage done to St. Cloud by the bombs of Mont Valérien is very inconsiderable. A portion of the Palace and a few houses were in ruins, but that was all. There is a large barrack there, which the soldiers assured me is lit up every night, and why this building has not been shelled, neither they nor I could understand. The newspapers say that the Prussians have guns on the unfinished redoubt of Brinlerion; it was not above 1,000 yards from where I was standing, but with my glass I could not make out that there were any there. Several officers with whom I spoke said that it was very doubtful. On my return, my cabman, who had got over his liquor, wanted double his fare. "For myself," he said, "I am a Frenchman, and I should scorn to ask for money for running a risk of being shot by a *canaille* of a German, but think of my horse;" and then he patted the faithful steed, whom I may possibly have the pleasure to meet again, served up in a sauce piquante.

The newspapers, almost without exception, protest against the mediation of England and Russia, which they imagine is offered by these Powers. "It is too late," says the organ of M. Picard. "Can France accept a mediation which will snatch from her the enemy at the moment when victory is certain?"

October 25th.

Has General Trochu a plan?—if so, what is it? It appears to me, as Sir Robert Peel would have said, that he has only three courses to pursue: first, to do nothing, and to capitulate as soon as he is starved out; this would, I reckon, bring the siege to an end in about two months: secondly, to fight a battle with all his disposable forces, which might be prolonged for several days, and thus risk all upon one great venture: thirdly, to cut his way out of Paris with the line and the Mobiles. The two united would form a force of about 150,000 men, and supported by 500 cannon, it may reasonably be expected that the Prussian lines would be pierced. In this case a junction might be effected with any army which exists in the provinces, and the combined force might throw itself upon the enemy's line of communications. In the meantime Paris would be defended by its forts and its ramparts. The former would be held by the sailors and the mobilized National Guards of Paris, the latter by the Sedentary Garde Nationale. Which of these courses will be adopted, it is impossible to say; the latter, however, is the only one which seems to present even a chance of ultimate success. With respect to the second, I do not think that the Mobiles could stand for days or even for hours against the artillery and musketry force of their opponents. They are individually brave, but like all raw troops they become excited under fire, shoot wildly, then rush forward in order to engage in a hand-to-hand encounter, and break before they reach the Prussian lines. In this respect the troops of the line are not much better.

The Prussian tactics, indeed, have revolutionized the whole system of warfare, and the French, until they have learnt them, will always go to the wall.

Every day that this siege lasts, convinces me more and more that General Trochu is not the right man in the right place. He writes long-winded letters, utters Spartan aphorisms, and complains of his colleagues, his generals, and his troops. The confidence which was felt in him is rapidly diminishing. He is a good, respectable, honest man, without a grain of genius, or of that fierce indomitable energy which sometimes replaces it. He would make a good Minister of War in quiet times, but he is about as fit to command in the present emergency as Mr. Cardwell would be. His two principal military subordinates, Vinoy and Ducrot, are excellent Generals of Division, but nothing more. As for his civilian colleagues, they are one and all hardly more practical than Professor Fawcett. Each has some crotchet of his own, each likes to dogmatize and to speechify, and each considers the others to be idiots, and has a small following of his own, which regards him as a species of divinity. They are philosophers, orators, or legists, but they are neither practical men nor statesmen. I understand that General Trochu says, that the most sensible among them is Rochefort.

We want to know what has become of Sergeant Truffet. As the Prussians are continually dinning it into Europe that the French fire on their flags of truce, the following facts, for the truth of which I can vouch, may, perhaps, account for it; if, indeed, it has ever occurred. A few days ago, some French soldiers, behind a barricade a little in advance of the Moulin Sagui, saw a Bavarian crawl towards them, waving a white flag. When he stopped, the soldiers called to him to come forward, but he remained, still waving his flag. Sergeant Truffet then got over the barricade, and went towards him. Several Germans immediately rushed forward, and sergeant, flag, and Germans, disappeared within the enemy's lines. The next day, General Vinoy sent an officer to protest against this gross violation of the laws of war, and to demand that the sergeant should be restored. The officer went to Creteil, thence he was sent to Choisy le Roi, where General Jemplin (if this is how he spells his name) declined to produce the sergeant, who, he said, was a deserter, or to give any explanation as to his whereabouts. Now Truffet, as his companions can testify, had not the remotest intention to desert. He was a good and steady soldier. He became a prisoner, through a most odious stratagem, and a Prussian general, although the facts have been officially brought before him, has refused to release him. The Germans are exceedingly fond of trumping up charges against the French, but they have no right to expect to be believed, until they restore to us our Truffet, and punish the Bavarians who entrapped him by means of a false flag of truce.

The subscription for the 1500 cannon hangs fire. The question, however, whether both cannon and Chassepots can be made in Paris is solved, as the private workshops are making daily deliveries of both to Government. At the commencement of the siege it was feared that there would not be enough projectiles; these, also, are now being manufactured. For the last week, the forts have been firing at everything and anything. The admirals in command say that the sailors lose themselves so, that they are obliged to allow them to fire more frequently than is absolutely necessary.

I have been endeavouring to form an estimate of the absolute cost in money of the siege, per diem. The National Guard receive in pay 24,000*l.*, rations to themselves and families amount to about 10,000*l.*, the Mobiles do not cost less than 30,000*l.* Unproductive industries connected with the war, about 15,000*l.* Rations to the destitute, 5000*l.* When, in addition to these items, it is remembered that every productive industry is at a standstill, it is no exaggeration to say that Paris is eating its head off at the rate of 200,000*l.* per diem.

Flourens has been re-elected commander-in-chief of five battalions of Belleville National Guards. The Government, however, declines to recognize this cumulative command. The "Mayor" writes a letter to-day to the *Combat* denouncing the Government, and demanding that the Republic "should decree victory," and shoot every unsuccessful general. Blanqui says that he lost his election as commander of a battalion, through the intrigues of the Jesuits. It was proposed on Saturday, at a club, to make a demonstration before the Hôtel de Ville, in favour of M. Mottu, the Mayor of the eleventh arrondissement, who was dismissed on account of his crusade against crucifixes. An amendment, however, was carried, putting it off until famine gives the friends of a revolution new adherents. Crucifixes were denounced by an orator in the course of the evening, as "impure nudities, which ought not to be suffered in public places, on account of our daughters."

The great meat question is left to every arrondissement to decide according to its own lights. As a necessary consequence of this, while in one part of Paris it takes six hours to get a beef-steak, in others, where a better system of distribution prevails, each person can obtain his ration of 100 grammes without any extraordinary delay. Butter now costs 18fr. the pound. Milk is beginning to get scarce. The "committee of alimentation" recommends mothers to nourish their babies from what Mr. Dickens somewhere calls "nature's founts."

I had a conversation yesterday with one of the best writers on the French press, and I asked him to tell me what were the views of the sensible portion of the population respecting the situation. He replied, "We always were opposed to the Empire; we knew what the consequences eventually would be. The deluge has overtaken us, and we must accept the consequences. In Paris, few who really are able to form a just estimate of our resources, can expect that the siege can have any but a disastrous termination. Everyone, however, has lost so much, that he is indifferent to what remains. We feel that Paris would be disgraced if at least by a respectable defence she does not show that she is ready to sacrifice herself for France." "But," I said, "you are only putting off the inevitable hour at a heavy cost to yourself." "Perhaps," he replied, "we are not acting wisely, but you must take into consideration our national weaknesses; it is all very well to say that we ought to treat now, and endeavour to husband our resources, so as to take our revenge in twenty years, but during that twenty years we should not venture to show ourselves abroad, or hold up our heads at home." "In the end, however, you must treat," I said. "Never," he replied. "Germany may occupy Alsace and Lorraine, but we will never recognise the fact that they are no longer French." "I hardly see," I said, "that this will profit you." "Materially, perhaps not," he answered, "but at least we shall save our honour." "And what, pray, will happen after the capitulation of Paris?" "Practically," he replied, "there is no Government in France, there will not be for about two years, and then, probably, we shall have the Orleans princes." The opinions enunciated by this gentleman are those of most of the *doctrinaires*. They appear to be without hope, without a policy, and without any very definite idea how France is to get out of the singularly false position in which the loss of her army, and the difficulty of her people to accept the inevitable consequences, have placed her. My own impression is, that the provinces will in the end insist upon peace at any cost, as a preliminary step towards some regular form of government, and the withdrawal of the German troops, whose prolonged occupation of department after department must exhaust the entire recuperative resources of the country.

October 27th.

At an early hour yesterday morning, about 100 English congregated at the gate of Charenton *en route* for London. There were with them about 60 Americans, and 20 Russians, who also were going to leave us. Imagine the indignation of these "Cives Romani," when they were informed that, while the Russians and the Americans would be allowed to pass the Prussian outposts, owing to the list of the English wishing to go not having reached Count Bismarck in time, they would have to put off their journey to another day. The guard had literally to be turned out to prevent them from endeavouring to force their way through the whole German army. I spoke this morning to an English butler who had made one of the party. This worthy man evidently was of opinion that the end of the world is near at hand, when a butler, and a most respectable person, is treated in this manner. "Pray, sir, may I ask," he said, with bitter scorn, "whether her Majesty is still on the throne in England?" I replied, "I believed that she was." "Then," he went on, "has this Count Bismarck, as they call him, driven the British nobles out of the House of Lords? Nothing which this feller does would surprise me now." Butler, Chargé d'Affaires, and the other *cives*, are, I understand, to make another start, as soon as the "feller" condescends to answer a letter which has been forwarded to him, asking him to fix a day for their departure.

We are daily anticipating an attack on the Southern side of the city. The Prussians are close into the forts on their line from Meudon to Choisy-le-Roi. Two days ago it was supposed that they were dragging their siege guns to batteries which they had prepared for them, notwithstanding our fire, which until now we proudly imagined had rendered it impossible for them to put a spade to the ground. Our generals believe, I know not with what truth, that the Prussians have only got twenty-six siege guns. If they are on the plateau of Meudon, and if they carry, as is asserted, nine kilometres, a large portion of the city on the left bank of the Seine will be under fire. On our side we have approached so close to the villages along the Prussian line in this direction that one side or the other must in self-defence soon make an attack. The newspapers of yesterday morning having asserted that Choisy-le-Roi was no longer occupied by the enemy, I went out in the afternoon to inspect matters. I got to the end of the village of Vitry, where the advanced posts, to whom I showed my pass, asked me where I wanted to go. I replied, to Choisy-le-Roi. A corporal pointed to a house at some distance beyond where we were standing. "The Prussians are in that house," he said. "If you like, you can go forward and look at them; they are not firing." So forward I went. I was within a hundred yards of the house when some francs tireurs, hid in the field to the right of the road, commenced firing, and the Fort d'Ivry from behind opened fire. The Prussians on their side replied with their needle-guns. I got behind a tree, feeling that my last hour was come. There I remained about half an hour, for whenever I moved a bullet came whizzing near me. At last a thought, a happy thought, occurred to me. I rolled myself into a ditch, which ran alongside the road, and down this ditch I crept until I got close to the barricade, over which I climbed with more haste than dignity. The soldiers were greatly amazed at my having really believed a statement which I had read in the newspapers, and their observations respecting the Parisians and their "organs" were far from complimentary. On my way back by Montrouge, I stopped to gossip with some Breton Mobiles. They, too, spoke with the utmost scorn of the patriots within the walls. "We are kept here," they said, "to defend these men, all of whom have arms like us; they live comfortably inside the ramparts, whilst the provinces are being ravaged." These Breton Mobiles are the idols of the hour. They are to the Republic what the Zouaves were to the Empire. They are very far, however, from reciprocating the admiration which the Republicans entertain for them. They are brave, devout, credulous peasants, care far more for Brittany than they do for Paris, and regard the individuals who rule by the grace of Paris with feelings the reverse of friendly. The army and the Mobiles, indeed, like being cooped up here less and less every day, and they cannot understand why the 300,000 National Guards who march and drill in safety inside the capital do not come outside and rough it like them. While I was talking to these Bretons one of them blew his nose with his handkerchief. His companions apologised to me for this piece of affectation. "He is from Finisterre," they said. In Finisterre, it appears, luxury is enervating the population, and they blow their noses with handkerchiefs; in other parts of Brittany, where the hardy habits of a former age still prevail, a more simple method is adopted.

The volunteering from the National Guard for active service has been a failure. 40,000 men were required; not 7,000 have sent in their names. The Ultras say that it is a scheme to get rid of them; the bourgeoisie say nothing, but volunteer all the less. The fact is, the siege as far as regards the Parisians has been as yet like hunting—all the pleasure of war, with one per cent. of the danger; and so long as they can help it they have no intention to increase that per-centage. As for the 1,500 cannon, they have not yet been made; but many of them have already been named. One is to be called the "Jules Favre," one the "Populace." "We already hear them thunder, and see the Prussians decimated," says the *Temps*, and its editor is not the first person who has counted his chickens before they are hatched.

All yesterday afternoon and evening the Fort of Issy, and the battery of the Bois de Boulogne, fired heavily on Brinborion and Meudon, with what result no one knows. Yesterday morning the *Combat* announced that Marshal Bazaine was treating for the surrender of Metz in the name of Napoleon. The Government was interviewed, and denied the fact. In the evening the *Combat* was burnt on the Boulevards. The chief of General Ducrot's staff has published a letter protesting against the assertions of certain journals that the fight at Malmaison produced no results. On the contrary, he says it gained us sixty square kilometres of ground in the plain of Genevilliers.

CHAPTER IX.

October 28th.

I SEE at a meeting of the mayors, the population of Paris is put down at 2,036,000. This does not include the regular army, or the Marines and Mobiles outside and within the lines. The consumption of meat, consequently, at the rate of 100 grammes per diem, must amount to between 400,000 and 500,000lbs. per diem. Although mutton according to the tariff is cheaper than beef, I rarely see any at the restaurants. This tells its own tale, and I imagine that in three weeks from now at the very latest fresh meat will have come to an end.

I am reluctantly coming to the conclusion that there is no more fight in the working men than in the bourgeois. The National Guard in Montmartre and Batignolles have held an indignation meeting to protest against their being employed in the forts. A law was passed on August 10 calling under arms all unmarried men between 25 and 40. In Paris it has never been acted on; it would, however, be far better to regularly enrol this portion of the National Guard as soldiers than to ask for volunteers. As long as these "sedentary" warriors can avoid regular service, or subjecting themselves to the discipline and the hardships of real soldiers, they will do so. Before the Pantheon, the mayor of an arrondissement sits on a platform, writing down the names of volunteers. Whenever one makes his appearance, a roll of drums announces to his fellow-citizens that he has undertaken to risk his valuable life outside the ramparts. It really does appear too monstrous that the able-bodied men of this city should wear uniforms, learn the goose-step, and refuse to take any part in the defence within shot of the enemy. That they should object to be employed in a campaign away from their homes, is hardly in accordance with their appeal to the provinces to rise *en masse* to defend France, but that they should decline to do anything but go over every twelve days to the ramparts, is hardly fighting even for their own homes. Surely as long as the siege lasts they ought to consider that the Government has a right to use them anywhere within the lines of investment. They make now what they call military promenades, that is to say, they go out at one gate, keep well within the line of the forts, and come in at another gate. Some of the battalions are ready to face the enemy, although they will not submit to any discipline. The majority, however, do not intend to fight outside the ramparts. I was reading yesterday the account of a court-martial on one of these heroes, who had fallen out with his commanding officer, and threatened to pass his sword through his body. The culprit, counsel urged, was a man of an amiable, though excitable disposition; the father of two sons, had once saved a child from drowning, and had presented several curiosities to a museum. Taking these facts into consideration, the Court condemned him to six days' imprisonment, his accuser apologised to him, and shook hands with him. What is to be expected of troops when military offences of the grossest kind are treated in this fashion? I know myself officers of the Garde Mobile, who, when they are on duty at the ramparts, quietly leave their men there, and come home to dinner. No one appears to consider this anything extraordinary. Well may General Trochu look up to the sky when it is overcast, and wish that he were in Brittany shooting woodcocks. He has undertaken a task beyond his own strength, and beyond the strength of the greatest general that ever lived. How can the Parisians expect to force the Prussians to raise the siege? They decline to be soldiers, and yet imagine that in some way or other, not only is their city not to be desecrated by the foot of the invader, but that the armies of Germany are to be driven out of France.

October 30th.

We really have had a success. Between the north-eastern and the north-western forts there is a plain, cut up by small streams. The high road from Paris to Senlis runs through the middle of it, and on this road, at a distance of about six kilometres from Paris, is the village of Bourget, which was occupied by the Prussians. It is a little in advance of their lines, which follow a small river called the Morée, about two kilometres in the rear. At 5 A.M. last Friday Bourget was attacked by a regiment of Francs-tireurs and the 9th Battalion of the Mobiles of the Seine. The Prussians were driven out of it, and fell back to the river Morée. During the whole of Friday the Prussian artillery fired upon the village, and sometimes there was a sharp interchange of shots between the advanced posts. On Friday night two attacks in considerable force were directed against the position, but both of them failed. At nine on Saturday morning, after a very heavy artillery fire from the batteries at Stains and Dugny, which was replied to from the forts of Aubervilliers and l'Est, La Briche and St. Denis, heavy masses of infantry advanced from Staines and Gonesse. When they approached the village the fire which was concentrated on them was so heavy that they were obliged to fall back. At about twelve o'clock I went out by the gate of La Villette. Between the ramparts and the Fort of Aubervilliers there were large masses of troops held in reserve, and I saw several battalions of National Guards among them, belonging, I heard, to the Volunteers. I pushed on to an inn situated at the intersection of the roads to Bourget and Courneuve. There I was stopped. It was raining hard, and all I could make out was that Prussians and French were busily engaged in firing, the former into Bourget, the latter into Stains and Dugny. It appears to have been feared that the Prussians would make an attack from Bourget upon either St. Denis or Aubervilliers; it was discovered, however, that they had no batteries there. Whether we shall be able to hold the position, or whether, if we do, we shall derive any benefit from it beyond having a large area in which to pick up vegetables, time alone will prove. On returning into Paris I came across in the Rue Rivoli about 200 patriots of all ages, brandishing flags and singing patriotic songs. These were National Guards, who had been engaged in a pacific demonstration at the Hôtel de Ville, to testify their affection to the Republic, and to demonstrate that that affection should be reciprocated by the Republic in the form of better arms, better pay, and better food. They had been harangued by Rochefort and Arago. I see by this morning's paper that the latter requested them to swear that not only would they drive the Prussians out of France, but that they would refuse to treat with any Government in Germany except a Republican one.

A decree of General Trochu converts the Legion of Honour into a military decoration. The journalists of all colours are excessively indignant at this, for they all expect, when the party which they support is in power, to be given this red ribbon as a matter of course. It has been so lavishly distributed that anyone who has not got it is almost obliged to explain why he is without it, in the way a person would excuse himself if he came into a drawing-room without a coat.

The theatres are by degrees reopening. In order not to

shock public opinion, the programmes of their entertainments are exceedingly dull. Thus the Comédie Française bill of fare for yesterday was a speech, a play of Molière's without costumes, and an ode to Liberty. I can understand closing the theatres entirely, but it seems to me absurd increasing the general gloom, by opening them in order to make the audiences wish that they were closed. Fancy, for an evening's entertainment, a speech from Mr. Cole, C.B.; the play of *Hamlet* played in the dresses of the present century; and an ode from Mr. Tupper.

A few days ago the newspapers asserted that M. Thiers had entered Paris, having been provided with a safe conduct by the King of Prussia. It is now said that he is not here yet, but that he shortly will be. Of course if Count Bismarck allows him to come in, he does so rather in the interests of Prussia than of France. I cannot believe myself that, unless Prussia has given up the idea of annexing Alsace and Lorraine to Germany, negotiation will be productive of good results. If Metz can be taken, if the armies of the provinces can be defeated, and if the provisions within the city become less plentiful than they are now, then perhaps the Parisians will accept the idea of a capitulation. At present, however, the very large majority believe that France must eventually conquer, and that the world is lost in wonder and admiration of their attitude. The siege is one long holiday to the working classes. They are as well fed as ever they were, and have absolutely nothing to do except to play at soldiers. Although the troops are unable to hold the villages within the fire of their forts, they are under the delusion that—to use the favourite expression—the circle in which we are inclosed is gradually but surely being enlarged. I was this morning buying cigars at a small tobacconist's. "Well," said the proprietor of the shop to me, "so we are to destroy the Prussians in twenty days." "Really," I said. "Yes," he replied, "I was this morning at the Mairie; there was a crowd before it complaining that they could not get meat. A gentleman—a functionary—got upon a stool. 'Citizens and citizenesses,' he said, 'be calm; continue to preserve the admirable attitude which is eliciting the admiration of the world. I give you my honour that arrangements have been made to drive the Prussians away from Paris in twenty days.' Of course," added my worthy bourgeois, "this functionary would not have spoken thus had the Government not revealed its plans to him." At this moment a well dressed individual entered the shop and asked for a subscription for the construction of a machine which he had invented to blow up the whole Prussian army. I expected to see him handed over to a policeman, but instead of this the bourgeois gave him two francs! What, I asked, is to be expected of a city peopled by such credulous fools?

A dispute is going on as to the relative advantages of secular and religious education. The Mayor of the 23rd arrondissement publishes to-day an order to the teachers within his domains, forbidding them to take the children under their charge to hear mass on Sundays. The municipality has also published a decree doubling the amount contributed by the city to the primary schools. Instead of eight million francs it is to be henceforward sixteen millions. This is all very well, but surely it would be better to put off questions affecting education until the siege is over. The alteration in the nomenclature of the streets also continues. The Boulevard Prince Eugène is to be called the Boulevard Voltaire, and the statue of the Prince has been taken down, to be replaced by the statue of the philosopher; the Rue Cardinal Fesch is to be called the Rue de Chateaudun. The newspapers also demand that the Rue de Londres should be rebaptised on the ground that the name of Londres is detested even more than Berlin. "If Prussia" (says one writer) "wages against us a war of bandits and savages, it is England which, in the gloom of its sombre country houses, pays the Uhlans who oppress our peasants, violate their wives, massacre our soldiers, and pillage our provinces. She rejoices over our sufferings."

The headquarters of the Ambulance Internationale are to move to-morrow from the Palais de l'Industrie to the Grand Hotel. In the Palais it was impossible to regulate the ventilation. It was always either too hot or too cold. Another objection to it which was urged by the medical men was, that one-half of it served as a store for munitions of war.

4 P.M.

So we have been kicked neck and crop out of Bourget. I have got such a cold that I have been lying up to-day. A friend of mine has just come in, and tells me that at eight this morning a regiment on their way to Bourget found the Mobiles who were in it falling back. Some Prussian troops appeared from between Stains and Courneuve, and attempted to cut off the retreat. Whether we lost any cannon my friend does not know. He thinks not. Some of our troops were trapped, the others got away, and fell back on the barricades in front of Aubervilliers. My friend observes that if it was not a rout, it was extremely like one. He thinks that we were only allowed to get into Bourget in order to be caught like rats in a trap. When my friend left the forts were firing on Pierrefitte and Etains, and the Prussians were established in front of Bourget. My friend, who thinks he has a genius for military matters, observes that we ought to have either left Bourget alone, or held it with more troops and more artillery. The Mobiles told him that they had been starving there for forty-eight hours, and only had two pieces of 12, two of 4, and one mitrailleuse. The Prussians had brought up heavy guns, and yesterday they established a battery of twenty-one cannon, which cannonaded the village.

October 31st.

Yesterday evening until eleven o'clock—a late hour now for Paris—the Boulevards were crowded. Although the news that Bourget had been retaken by the Prussians had been *affiché* at the Mairies, many who asserted it were at first treated as friends of Prussia. Little by little the fact was admitted, and then every one fell to denouncing the Government. To-day the official bulletin states that we retreated in good order, leaving "some" prisoners. From what I hear from officers who were engaged, the Mobiles fought well for some time, although their ammunition was so wet that they could only fire twelve shots with their cannon, and not one with their mitrailleuse. When they saw that they were likely to be surrounded, there was a stampede to Aubervilliers and to Drancy, the latter of which was subsequently evacuated. To-day we have two pieces of news—that M. Thiers entered Paris yesterday, and that Metz has fallen. The *Journal des Débats* also publishes copious extracts from a file of provincial papers up to the 26th, which it has obtained.

I hear that M. Thiers advises peace on any terms. The Government of Paris are in a difficult position. They have followed in the course of Palikao. By a long *suggestio falsi et suppressio veri* they have led the population of this city to believe that the position of France has bettered itself every day that the siege has lasted. We have been told that Bazaine could hold out indefinitely, that vast armies were forming in the provinces, and would, before the middle of November, march to the relief of Paris; that the investing army was starving, and that it had been unable to place a single gun in position within the range of the forts; that we had ample provisions until the month of February, and that there would not be the slightest difficulty in introducing convoys. Anyone who ventured to question these facts was held up to public execration. General Trochu announced that he had a "plan," and that if only he were left to carry it out, it must result in success. All this time the General and the members of the Government, who were at loggerheads with each other, privately confessed to their friends that the situation was growing every day more critical.

The attempt to obtain volunteers from the population of the capital for active service outside the gates has resulted in a miserable failure, and the Government does not even venture to carry out the law, which subjects all between twenty-five and thirty-five to enrolment in the army. With respect to public opinion, all are opposed to the entry of the Prussians into Paris, or to a peace which would involve a cession of territory; but many equally object to submitting either to real hardship or real danger. They hope against hope that what they call their "sublime attitude" will prevent the Prussians from attacking them, and that they may pass to history as heroes, without having done anything heroic. I had thought that the working men would fight well, but I think so no longer. Under the Empire they got high wages for doing very little. Since the investment of the capital, they have taken their 1fr. 50c. and their rations for their families, and done hardly anything except drill, gossip, and about once a week go on the ramparts. So fond they are of this idle existence, that although workshops offer 6fr. a day to men, they cannot obtain hands. With respect to provisions, as yet the poorer classes have been better off than they ever were before. Every one gets his 50 or 100 grammes of meat, and his share of bread. Those persons alone who were accustomed to luxuries have suffered from their absence. Meat of some kind is, however, to be obtained by any person who likes to pay for it about twice its normal value. So afraid is the Government of doing anything which may irritate the population, that, contrary to all precedent, the garrison and the wounded alone are fed with salt meat. What the result of M. Thiers' mission will be, it is almost impossible to say. The Government will be anxious to treat, and probably it will put forward feelers to-morrow to see how far it may dare go. Some of its members already are endeavouring to disconnect themselves from a capitulation, and, if it does take place, will assert that they were opposed to it. Thus, M. Jules Favre, in a long address to the mayors of the banlieus yesterday, goes through the old arguments to prove that France never desired war.

This gentleman is essentially an orator, rather than a statesman. When he went to meet Count Bismarck at Ferrières, he was fully prepared to agree to the fortresses in Alsace and Lorraine being rased; but when he returned, the phrase, "*Ni un pouce du territoire, ni une pierre des forteresses,*" occurred to him, and he could not refrain from complicating the situation by publishing it.

To turn for a moment to less serious matters. I never shall see a donkey without gratefully thinking of a Prussian. If anyone happens to fall out with his jackass, let me recommend him, instead of beating it, to slay and eat it. Donkey is now all the fashion. When one is asked to dinner, as an inducement one is told that there will be donkey. The flesh of this obstinate, but weak-minded quadruped is delicious—in colour like mutton, firm and savoury. This siege will destroy many illusions, and amongst them the prejudice which has prevented many animals being used as food. I can most solemnly assert that I never wish to taste a better dinner than a joint of a donkey or a *ragout* of cat—*experto crede.*

November 1st.

We have had an exciting twenty-four hours. The Government of the National Defence has in the course of yesterday been deposed, imprisoned, and has again resumed the direction of public affairs. I went yesterday, between one and two o'clock, to the Hôtel de Ville. On the place before it there were about 15,000 persons, most of them National Guards from the Faubourgs, and without arms, shouting, " Vive la Commune! Point d'armistice!" Close within the rails along the façade there were a few Mobiles and National Guards on duty. One of the two great doorways leading into the hotel was open. Every now and then some authority appeared to make a speech which no one could catch; and at most of the windows on the first floor there was an orator gesticulating. The people round me said that the mayors of Paris had been summoned by Arago, and were in one room inside deliberating, whilst in another was the Government. I managed to squeeze inside the rails, and stood near the open door. At about 2·30 the Mobiles who guarded it were pushed back, and the mob was forcing its way through it, when Trochu appeared, and confronted them. What he said I could not hear. His voice was drowned in cries of " A bas Trochu!" Jules Simon then got on a chair, to try the effect of his eloquence; but in the midst of his gesticulations a body of armed men forced their way through the entrance, and with about 300 of the mob got inside the Hotel. Just then three or four shots were fired. The crowd outside scampered off, yelling " Aux armes!" and running over each other. I thought it more prudent to remain where I was. Soon the mob returned, and made a rush at both the doors; for the one which had been open had been closed in the interval. This one they were unable to force, but the other, which leads up a flight of steps into the great covered court in the middle of the building, yielded to the pressure, and through it I passed with the crowd; whilst from the windows above slips were being thrown out with the words " Commune décrétée—Dorian president" on them. The covered court was soon filled. In the middle of it there is a large double staircase leading to a wide landing, from which a door and some windows communicate with a long salle.

This, too, was invaded, and for more than two hours I remained there. The spectacle was a curious one—everybody was shouting, everybody was writing a list of a new Government and reading it aloud. In one corner a man incessantly blew a trumpet, in another a patriot beat a drum. At one end was a table, round which the mayors had been sitting, and from this vantage ground Felix Pyat and other virtuous citizens harangued, and, as I understood, proclaimed the Commune and themselves, for it was impossible to distinguish a word. The atmosphere was stifling, and at last I got out of a window on to the landing in the courtyard. Here citizens had established themselves everywhere. I had the pleasure to see the "venerable" Blanqui led up the steps by his admirers. This venerable man had, *horresca referens,* been pushed up in a corner, where certain citizens had kicked his venerable frame, and pulled his venerable white beard, before they had recognised who he was. By this time it appeared to be understood that a Government had been constituted, consisting of Blanqui, Ledru-Rollin, Delescluze, Louis Blanc, Flourens, and others. Flourens, whom I now perceived for the first time, went through a corridor, with some armed men, and I and others followed him. We got first into an antechamber, and then into a large room, where a great row was going on. I did not get farther than close to the door, and consequently could not well distinguish what was passing, but I saw Flourens standing on a table, and I heard that he was calling upon the members of the Government of National Defence, who were seated round it, to resign, and that Jules Favre was refusing to do so. After a scene of confusion, which lasted half an hour, I found myself, with those round me, pushed out of the room, and I heard that the old Government had been arrested, and that a consultation was to take place between it and the new one. Feeling hungry, I now went to the door of the Hôtel to get out, but I was told I could not do so without a permission from the citizen Blanqui. I observed that I was far too independent a citizen myself to ask any one for a permit to go where I liked, and as I walked on the citizen sentinel did not venture to stop me. As I passed before Trochu's head-quarters at the Louvre I spoke to a captain of the Etat-Major, whom I knew, and whom I saw standing at the gate. When he heard that I had just come from the Hôtel de Ville, he anxiously asked me what was going on there, and whether I had seen Trochu. General Schmitz, he said, had received an order signed by the mayors of Paris to close the gates of the town, and not on any pretext to let any one in or out. At the Louvre he said all was in confusion, but he understood that Picard had escaped from the Hôtel de Ville, and was organizing a counter-movement at the Ministry of Finance. Having dined, I went off to the Place Vendôme, as the *générale* was beating. The National Guards of the quarter were hurrying there, and Mobile battalions were marching in the same direction. I found on my arrival that this had become the head-quarters of the Government; that an officer who had come with an order to Picard to go to the Hôtel de Ville, signed by Blanqui, had been arrested. General Tamisier was still a prisoner with the Government. Soon news arrived that a battalion had got inside the Hôtel de Ville and had managed to smuggle Trochu out by a back door. Off I went to the Louvre. There Trochu, his uniform considerably deteriorated, was haranguing some battalions of the Mobiles, who were shouting "Vive Trochu!" Other battalions were marching down the Rue Rivoli to the Hôtel de Ville. I got into a cab and drove there. The Hôtel was lit up. On the "place" there were not many persons, but all round it, in the streets, were Mobiles and Bourgeois National Guards, about 20,000 in all. The Hôtel was guarded, I heard, by a Belleville battalion, but I could not get close in to interview them. This lasted until about two o'clock in the morning, when the battalions closed in, Trochu appeared with his staff, and in some way or other, for it was so dark, nothing could be seen, the new Government was ejected; M. Jules Favre and his colleagues were rescued. M. Delescluze, who was one of the persons there, thus describes what took place : " A declaration was signed by the new Government declaring that on the understanding that the Commune was to be elected the next day, and also the Provisional Government replaced by an elected one, the citizens designed at a public meeting to superintend these elections withdrew." This was communicated first to Dorian, who appears to have been half a prisoner, half a friend; then to the members of the old Government, who were in honourable arrest; then to Jules Ferry outside. A general sort of agreement appears then to have been made, that bygones should be bygones. The Revolutionists went off to bed, and matters returned to the point where they had been in the morning. Yesterday evening a decree was placarded, ordering the municipal elections to take place to-day, signed Etienne Arago; and to-day a counter-decree, signed Jules Favre, announces that this decree appeared when the Government was *gardé à vue*, and that on Thursday next a vote is to be taken to decide whether there is to be a Commune or not.

To-day the streets are full of National Guards marching and counter-marching, and General Tamisier has held a review of about 10,000 on the Place Vendôme. Mobile battalions also are camped in the public squares. I went to the Hôtel de Ville at about one o'clock, and found Mr. Washburne there. We both came to the conclusion that Trochu had got the upper hand. Before the Hôtel de Ville there were about 5,000 Mobiles, and within the building everything appeared quiet. Had General Trochu been a wise man he would have anticipated this movement, and not rendered himself ridiculous by being imprisoned with his council of lawyers and orators for several hours by a mob. The working men who performed this feat seemed only to be actuated by a wild desire to fight out their battle with the Prussians, and not to capitulate. They appear to wish to be led out, and imagine that their undisciplined valour would be a match for the German army. They showed their sense by demanding that Dorian should be at the head of the new Government. He is not a Demagogue, he has written no despatches, nor made any speeches, nor decreed any Utopian reforms after the manner of his colleagues. But, unlike them, he is a practical man of business, and this the working men have had discernment enough to discover. They are hardly to be blamed if they have accepted literally the rhetorical figures of Jules Favre. When he said that, rather than yield one stone of a French fortress, Paris would bury itself beneath its ruins, they believed it. I need hardly say that neither the Government nor the bourgeoisie have the remotest intention to sacrifice either their own lives or their houses merely in order to rival Saragossa. They have got themselves into a ridiculous position by their reckless vaunts, and they have welcomed M. Thiers, as an angel from heaven, because they hope that he will be able to save them from cutting too absurd a figure. He left yesterday at three o'clock, and I understand he has full powers to negotiate an armistice upon any terms which will save the *amour-propre* of the Parisians. I should not be surprised, however, if the Government continues to resist until the town is in real danger or has suffered real privations. If the Parisians take it into their heads that they will be able to palm themselves off as heroes by continuing for a few weeks longer their passive attitude of opposition, they will do so. What inclines them to submit to conditions now, is not so much the capitulation of Bazaine, as the dread that by remaining much longer isolated they will entirely lose their hold on the Provincials. That these Helots should venture to express their opinions, or to act except in obedience to orders from the capital, fills them with indignation.

November 2nd.

The Government has issued the following form, on which the vote is to be taken to-morrow: " Does the population of Paris maintain, Yes or No, the powers of the Government of National Defence ? "

The Ultras bitterly complain that the members of the Government agreed to the election of a Commune, on the recommendation of all the mayors, and that now they are going back from their concession, and are following in the steps of the Empire and taking refuge in a Plebiscite. They, therefore, recommend their friends to abstain from voting. The fact is, that the real question at issue is, whether Paris is to resist to the end, or whether it is to fall back from the determination to do so, which it so boldly and so vauntingly proclaimed. The bourgeois are getting tired of marching to the ramparts, and making no money; the working-men are thoroughly enjoying themselves, and are perfectly ready to continue the *status quo*. I confess I rather sympathise with the latter. They may not be over wise, but still it seems to me that Paris ought to hold out as long as bread lasts, without counting the cost. She had invited the world to witness her heroism, and now she endeavours to back out of the position which she has assumed. I have not been down to Belleville to-day, but I hear that there and in the other outer Faubourgs there is great excitement, and the question of a rising is being discussed. Flourens and some other commanders of battalions have been cashiered, but they are still in command, and no attempt is being made to oblige them to recognise the decree. Rochefort has resigned his seat in the Government, on the ground that he consented to the election of the Commune. The general feeling among the shopkeepers seems to be to accept an armistice on almost any terms, because they hope that it will lead to peace. We will take our revenge, they say, in two years. A threat which simply means that if the French army can fight then, they will again shout "*à Berlin!*" M. Thiers is still at Versailles. There appears to be a tacit truce, but none knows precisely what is going on. A friend of mine saw General Trochu yesterday on business, and he tells me that this worthy man was then so utterly prostrated that he did not even refer to the business which he had come to transact. Never was a man more unfit to defend a great capital. "Why do you not act with energy against the Ultras?" said my friend. "I wish," replied Trochu, "to preserve my power by moral force." This is all very well, but can the commander of a besieged town be said to have preserved his power when he allows himself to be imprisoned by a mob for six hours, and then does not venture to punish its leaders? Professor Fustel de Coulanges has written a reply to Professor Mommsen. He states the case of France with respect to Alsace very clearly. "Let Prussia double the war-tax she imposes on France, and give up this iniquitous scheme of annexation," ought to be the advice of every sincere friend of peace. In any case, if Alsace and Lorraine are turned with the German Rhine Provinces into a neutral State, I do hope that we shall have the common sense not to guarantee either its independence or its neutrality. If we do so, within ten years we shall infallibly be dragged into a Continental war. We have a whim about Belgium, one day it will prove a costly one; we cannot, however, afford to indulge in many of these whims.

CHAPTER X.

November 3rd.

THE vote is being taken to-day whether the population of Paris maintains in power the Government of National Defence. On Saturday each of the twenty arrondissements is to elect a Mayor and four adjuncts, who are to replace those nominated by the Government. Of course the Government will to-day have a large majority. Were it to be in the minority the population would simply assert that it wishes to live under no Government. This plébiscite is in itself an absurdity. The real object, however, is to strengthen the hands of the depositories of power, and to enable them to conclude an armistice, which would result in a Constituent Assembly, which would free them from the responsibility of concluding peace on terms rather than accept which they proudly asserted a few weeks ago they would all die. The keynote of the situation is given by the organs of public opinion, which until now have teemed with articles calling upon the population of the capital to bury itself beneath its ruins, and thus by a heroic sacrifice to serve as an example to the whole of France. To-day they say, " It appears that the provinces will not allow Paris to be heroic. They wish for peace; we have no right to impose upon them our determination to fight without hope of victory." ✳The fact is that the great mass of the Parisians wish for peace at any price. Under the circumstances I do not blame them. No town is obliged to imitate the example of Moscow. If, however, it merely intends to submit to a blockade, and to practically capitulate on terms which it scouted at first, before any of its citizens have been even under fire, and before its provisions are exhausted, it would do well not to call upon the world to witness its sublimity. My impression is that on one point alone the Parisians will prove obstinate, and that is if the Prussians insist upon occupying their town; upon every other they will only roar like "sucking doves." Rather than allow the German armies to defile along the Boulevards, they would give up Alsace, Lorraine, and half a dozen other provinces. As regards the working-men, they have far more go in them than the bourgeois, and if the Prussians would oblige them by assaulting the town, they would fight well in the streets; but with all their shouts for a sortie, I estimate their real feelings on the matter by the fact that they almost unanimously, on one pretext or another, decline to volunteer for active service outside the ramparts.

The elections on Saturday, says M. Jules Favre, will be a "negation of the Commune." By this I presume he means that the elected Mayors and their adjuncts will only exercise power in their respective arrondissements, but that their collective action will not be recognised. As, however, they will be the only legally elected body in Paris, and as, undoubtedly, they will frequently meet together, it is very probable that they will be able to hold their own against the Government. The word "Commune" is taken from the vocabulary of the first Revolution. During the Reign of Terror the Municipality was all powerful, and it styled itself a "Commune." By "Commune," consequently, is simply meant a municipality which is strong enough to absorb tacitly a portion of the power legally belonging to the Executive.

The Government now meets at one or other of the ministries. At the Hôtel de Ville Etienne Arago still reigns. Being a member of the Government himself, he cannot well be turned out by his own colleagues, but they distrust him, and do not clearly know whether he is with them or against them. Yesterday, several battalions were stationed round the hotel. Arago came out to review them. He was badly received, and the officers let him understand that they were not there to be reviewed by him. Soon afterwards General Tamisier passed along the line, and was greeted with shouts of "A bas la Commune!"

I am sorry for Trochu; he is a good, honourable, high-minded man; somewhat obstinate, and somewhat vain; but actuated by the best intentions. He has thrust himself into a hornet's nest. In vain he now plaintively complains that he has made Paris impregnable, that he cannot make sorties without field artillery, and that he is neither responsible for the capitulation of Metz, nor the rout the other day at Bourget. What, then, say his opponents with some truth, was your wonderful plan? Why did you put your name to proclamations which called upon us, if we could not conquer at least to die? Why did you imprison as calumniators those who published news from the provinces, which you now admit is true? It is by no means easy for him or his colleagues to reply to these questions.

General Bellemare has been suspended. He, it appears, is to be the scapegoat of the Bourget affair. I hear from the Quartier-Général that the real reason why the artillery did not arrive in time to hold this position was, not because Bellemare did not ask for it, but because he could not get it. Red tape and routine played their old game. At St. Denis none could be sent because St. Denis is within the "territorial defence of Paris," and Bourget is not. In vain Bellemare's officers went here and there. They were sent from pillar to post, from one aged General to another, and at eleven o'clock on the day when Bourget was taken, after the troops had been driven out of it, the artillery, every formality having been gone through, was on its way to the village. It is pleasant, whilst one is cut off from the outer world, to be reminded by these little traits of one's native land, its War-Office and its Horse-Guards.

I was out yesterday afternoon along our southern advanced posts. A few stray shots were occasionally fired by Francs-tireurs; but there seemed to be a tacit understanding that no offensive operations should take place. The fall of the leaves enables us to distinguish clearly the earthworks and the redoubts which the Prussians have thrown up. I am not a military man, but my civilian mind cannot comprehend why Vanves and Montrouge do not destroy with their fire the houses occupied on the plateau of Chatillon by the Prussians. I asked an officer, who was standing before Vanves, why they did not. He shrugged his shoulders, and said, "It is part of the plan, I suppose." Trochu is respected by the troops, but they have little confidence in his skill as a commander. In the evening I went to the Club Rue d'Arras, which is presided over by the "venerable" Blanqui in person, and where the ultras of the Ultras congregate. The club is a large square room, with a gallery at one end and a long tribune at the other. On entering through a baize door one is called upon to contribute a few sous to the fund for making cannon. When I got there it was about 8·30. The venerable Blanqui was seated at a table on the tribune; before him were two assessors. One an unwholesome citizen, with long blond hair hanging down his back, the other a most truculent-looking ruffian. The hall was nearly full; many were in blouses, the rest in uniform; about one-fifth of the audience was composed of women, who either knitted, or nourished the infants which they held in their arms. A citizen was speaking. He held a list in his hand of a new Government. As he read out the names some were applauded, others rejected. I had found a place on a bench by the side of a lady with a baby, who was occupied, like most of the other babies, in taking its supper. Its food, however, apparently did not agree with it, for it commenced to squall lustily. "Silence," roared a hundred voices, but the baby only yelled the louder. " Sit upon it," observed some energetic citizens, looking at me, but not being a Herod, I did not comply with their order. The mother became frightened lest a *coup d'état* should be made upon her offspring, and after turning it up and solemnly smacking it, took it away from the club. By this time orator No. 1 had been succeeded by orator No. 2. This gentleman, a lieutenant in the National Guard, thus commenced. " Citizens, I am better than any of you. (Indignant disapproval.) In the Hôtel de Ville on Monday I told General Trochu that he was a coward." (Tremendous shouts of " You are a liar," and men and women shook their fists at the speaker.) Up rose the venerable Blanqui. There was a dead silence. "I am master here," he said; "when I call a speaker to order he must leave the tribune, until then he remains." The club listened to the words of the sage with reverential awe, and the orator was allowed to go on. " This, perhaps, no one will deny," he continued. " I took an order from the Citizen Flourens to the public printing establishment. The order was the deposition of the Government of National Defence "—(great applause)—and satisfied with his triumph the lieutenant relapsed into private life. After him followed several other citizens, who proposed resolutions, which were put and carried. I only remember one of them, it was that the Jesuits in Vaugirard (a school) should at once be ejected from the territories of the Republic. At ten o'clock the venerable Blanqui announced that the sitting was over, and the public noisily withdrew. An attempt has been made by the respectable portion of the community to establish a club at the Porte St. Martin Theatre, where speakers of real eminence nightly address audiences. I was there a few evenings ago, and heard A. Coquerel and M. Lebueier, both Protestant pastors, deliver really excellent speeches. The former is severe and demure, the latter a perfect Boanerges. He frequently took up a chair and dashed it to the ground to emphasise his words. This club is usually presided over by M. Cernuschi, a banker, who was in bad odour with the Imperial Government for having subscribed a large sum for the electoral campaign against the Plébiscite. Another club is held at the Folies Bergères, an old concert-hall, something like the Alhambra. The principal orator here is a certain Falcet, a burly athlete, who was, I believe, formerly a professional wrestler. Here the quality of the speeches is poor, the sentiments of the speakers mildly Republican. At the Club Montmartre the president is M. Tony Reveillon, a journalist of some note. The assessors are always elected. A person proposes himself, and the President puts his name to the audience. Generally a dozen are rejected before the two necessary to make the meeting in order are chosen. Every time I have been there an old man—I am told an ex-professor in a girls' school—has got up, and with great unction blessed the National Guards—the "heroic defenders of our homes." Sometimes he is encored several times; and were his audience to let him, I believe that he would continue blessing the "heroic defenders" until the next morning. The old gentleman has a most reverent air, and I should imagine in quiet times goes about as a blind man with a dog. He was turned out of the school in which he was a professor—a profane disbeliever in all virtue assures me— for being rather too affectionate towards some of the girls. "I like little girls—big ones, too," Artemus Ward used to say, and so it appears did this worthy man. Besides the clubs which I have mentioned, there are above 100 others. Most of them are kept going by the sous which are collected for cannon, or some other vague object. Almost all are usually crowded; the proceedings at most of them are more or less disorderly; the resolutions carried more or less absurd, and the speeches more or less bad. With the exception of the Protestant pastors, and one or two others, I have not heard a single speaker able to talk connectedly for five minutes. Wild invectives against the Prussians, denunciations against Europe, abuse of every one who differs from the orator, and the very tallest of talk about France—what she has done, what she is doing, and what she will do—form the staple of almost all the speeches.

Evening.

I went down to Belleville this afternoon. Everything was quiet. The people, as usual, in the streets doing nothing. If you can imagine the whole of Southwark paid and fed by the Government, excused from paying rent, arrayed in kepis and some sort of uniform, given guns, and passing almost all the time gossiping, smoking, and idling, you will be able to form a correct notion of the aspect of Belleville and the other outer faubourgs. The only demonstration I have heard of has been one composed of women, who marched down the Rue du Temple behind a red flag, shouting " Vive la Commune." As far as is yet known, about one-seventh of the population have voted "No." The army and the Mobiles have almost all voted "Yes." A friend of mine, who was out driving near Bobigny, says he was surrounded by a Mobile regiment, who were anxious to know what was passing in Paris. He asked them how they had voted. "For peace," they replied. "If the National Government wish to continue the war, they must come out here and fight themselves." Many battalions have issued addresses to the Parisians saying that they will not fight for a Commune, and that the provinces must have a vote in all decisions as to the future destinies of France. General Vinoy also has issued an order to the 13th Corps d'Armée, declaring that if the peace of Paris is disturbed he will march at their head to put down disorders.

November 5th.

That Paris is prudent to seize upon the first loop-hole to get out of the position into which she has inconsiderately thrust herself is most certain. Never for a moment did I believe that the Parisians, indifferent to all but honour, would perish to the last man rather than give up one inch of territory, one stone of a fortress. Heroic constancy and endurance under misfortune are not improvised. A population, enervated by twenty years of slavery, corruption, and luxury, is not likely to immolate itself for country, like the Spartans at Thermopylæ. People who mean to die do not sign a preliminary round-robin to do so. Real fighting soldiers do not parade the streets behind half-a-dozen fantastically dressed *vivandières*. When in a town of 2,000,000 inhabitants not above 12,000 can be found ready to submit to military discipline, and to go outside an inner line of fortifications, it is ridiculous to expect a defence like that of Saragossa. We are under the impression to-day that an armistice will be signed to-morrow. No one affects even to doubt that the word means peace. The bourgeoisie are heartily tired of playing at soldiers, the game has lost its novelty, and the nights are too cold to make an occasional pic-nic to the fortifications agreeable any longer. Besides, business is business, and pleasant as it may be to sit arrayed in uniform behind a counter, in the long run customers are more remunerative, if not so glorious. The cry for peace is universal, the wealthy are lusting after the flesh-pots of Egypt, the hotel-keepers are eagerly waiting for the rush of sight-seers, and the shopkeepers are anxious to make up for lost time by plundering friend and foe. The soldiers, although Trochu is popular with them, have neither faith nor confidence in his generalship. The Mobiles and peasants recently from their villages wish to go home, and openly tell the Parisians that they have no intention to remain out in the cold any longer on salt beef, whilst the heroic citizens are sleeping quietly in their houses, or in barracks, and gorging themselves with fresh provisions. As for the working-men, they are spoiling for a fight in the streets, either with the Prussians, or, if that cannot be, with anyone else. They are, however, so thoroughly enjoying themselves, doing nothing, and getting paid for doing it, that they are in too good a temper to be mischievous. The new Prefect of the Police has arrested Felix Pyat and other leaders of the riot of last Monday. Flourens and the venerable Blanqui are only not in prison because they are in hiding. The mayors of the different arrondissements are being elected to-day, but no one seems to trouble himself about the election.

The vote of Thursday has somewhat surprised the bourgeoisie. That one-seventh of the population should have registered their deliberate opinion that they prefer no Government to that under which they are living is by no means a reassuring fact, more particularly when this seventh consists of "men of action," armed with muskets, and provided with ammunition. As long as the Line and the Mobiles remain here, Trochu will be able, if he only acts with firmness, to put down all tendencies to disorder; but were there to be a fight between the friends of the Government among the Garde Mobile and its opponents, I am not certain that the former would have the upper hand. As it is, the Hôtel de Ville and the Louvre are guarded by Breton battalions of the Mobile, and Vinoy has announced that if there is a disturbance he will at once march to the aid of the Government at the head of his division. Many complaints are made about the mode in which the vote was taken on Thursday; some of them appear to me to be just. The fact is, that Frenchmen have not the most elementary notion of fair play in an election. No matter what body of men are in power, they conceive that they have a perfect right to use that power to obtain a verdict in their favour from their fellow-citizens. Tried by our electioneering code, every French election which I ever witnessed would be annulled on the ground of "intimidation" and "undue influence."

Evening.

No news yet about the armistice. I hear that it is doubtful whether it will be signed, but no doubt respecting it seems to disquiet the minds of the Parisians. I cannot help thinking that they have got themselves again into a fool's paradise. Their newspapers tell them that the Neutral Powers are forcing Prussia to be reasonable, and that Bismarck is struck with awe at the sight of our "heroic attitude." As for his not accepting any terms which we may put forward, the idea does not enter the mind of any one. I must say, however, that there is a vague feeling that perhaps we are not quite so very sublime as we imagine. Even to pay a war indemnity seems to be a concession which no one anticipated. For the first time since I have known the Parisians, they are out of conceit with themselves. "If Prussia forces us to make peace now, in five years we will crush her," is the somewhat vague threat with which many console themselves. Others say that on the conclusion of peace they will leave France; but whether this is intended to punish France, Prussia, or themselves, I do not know. Others boldly assert that they are prevented from immolating themselves by the Neutral Powers. It is the old story of "hold me back, don't let me get at him." One thing, however, is certain, that the capture of Bazaine, the disaster at Bourget, the row at the Hôtel de Ville, the Prussian cannon on the heights of

Meudon, and the opportune arrival of Thiers, have made this population as peaceful to-day, as they were warlike a few weeks ago.

I really am sorry for these vain, silly, gulled humbugs among whom I am living. They have many amiable qualities, although, in trying to be Spartans, they have mistaken their vocation. They are, indeed, far too agreeable to be Spartans, who in private life must have been the most intolerable of bores. It is a sad confession of human weakness, but, as a rule, persons are not liked on account of their virtues. Excessively good people are—speaking socially—angular. Take, for instance, the Prussians; they are saints compared with the French. They have every sort of excellence: they are honest, sober, hard-working, well-instructed, brave, good sons, husbands, and fathers; and yet all this is spoilt by one single fault—they are insupportable. Laugh at the French, abuse them as one may, it is impossible to help liking them. Admire, respect the Prussians as one may, it is impossible to help disliking them. I will venture to say that it would be impossible to find 100 Germans born south of the Main who would declare, on their honour, that they prefer a Prussian to a Frenchman. The only Prussian I ever knew who was an agreeable man was Bismarck. All others with whom I have been thrown— and I have lived for years in Germany—were proud as Scotchmen, cold as New Englanders, and touchy as only Prussians can be. I once had a friend among them. His name was Buckenbrock. Inadvertently I called him Butterbrod. We have never spoken since. A Prussian lieutenant is the most offensive specimen of humanity that nature and pipeclay have ever produced. Apart from all political considerations, the supremacy of this nation in Europe will be a social calamity, unless France, like vanquished Greece, introduces the amenities of society among these pedants, squires, and martinets.

What, however, is to be done for the French? Nothing, I am afraid. They have brought their troubles on their own heads; and, to use an Americanism, they must face the music. Even at this late moment they fail to realise the fact that they ever will be called upon to endure any real hardships, or that their town ever really will be bombarded. I was watching the crowd on the Boulevards this afternoon. It was dispirited because it had for twenty-four hours set its heart upon peace, and was disappointed like a child who cannot get the toy it wants; but I will venture to say, not one person in his heart of hearts really imagined that perhaps within a week he might be blown up by a bomb. They either will not or cannot believe that anything will happen which they do not desire. Facts of this kind must be palpably brought home to them before they will even imagine that they are possible.

The army has been re-organized by that arch organizer Trochu. According to this new plan, the whole armed force is divided into three armies. The first comprises the National Guards; the second, under General Ducrot, is what may be called the active army; it consists of three corps, commanded respectively by Generals Vinoy, d'Exea, and Renault. The third comprises all the troops in the forts, in the cottages adjacent to the forts, which have to be occupied for their defence, and the fourth commanded by Trochu. The second army will have four cannon to each thousand men, and will be used to effect a sortie, if possible. This new arrangement is not well received by military men. Both among soldiers and officers, General Vinoy is far more popular than any other general; he is a sort of French Lord Clyde. Until now he had a co-ordinate command with Ducrot. That he should be called upon to serve under him is regarded as an injustice, more particularly because Ducrot is an intimate personal friend of Trochu. Ducrot and Trochu believe in themselves, and believe in each other; but no one else believes in them. They certainly have not yet given the slightest evidence of military capacity, except by criticising what has been done by others. Now, at last, however, Trochu will have an opportunity to carry out his famous plan, by which he asserts that he will raise the blockade in fourteen days, and of which he has given the fullest details in his will. Ridicule kills in France—and since this eminent General, as an evidence that he had a plan, appealed to the will which he had deposited with his lawyer, he lost all influence. I need not say that this influence has not been restored by the absurd arrest to which he was subjected by Messrs. Flourens and Blanqui.

November 6th.

So we have declined the armistice. The Government deliberated exactly five minutes over the question. The *Journal Officiel* says:—" Prussia expressly refused to entertain the question of revictualment, and only admitted under certain reserves the vote of Alsace and Lorraine." No further details are given. An opportunity has been lost, which may never recur. Public opinion was disposed to accept a cessation of the siege on almost any terms. General Trochu, however, and his colleagues had not the civic courage to attach their names to a document which would afterwards have been cast in their teeth. A friend of mine, a military man, saw Trochu late last night. He strongly urged him to accept the armistice, but in vain. "What do you expect will occur? You must know that the position is hopeless," said my friend. "I will not sign a capitulation," was all he could get from Trochu. This worthy man is as obstinate as only weak men can be; his colleagues, as self-seeking as only French politicians can be. The news that the armistice had been rejected, fell like a thunderclap upon the population. I never remember to have witnessed a day of such general gloom since the commencement of the siege. The feeling of despair is, I hear, still stronger in the army. Were the real condition of things outside known, I am certain that the Government would be forced to conclude an armistice, on no matter what terms. I happened to come across to-day a file of English newspapers up to the 22nd ult., and I fully realised how all intelligence from without has been distorted by the Government to serve its own purposes. Now a few days ago, these very papers had been lent to Trochu. He read them, kept them two days to show some of his colleagues, and then returned them. One single extract was published by the *Journal Officiel*—a German report upon the defences of Paris. No man in the House of Commons is more fond of special pleading than Sir Roundell Palmer. When anyone complains of it, the reply is, that he teaches some children their catechism on Sundays. Now, when anyone ventures to question the veracity of Trochu, one is told that he has adopted his brother's children.

According to measurements which have been made, the Prussian batteries at Sèvres and Meudon will carry to the Champ de Mars. From Montretout their guns would throw shells into the Champs Elysées; but we think that Valérien will silence them as soon as they open. Meat is getting more and more scarce every day. That great moralist, Dr. Johnson, said that he should prefer to dine with a Duke than the most agreeable of Commoners. I myself at present should prefer to dine with a leg of mutton than the most agreeable of human beings—Duke or Commoner. I hear, on what I believe to be good authority, that we shall see the end of our fresh meat on or about the 20th of this month.

Yesterday, all the hidden stores which had been hoarded up with an eye to a great profit were thrown on the market. To-day they have again disappeared. Lamb is, however, freely offered for sale, and curiously enough, at the same time, live dogs are becoming scarce.

Several Ultras have been elected mayors of the different arrondissements; among them Citizen Mottu, who was turned out of his mayorship about a fortnight ago because he refused to allow any child to attend a place of worship except with his own consent. It is all very well for M. Jules Favre to say that the election of mayors is a negation of a Commune. As I understand it, a Commune is but a council of elected mayors. If the Government loses its popularity, the new mayors will become a Commune. The more, however, the majority desire peace, the less likely will they be to throw themselves into the arms of Citizen Mottu and his friends, who are all for war *à outrance*.

Monday, November 7th.

The newspapers of to-day, with the exception of the Ultra organs, are loud in their expressions of regret that the armistice has not been agreed to. The Government gives no further details, but yesterday afternoon M. Jules Favre informed several members of the press who "interviewed" him, that Prussia refused to allow the introduction of provisions into Paris during the duration of the armistice. I have long ceased believing any assertion of a member of the French Government, unless supported by independent evidence. But if this be really true, I must say that Count Bismarck has been playing a game with the Neutral Powers, for it can hardly be expected that Paris would consent to suspend all military operations against the Prussians, whilst their process of reducing the town by starvation was uninterrupted. Besides, as such a condition would have amounted practically to a capitulation, it would have been more frank on the part of Count Bismarck to have submitted the question in that form. I anticipate very shortly a sortie in force. An attempt will be made with the Second Army to pierce the Prussian lines. There appears no reason to doubt that it will fail, and then the cry for peace will become so strong that the Government will be obliged to listen seriously to it.

General Trochu's new organization is severely criticised. I hear from military men that he elaborated it himself with his personal friends. So secret was it kept, that the Minister of War knew nothing about it until it appeared in the *Journal Officiel* yesterday. After the scene of last Monday General Vinoy reproached Trochu for having tamely submitted to arrest and insult by a mob for several hours, and strongly hinted that a French general owed it to his cloth not to allow his decorations to be torn from his heart. It is said by General Vinoy's friends that those observations are mainly the cause why he has been deprived of his independent command, and placed under the orders of General Ducrot, with respect to whose evasion from Sedan many French officers shake their heads.

I cannot help thinking that the result of the vote of the army on Thursday last is only relatively correct. Line, Mobile, and Marines do not amount to 250,000 men, unless I am very much mistaken. The Second Army, under Ducrot, will number about 110,000 men.

The English at last are about to leave. They are very indignant at having been, as they say, humbugged so long, and loud in their complaints against their Embassy. I do not think, however, that the delay has been the fault either of Colonel Claremont or of Mr. Wodehouse. These gentlemen have done their best, but they were unable to get the Prussian and French authorities to agree upon a day for the exodus. On the one hand, to send to Versailles to receive an answer took forty-eight hours; on the other, from the fact that England had not recognized the Republic, General Trochu could not be approached officially. Colonel Claremont happens to be a personal friend of his, and it is, thanks to his exertions, coupled with those of Mr. Washburne, that the matter has at length been satisfactorily arranged. I need hardly observe that the Foreign-office has done its best to render the question more complicated. It has sent orders to Mr. Wodehouse to provide for the transport of British subjects, without sending funds, and having told Lord Lyons to take the archives with him, it perpetually refers to instructions contained in despatches which it well knows are at Tours.

Mr. Washburne remains. He has done his best to induce the Government to agree to an armistice, and has clearly told them that they ought not to sacrifice Paris without a prospect of a successful issue. He is in despair at their decision, and anticipates the worst. In the interests of humanity it is greatly to be regretted that Lord Lyons should have received orders to quit Paris. The personal consideration in which he was held, and the great influence which it gave him, would have been invaluable during the negotiations of the last few days.

November 8th.

I was once in love. The object of my affections had many amiable qualities. I remember I thought her an angel; but when she was crossed, she used to go up into her room and say that she would remain there without eating until I yielded the point at issue between us. As I was invariably right and she was invariably wrong, I could not do this; but, pitying the weakness of her sex, and knowing its obstinacy, I usually managed to arrange matters in a way which allowed her to emerge from her retreat without any great sacrifice of *amour propre*. The Parisians remind me of this sentimental episode of my existence; they have mounted a high pedestal, and called upon the world to witness that no matter what may be the danger to which they are exposed, they will not get off it, unless they obtain what they want; that they will obtain it, they find is most improbable, and they are anxiously looking around for some one to help them down, without being obliged absolutely "to swallow their own words." They had hoped that the armistice which was proposed by the neutrals would in some way get them out of their difficulty; and, as the siege still continues, they are exceedingly indignant with their kind friends. "They have," say the papers, "loosened one mainspring of sacrifice. If we had fully determined to perish, rather than yield, if we do not, it will be the fault of Russia, Austria, and England." Be the cause what it may, the "mainspring of sacrifice" most assuredly is not only loosened, but it has run down, and, unless some wonderful success occurs shortly, it will never be wound up again. As long as it could be supposed that cannon and musketry would only do their bloody work outside the exterior forts, and that Paris might glory in a "heroic attitude" without suffering real hardships or incurring real danger, the note of defiance was loud and bold. As it is, the Government is obliged to do its utmost to keep their courage up to the sticking point. These foolish people really imagined that, like them, the world regarded their city as a species of sacred Jerusalem, and that public opinion would never allow the Prussians either to bombard it, or to expose the high priests of civilization who inhabit it to the realities of war. It is necessary to live here to understand the strength of this feeling. In England, little attention is paid to the utterances of French newspapers, but the Parisians, more profoundly ignorant of foreign politics than the charity school boys of an English village, were under the flattering delusion that we, in common with every other nation, lived alone to merit their favourable opinion. They find now, to their profound astonishment, that beyond a barren sympathy, founded upon a common humanity, no one regards Paris as different to any other great city, and that, if they choose to convert it into an intrenched camp for their armies, they must meet the consequences. Either they must accept the victor's terms of peace or they must fight the Prussians. The reality of the situation is by degrees coming home to them. From the general tone of the conversations I hear, I am inclined to think that, in their hearts, they admit that Alsace, if not Lorraine, is irretrievably lost. Words have a great influence over them, and they find consolation for this loss of territory in the phrase that Alsace will annex a portion of Germany, and not be annexed to Germany. It is admitted also that sooner or later, an indemnity must be paid in money to Prussia. The newspapers, who were the loudest in their praises of M. Jules Favre's language at Ferrières, now complain that nothing is to be gained by bombast, and that it is ridiculous of him to talk about "France" proposing "conditions of peace" which must be unacceptable to Prussia. The main grounds for continued resistance are the personal ambition of the members of the Government, who well know that if they sign an armistice, which is tantamount to peace, they will hereafter be made scapegoats, and be told that the Parisians were balked of their desire to perish to the last man; the mulish obstinacy of Trochu; and the dread of the capital losing its supremacy over the Provinces. Of course, there are some who wish to fight on to the bitter end. The "Ultras" hope to found on a war *à outrance* a democratic republic, and dream of the successes of the First Revolution. The politicians hardly know what they want. Their main idea is to keep up for their own purposes that centralization which has so long been the bane of this country. If they agree to terms before Paris has given France an example of heroism, they fear that her supremacy will be compromised; if they allow the insulation to continue, they fear that the Provinces will accustom themselves to independent action; if a Constituent Assembly be elected whilst free communication between Paris and the rest of France is interrupted, they fear that this Assembly will consist of local candidates rather than those, as has heretofore been the case in all French Legislative Chambers, who are imposed upon the departments by a central organization in the capital.

The position of the Government is a singular one. They obtained last Thursday a large majority on their plebiscite, because it was fully understood that "oui" meant peace; indeed, on many bulletins, the words "and peace" were added to the "oui." They have imprisoned the leaders of those who revolted to the cry of "no armistice!" Their friends the bourgeois trusted to them to put off the municipal elections until after the war, and they rallied to their defence to the cry of "no Commune!" In each arrondissement a mayor and two adjuncts have been elected, and these mayors and adjuncts have only to meet together in order to assume that right to interfere in public affairs which converts a municipality into a commune. In Belleville the elected mayor is a prisoner, and his two adjuncts, Flourens and Milliere, are in hiding. In the nineteenth arrondissement M. Delescluze, by far the most able of the Ultras, is mayor. Contrary to the wishes, consequently, of their adherents, we are to have no armistice, and we probably shall have a commune. The Ultras are persecuted, but their programme is adopted.

There appears to be a tacit truce between all parties within the city until Trochu has made some attempt to carry out his famous plan. For the last fortnight the Government has not published any news which it may have received from the Provinces. M. Thiers has either made no report upon their condition, or it has been concealed. M. Jules Favre, in his despatch to the envoys abroad, enters into no details, and confines himself to the simple announcement, that the armistice was not concluded because Count Bismarck would not allow Paris to be revictualled during the twenty-five days which it was to last. Our anxiety for news respecting what is passing outside has to be satisfied with the following words, which fell from the lips of M. Thiers : " I have seen the Army of the Loire and the Prussian Guard ; man to man I prefer the former." The *Débats* and some other journals contain extracts from the English newspapers up to the 22nd ult. I observe that everything which tells against France is suppressed, and what is published is headed with a notice, that as the source is English the truth is questionable. Thus does the press, while abusing the Government for keeping back intelligence, fulfil its mission.

The plan for the redistribution of the troops, and their change from one corps to another, which was announced on Sunday in a decree signed Trochu, has not yet been carried out. Its only effect has been as yet to render confusion twice confounded. Its real object, I hear, was to place General Ducrot in command of the left bank of the Seine, instead of General Vinoy, because it is expected that the fighting will be on that side of the river. So indignant is General Vinoy at being placed under the orders of General Ducrot, that he threatens to give in his resignation on the ground that by military law no officer can be called to serve under a general who has capitulated, and who has not been tried before a court-martial. The dispute will, I imagine, in some way or other, be arranged, without its coming before the public. General Vinoy's retirement would produce a bad effect on the army ; for, both with officers and men, he is far more popular than either Ducrot or Trochu. He passes as a fighting general ; they pass as writing generals. As for Trochu, to write and to talk is with him a perfect mania. "I have seen him on business," said a superior officer to me, "a dozen times, but I never have been able to explain what I came for ; he talked so incessantly that I could not put in a word."

I was out this morning along the Southern outposts, the forts were firing intermittently. At Cachau there was a sharp interchange of shots going on between the Prussian sentinels and Mobiles. It is a perfect mystery to me how the Prussians have been allowed to establish themselves at Clamart and at Chatillon, which are within range of the guns of these forts. Our famous artillerists do not appear to have prevented them from establishing batteries exactly where they are most dangerous to us. General Trochu has not confided to me his celebrated plan, but I am inclined to think, that whatever it may have been, he will do well to put it aside, and to endeavour to dislodge the enemy in Chatillon and the adjacent villages, before their batteries open fire. I suggested this to an officer, and he replied that the troops, thanks to the decree of Sunday, hardly knew who commanded them, or where they were to be stationed—"On paper," he added, "I and my battalion are at La Malmaison." As for the sortie, which is to revictual Paris, by forcing the Prussian lines, it is simply absurd to talk of it. If Trochu attempts it, the result must be disastrous, and *coûte qui coûte*, the political exigences of the situation render it absolutely necessary that at least apparent success must crown our next encounter with the enemy. The next thing would be to hold our own, as long as the provisions last, and trust to the chapter of accidents; but this is impossible in the present temper of both soldiers and citizens. General Trochu has insisted so loudly that, if not interfered with, he would not only keep the enemy out of Paris, but raise the siege—that he must do something to redeem his pledge.

We have almost forgotten our troubles, in hearing that King William, "to recompense his soldiers and reward their valour," has made his son and his nephew Field Marshals. We wish to know whether, if they take Paris, he will reward them, by declaring himself infallible, and giving "our Fritz" a few million francs. With fear and trembling we ask whether the success of the Bavarians will be recognized by their monarch being allowed to inflict on us the operas of his friend Wagner.

A new industry has sprung up in Paris. A manufactory has been discovered, in which Prussian casques and sabres were being made. It was at first thought that the owner was engaged in a dark conspiracy, but, upon being arrested, he confessed that he was endeavouring to meet the demand for trophies from the fields of battle. In one room of the house of this ingenious speculator, a large number of forged letters were found, from mothers, sisters, and brides, to their relations in the army before Paris: these, he explained, were to be sold, warranted from the pocket of a German corpse.

Has Gambetta contracted with a London firm for a loan of 250 millions at 42? The financial world here is in a state of the greatest agitation about a statement to this effect, which has been discovered in an English newspaper. The Government officially declare that it knows nothing about the matter. It is a curious sign of the universal belief of any one in official utterances, that this denial is regarded as very questionable evidence against the loan having been made. What puzzles us is, that the Trente is at 53—why then was this new loan issued at 42? An attempt has been made to oblige those persons left in charge of houses occupied by foreigners here, to pay the tax upon absents. An energetic protest, however, of Mr. Washburne, has saved Americans from this extortion.

CHAPTER XI.

Wednesday, November 9th.

I BOUGHT a dozen newspapers this morning. ⟨Every one of them, with the exception of the *Gaulois*, in more or less covert language, insists upon peace upon any terms.⟩ Our "main-spring" not only has run down, but is broken. The complaints, too, against the Government for concealing all news it has received from the provinces, and for giving no details respecting the negotiations with respect to the armistice, are most outspoken. M. Edmond About, in the *Soir* of last night, insists that we ought to have agreed to the armistice, even without a revictualment; and such appears to be the opinion of almost everyone. Poor M. Jules Favre, who a few weeks ago was lauded to the skies for having so nobly expressed the ideas of his countrymen, when he said that rather than yield one foot of territory, one stone of a fortress, they would all perish, is now abused for having compromised the situation, and made it difficult to treat, by his mania for oratorical clap-trap. In the *Figaro*, Villemessant blunders through three columns over being again disappointed in his expectations of embracing his wife, and plaintively tells "William" that though he may not be anxious to see "his Augusta," this is no reason why he, Villemessant, should not be absolutely wild to see Madame. A more utter and complete collapse of all "heroism" I never did witness.

General Trochu has, with his usual intelligence, seized

this moment to issue a decree, mobilizing 400 men from each battalion of the National Guard. First, volunteers; secondly, unmarried men, between 25 and 35 years; thirdly, unmarried men, between 35 and 45; fourthly, married men between 25 and 35; fifthly, married men, between 35 and 45, are successively to be called upon to fill up the contingent. The Vinoy affair has been settled by the appointment of the General to the command of the Third Army. The following statistics of the annual consumption of meat by Paris will give some idea of the difficulty of revictualling it:—oxen, 156,680; bulls, 66,028; cows, 31,095; calves, 120,275; sheep, 916,388. Meat is now distributed every three days. I hear that on the present scale of rationing there is enough for five more distributions. We shall then fall back on horses, and our own salt provisions; the former will perhaps last for a week, as for the latter it is impossible to give any accurate estimate. We have, however, practically unlimited supplies of flour, wine, and coffee; if consequently the Parisians are ready to content themselves with what is absolutely necessary to support existence, the process of starving us out will be a lengthy one.

November 14th.

"Wanted, 10,000 Parisians ready to allow themselves to be killed, in order that their fellow-citizens may pass down to posterity as heroes!" The attempt to obtain volunteers having miserably failed, and fathers of families having declined to risk their valuable lives whilst one single bachelor remains out of reach of the Prussian guns, the Government has now issued a decree calling to arms all bachelors between the age of 25 and 35. If this measure had been taken two months ago it might have been of some use, but it is absurd to suppose that soldiers can be improvised in a few days. I must congratulate my friends here upon the astounding ingenuity which they show in discovering pretexts to avoid military service. It is as difficult to get them outside the inner ramparts as it is to make an old fox break cover. In vain huntsman Trochu and his first whip, Ducrot, blow their horns, and crack their whips; the wily reynard, after putting his nose outside his retreat, heads back, and makes for inaccessible fastnesses, with which long habit has made him familiar. That General Trochu will be able to beat the Prussians no one supposes; but if he can manage to get even 5,000 of the heroes who have for the last two months been professing a wish to die for the honour of their country under fire, he will have accomplished a most difficult feat.

For the last few days the newspapers, one and all, have been filled with details of the negotiations which were supposed to be going on at Versailles. Russia, it was said, had forwarded an ultimatum to the King of Prussia, threatening him with a declaration of war in case he persisted in besieging Paris, or in annexing any portion of French territory. Yesterday morning the *Journal Officiel* contained an announcement that the Government knew absolutely nothing of these negotiations. The newspapers are, however, not disposed to allow their hopes of peace to be destroyed in this manner, and they reply that "it being notorious that no member of the Government can speak the truth, their official denial proves conclusively the contrary of what it states." It is indeed difficult to know who or what to believe; all I know for certain is, that M. Jules Favre assured Mr. Washburne on Saturday night that since M. Thiers had quitted Paris he had had no communication with the outer world, and did not even know whether the Tours delegation was still there. Men may lie for a certain time, and yet be believed, but this "arm of war" has been so abused by our rulers, that at present their most solemn asseverations meet with universal incredulity—not, indeed, that the Parisians are cured of their mania for crediting every tale which comes to them from any other source—thus, for instance, every newspaper has contained the most precise details from eye-witnesses of a conflict which took place two nights ago before the battery of Hautes-Bruyères, in which our "braves Mobiles" took between two and three thousand prisoners, and slew hecatombs of the enemy. Now, I was both yesterday and the day before yesterday at the Hautes-Bruyères, and I can certify myself that this pretended battle never took place.

It is impossible to predict what will occur during the next fortnight. *Felix qui potuit rerum cognoscere causas.* General Trochu has this morning issued a lengthy address to the inhabitants of the city, informing them that, had it not been for their riotous conduct on Oct. 31 the armistice would have been concluded; and that now all that remains for them to do, is to "close their ranks and to elevate their hearts." "If we triumph, we shall have given our country a great example; if we succumb, we shall have left to Prussia an inheritance which will replace the First Empire in the sanguinary annals of conquest and violence; an inheritance of hatred and maledictions which will eventually prove her ruin." The great question which occupies all minds now is "the sortie." General Trochu and General Ducrot insist upon at least making an attempt to pierce the Prussian lines. All the other generals say that, as it cannot succeed, it is wrong to sacrifice life to no good purpose. This is how the matter is regarded by officers and soldiers. As for the National Guard, they distinctly say that they will be no parties to any such act of folly. Even in the councils of the Government there is a strong feeling against it; but General Trochu declines to allow the question, which he says is a purely military one, to be decided by the lawyers who are his colleagues. They, on their side, complain that the General never quits the Louvre, has surrounded himself with a number of clerical dandies as his aides-de-camp, whose religious principles may be sound, but whose knowledge of war is nil; and that if he wished to make a sortie he should not have waited until the Prussians had rendered its success impossible by completing their lines of investment. It is said that the attempt will be made along the post road to Orleans, it being now considered impossible, as was at first intended, to open communications by the Havre railroad. The general impression is either that the troops engaged in it will be driven back under the forts in confusion, or that some 50,000 will be allowed to get too far to return, and then will be netted like sparrows. It is not, however, beyond the bounds of possibility that the Prussians will not wait until our great administrator has completed his preparations for attack, but will be beforehand with him, and open fire upon the southern posts from their batteries, which many think would effectually reduce to silence the guns of Vanves, Issy, and of the advanced redoubts. These Prussian batteries are viewed with a mysterious awe. We fire on them, we walk about within less than a mile of them, and they maintain an ominous silence. On the heights of Chatillon it is said at the advanced posts that there are 108 siege guns in position; some of them we can actually distinguish without a glass, and yet not a shot comes from them. Yesterday, the gates of the Bois de Boulogne were opened, and a crowd of several thousand persons walked and drove round the lake. Over their heads one of the bastions was throwing shells into Montretout, but it seemed to occur to no one that Montretout might return the compliment, and throw a few shells, not over their heads, but into their midst. One of the most curious phases in this remarkable siege is, that the women seem to consider the whole question a political one, which in no way regards them—they neither urge the men to resist, nor clamour for peace. *Tros Tyriusque* seems much the same to them; a few hundreds have dressed themselves up as vivandières, the others appear to regret the rise in the price of provisions, but to trouble their heads about nothing else. If they thought that the cession of Alsace and Lorraine would reduce the price of butchers' meat, they would in a sort of apathetic way be in favour of the cession; but they are so utterly ignorant of everything except matters connected with their toilettes and M. Paul de Kock's novels, that they confine themselves to shrugging their shoulders and hoping for the best, and they support all the privations to which they are exposed owing to the siege without complaint and without enthusiasm. The word armistice being beyond the range of their vocabulary, they call it "l'aministie," and imagine that the question is whether or not King William is ready to grant Paris an amnesty. As Æneas and Dido took refuge in a cave to avoid a shower, so I for the same reason found myself with a young lady this morning under a porte cochère. Dido was a lively and intelligent young person, but I discovered in the course of our chance conversation that she was under the impression that the Russians as well as the Prussians were outside Paris, and that both were waging war for the King of Spain. Sedan, I also learnt, was in the neighbourhood of Berlin.

The *Temps* gives the following details of our provisions —Beef will fail in a week, horse will then last a fortnight; salt meat a further week; vegetables, dried fruits, flour, &c., about three weeks more. In this calculation I think that the stock of flour is understated, and that if we are contented to live on bread and wine we shall not be starved out until the middle of January. The ration of fresh meat is now reduced in almost all the arrondissements to thirty grammes a head. There is no difficulty, however, in obtaining for money any quantity of it in the restaurants. In the bouillons only one portion is served to each customer. Cats have risen in the market—a good fat one now costs twenty francs. Those that remain are exceedingly wild. This morning I had a salmis of rats—it was excellent—something between frog and rabbit. I breakfasted with the correspondents of two of your contemporaries. One of them, after a certain amount of hesitation, allowed me to help him to a leg of a rat; after eating it he was as anxious as a terrier for more. The latter, however, scornfully refused to share in the repast. As he got through his portion of salted horse, which rejoiced in the name of beef, he regarded us with horror and disgust. I remember when I was in Egypt that my feelings towards the natives were of a somewhat similar nature when I saw them eating rat. The older one grows the more tolerant one becomes. If ever I am again in Africa I shall eat the national dish whenever I get a chance. During the siege of Londonderry rats sold for 7s. each, and if this siege goes on many weeks longer, the utmost which a person of moderate means will be able to allow himself will be an occasional mouse. I was curious to see whether the proprietor of the restaurant would boldly call rat, rat in my bill. His heart failed him—it figures as a salmi of game.

November 15*th*.

We have passed from the lowest depths of despair to the wildest confidence. Yesterday afternoon a pigeon arrived covered with blood, bearing on its tail a despatch from Gambetta, of the 11th, announcing that the Prussians had been driven out of Orleans after two days' fighting, that 1,000 prisoners, two cannon, and many munition waggons had been taken, and that the 'pursuit was still continuing. The despatch was read at the Mairies to large crowds, and in the *cafés* by enthusiasts, who got upon the tables. I was in a shop when a person came in with it. Shopkeeper, assistants, and customers immediately performed a war dance round a stove; one would have supposed that the war was over and that the veracity of Gambetta is unimpeachable. But as though this success were not enough in itself, all the newspapers this morning tell us that "Chartres has also been retaken," that the army of Kératry has effected a junction with that of the Loire, and that in the North Bourbaki has forced the Prussians to raise the siege of Amiens. Everyone is asking when "they" will be here. Edmond About, in the *Soir*, eats dirt for having a few days ago suggested an armistice.

At the Quartier-Général I do not think that very great importance is attached to Gambetta's despatch, except as an evidence that the provinces are not perfectly apathetic. It is considered that very possibly the Prussians may have concentrated their whole available force round Paris, in order to crush our grand sortie when it takes place. General Trochu himself takes the most despondent view of the situation, and bitterly complains of the "spirit" of the army, the Mobiles, and the Parisians. This extraordinary commander imagines that he will infuse a new courage in his troops by going about like a monk of La Trappe, saying to every one, "Brother, we must die."

Mr. Washburne received yesterday a despatch from his Government—the first which has reached him since the commencement of the siege—informing him that his conduct in remaining at Paris is approved of. With the despatch there came English newspapers up to the 3rd. Extracts from them will, I presume, be published to-morrow. I passed the afternoon greedily devouring the news at the American Legation. It was a curious sight—the Chancellerie was crowded with people engaged in the same occupation. There were several French journalists, opening their eyes very wide, under the impression that this would enable them to understand English. A Secretary of Legation was sitting at a table giving audiences to unnumbered ladies who wished to know how they could leave Paris; or, if this was impossible, how they could draw on their bankers in New York. Mr. Washburne walked about cheerily shaking everyone by the hand, and telling them to make themselves at home. How different American diplomatists are to the prim old women who represent us abroad, with a staff of half-a-dozen dandies helping each other to do nothing, who have been taught to regard all who are not of the craft as their natural enemies. At the English Embassy Colonel Claremont and a porter now represent the British nation. The former, in obedience to orders from the Foreign Office, is only waiting for a reply from Count Bismarck to his letter asking for a pass to leave us. Whether the numerous English who remain here are then to look to Mr. Washburne or to the porter for protection I have been unable to discover.

M. Felix Pyat has been let out of prison. He says that he rather prefers being there than at liberty, for in his cell he can "forget that he is in a town inhabited by cowards," and devote himself to the works of M. Louis Blanc, which he calls the "Bibles of democracy."

Although Trochu is neither a great general nor a great statesman, he is a gentleman. I am therefore surprised that he allows obscene caricatures of the Empress to be publicly sold in the streets and exhibited in the kiosks. During the time that she occupied the throne in this most scandal-loving town, no scandal was ever whispered against her. She was fond, it is true, of dress, but she was a good mother and a good wife. Now that she and her friends are in exile, "lives of the woman Bonaparte" are hawked about, which in England would bring their authors under Lord Campbell's statute. In one caricature she is represented stark naked, with Prince Joinville sketching her. In another, called "the Spanish cow," she is made a sort of female Centaur. In another she is dancing the Can-can, and throwing her petticoats over her head, before King William, who is drinking champagne, seated on a sofa, while her husband is in a cage hung up to the wall. These scandalous caricatures have not even the merit of being funny, they are a reflection upon French chivalry, and on that of Trochu. What would he say if the Government which succeeds him were to allow his own wife to be insulted in this cowardly manner?

Anything more dreary than the Boulevards now in the evening it is difficult to imagine. Only one street lamp in three is lighted, and the *cafés*, which close at 10·30, are put on half-allowance of gas. To mend matters, everyone who likes is allowed to put up a shed on the side walk to sell his goods, or to collect a crowd by playing a dirge on a fiddle. The consequence is that the circulation is rendered almost impossible. I suggested to a high authority that the police ought at least to interfere to make these peripatetic musicians "move on," but he told me that, were they to do so, they would be accused of being "Corsicans and Reactionaries." These police are themselves most ludicrous objects; anyone coming here would suppose that they are members of some new sect of peripatetic philosophers; they walk about in pairs, arrayed in pea jackets with large hoods; and when it is wet they have umbrellas. Their business appears to be never to interfere with the rights of their fellow-citizens to do what they please, and so helpless do they look, that I believe if a child were to attack them, they would appeal to the passers-by for protection.

I see in an English paper of the 3rd that it is believed at Versailles that we have only fresh meat for twelve days. We are not so badly off as that. How many oxen and cows there still are I do not know; a few days ago, however, I counted myself 1,500 in a large pen. The newspapers calculate that at the commencement of the siege there were 100,000 horses in Paris, and that there are now 70,000; 30,000 will be enough for the army, consequently 40,000 can be eaten. The amount of meat on each horse averages 500 lb., consequently we have twenty million pounds of fresh horseflesh, a quantity which will last us for more than three months at the present rate of the meat consumption. These figures are, I think, very much exaggerated. I should say that there are not more than 40,000 horses now in Paris. The *Petites Voitures* (Cab) Company has 8,000, and offered to sell them to the Government a few days ago, but that proposal was declined. As regards salt meat, the Government keep secret the amount. It cannot, however, be very great, because it is only derived from animals which have been killed since the siege commenced. The stock of flour, we are told, is practically unlimited, and as no attempt is made to prevent its waste in pasty and fancy cakes, the authorities are acting apparently on this assumption.

The health of Paris is far from satisfactory, and when the winter weather regularly sets in there will be much sickness. No one is absolutely starving, but many are without sufficient nourishment. The Government gives orders for 10c. worth of bread to all who are in want, and these orders are accepted as money by all the bakers. In each arrondissement there are also what are called cantines économiques, where a mess of soup made from vegetables and a small quantity of meat can be bought for five centimes. Very little, however, has been done to distribute warm clothing among the poor, and when it is considered that above 100,000 persons have come into Paris from the neighbouring villages, most of whom are dependent upon public or private charity, it is evident that, even if there is no absolute want, there must be much suffering. Count Bismarck was not far wrong when he said that, if the siege be prolonged until our stock of provisions is exhausted, many thousands in the succeeding weeks will die of starvation. I would recommend those charitable persons who are anxious to come to the aid of this unfortunate country to be ready to throw provisions into Paris as soon as communications with England are reopened, rather than to subscribe their money to ambulances. All things considered, the wounded are well tended. In the hotel in which I am residing the Société Internationale has established its head-quarters. We have now 160 wounded here, and beds are prepared for 400. The ambulance occupies two stories, for which 500 francs a day are paid; and an arrangement has been made with the administration of the hotel to feed the convalescent for 2·50 francs per diem. As in all French institutions, there appear to me to be far too many officials; the corridors are pervaded with young healthy men, with the red cross on their arms, who are supposed to be making themselves useful in some mysterious manner, but whose main object in being here is, I imagine, to shirk military service. The ambulance which is considered the best is the American. The wounded are under canvas, the tents are not cold, and yet the ventilation is admirable. The American surgeons are far more skilful in the treatment of gun-shot wounds than their French colleagues. Instead of amputation they practise resection of the bone. It is the dream of every French soldier, if he is wounded, to be taken to this ambulance. They appear to be under the impression that, even if their legs are shot off, the skill of the Æsculapii of the United States will make them grow again. Be this as it may, a person might be worse off than stretched on a bed with a slight wound under the tents of the Far West.

The French have a notion that, go where you may, to the top of a pyramid or to the top of Mont Blanc, you are sure to meet an Englishman reading a newspaper; in my experience of the world, the American girl is far more inevitable than the Britisher; and, of course, under the Stars and Stripes which wave over the American tents she is to be found, tending the sick, and, when there is nothing more to be got for them, patiently reading to them or playing at cards with them. I have a great weakness for the American girl, she always puts her heart in what she is about. When she flirts she does it conscientiously, and when she nurses a most uninviting-looking Zouave, or Franc-tireur, she does it equally conscientiously; besides, as a rule, she is pretty, a gift of nature which I am very far from undervaluing.

November 16*th.*

It is reported in "official circles" that a second pigeon has arrived with intelligence from the French Consul at Bâle, that the Baden troops have been defeated, and that some of them have been obliged to seek refuge in Switzerland. The evident object of Trochu now is to get up the courage of our warriors to the sticking point for the grand sortie which is put off from day to day. The newspapers contain extracts from the English journals which came in the day before yesterday. By a process, in which we are adepts at believing everything which tells for us, and regarding everything which tells against us as a fabrication of perfidious Albion, we have consoled ourselves with the idea that "the situation is far better than we supposed." As for Bazaine, we cannot make up our minds whether we ought to call him a traitor or a hero. We therefore say as little about him as possible.

I have just come back from the southern outposts. The redoubts of Moulin Saqui and Hautes Bruyères were firing heavily, and the Prussians were replying from Chatillon. Their shrapnell, however, fell short, just within our advanced line. From the sound of the guns, it was supposed that they were only using field artillery. The sailors insist that the enemy has been unable to place his siege-guns in position, and that our fire knocks their earthworks to pieces. I am inclined to think that behind these earthworks there are masked batteries, for surely the Prussian Engineer officers cannot be amusing themselves with making earthworks for the mere pleasure of seeing them knocked to pieces. Anyhow they are playing a deep game, for, as far as I can hear, they have not fired a single siege-gun yet, either against our redoubts or forts.

November 19th.

Burke, in his work on the French Revolution, augured ill of the future of a country the greater number of whose legislators were lawyers. What would he have said of a Government composed almost exclusively of these objects of his political distrust? When history recounts the follies of the French Republic of 1870, I trust that it will not forget to mention that all the members of the Government, with the exception of one—six ministers, 13 under-secretaries of State, the Prefet of Police, 24 prefets and commissaries, sent into the provinces, and 36 other high functionaries—belonged to the legal profession. The natural consequence of this is that we cannot get out of "Nisi prius." Our rulers are unable to take a large statesmanlike view of the situation. They live from hand to mouth, and never rise above the expedients and temporizing policy of advocates. They are perpetually engaged in appealing against the stern logic of facts to some imaginary tribunal, from which they hope to gain a verdict in favour of their clients. Like lawyers in England, they entered public life to "get on." This is still the first object of each one of them; and as they are deputies of Paris, they feel that, next to themselves, they owe allegiance to their electors. To secure the supremacy of Paris over the provinces, and of their own influence over Paris, is the Alpha and Omega of their political creed. With an eye to the future, each of them has his own journal; and when any decree is issued which is not popular, the public is given to understand in these semi-official organs that every single member of the Government voted against it, although it passed by a majority.

It is somewhat strange that the military man who, by the force of circumstances, is the President of this Devil's own Government is by nature more of a lawyer than even if he had been bred up to the trade. His colleagues own in despair that he is their master in strength of lungs, and that when they split straws into two he splits them into four. In vain they fall back on their pens and indite letters and proclamations, their President out-letters and out-proclaims them. Trochu is indeed a sort of military Ollivier. He earned his spurs as a military critic, Ollivier as a civil critic. Both are clever, and eminently respectable in their private relations, and both are verbose, unpractical, and wanting in plain common sense. Ollivier had a plan, and so has Trochu. Ollivier complained when his plan failed, that it was the fault of every one except himself, and Trochu is already doing the same. Both protested against the system of rule adopted by their predecessors, and have followed in their steps. Both were advocates of publicity, and both audaciously suppressed and distorted facts to suit their convenience. Ollivier is probably now writing a book to prove that he was the wisest of ministers. Trochu, as soon as the siege is over, will write one to prove that he was the best of generals. Ollivier insisted that he could found a Liberal Government upon an Imperial basis, and miserably failed. Trochu declares that he, and he alone, can force the Prussians to raise the siege of Paris. When his plan has failed, as fail it in all probability will, he still, with that serene assurance which is the attribute of mediocrity, will insist that it ought to have succeeded. "*Victrix causa Diis placuit, sed victa Catoni.*" Those who knew him in Brittany tell me that long before he became a personage, "le plan de Trochu" was a standing joke throughout that province. The General, it appears, is fond of piquet; whenever he sat down to play he said, "j'ai mon plan." When he got up after losing the game, as was usually the case, he went away muttering, "Cependant, mon plan était bon." He seemed to have this word "plan" on the brain, for no one who ever played with him could perceive in his mode of handling the cards the slightest trace of a plan. The mania was harmless as long as its exhibition was confined to a game in which a few francs were to be won or lost, but it becomes most serious in its consequences when the destinies of a country are subordinated to it. At the commencement of the siege, General Trochu announced that he not only had a "plan," but that he had inscribed it in his will, which was deposited with his notary. An ordinary man would have made use of the materials at his command, and, without pledging himself to success, would have endeavoured to give the provinces time to organize an army of succour by harassing the Prussians, and thus preventing them from detaching troops in all directions. Instead of this, with the exception of some two or three harmless sorties, they have been allowed slowly to inclose us in a net of circumvallations. Our provisions are each day growing more scarce, and nothing is done except to heap up defensive works to prevent the town being carried by an assault, which there is no probability that the besiegers mean to attempt. Châtillon and Meudon were ill guarded, but ditches were cut along the Avenue de l'Impératrice. The young unmarried men in Paris were not incorporated until the 50th day of the siege, but two or three times a week they were lectured on their duties as citizens by their leader. If there is really to be a sortie everything is ready, but now the General hesitates—hints that he is not seconded, that the soldiers will not fight, and almost seems to regret at last his own theoretical presumption. "He trusted," said one of his generals to me, "first to the neutrals, then to the provinces, and now he is afraid to trust to himself." Next time a general is besieged in a town I should recommend him not to announce that he has a plan which must ensure victory, unless indeed it be a German town, where nothing which an official can do is considered ridiculous.

Benjamin Constant said of his countrymen that their heads could never contain more than one idea at once. A few days ago we were full of our victory at Orleans. Then came the question whether or not Bazaine was a traitor. To-day we have forgotten Bazaine and Orleans. The marching battalions of the National Guard are to have new coats, and we can talk or think of nothing else. The effect as yet of these marching battalions has been to disorganise the existing battalions. Every day some new decree has been issued altering their mode of formation. Perhaps the new coats will settle everything, and convert them into excellent soldiers. Let us hope it.

We are by no means satisfied with the news which has reached us through the English papers up to the 3rd. Thus the *Liberté*, after giving extracts from numbers of the *Pall Mall Gazette*, the *Daily News*, the *Daily Telegraph*, the *Sun*, the *Times*, and the *Standard*, accompanies them with the following reflections :—" We feel bound to protest in favour of the English press against the assertions of those who would judge the opinions of a great liberal nation by the wretched specimens which are under our eyes. Heaven be praised. The civilized world is not so degenerate that the ignoble conduct of Prussia fails to elicit universal reprobation." We have had two more pigeons, but Gambetta either cannot or will not let us know anything of importance. These two messengers confirm the news of the "victory of Orleans," and inform us that public opinion is daily pronouncing in favour of France, and that the condition of affairs in the provinces is most satisfactory. Such is the universal distrust felt now for any intelligence which emanates from an official source, that if Gambetta were to send us in an account of a new victory to-morrow, and if all his colleagues here were to swear to its truth, we should be in a wild state of enthusiasm for a few hours, and then disbelieve the whole story.

Small-pox is on the increase. The deaths last week from this disease amounted to 419; the general mortality to 1885—a number far above the average. The medical men complain of the amount of raw spirits which is drunk—particularly at the ramparts, and ascribe much of the ill health to this cause.

By the bye, the question of the treason of Bazaine turns with us upon what your correspondent at Saarbruck meant by the word "stores," which he says were discovered in Metz. If munitions of war, we say that Bazaine was a hero; if food, that he was a traitor.

If sieges were likely to occur frequently, the whole system of ambulances, as against military hospitals, would have to be ventilated. There are in Paris two hundred and forty-three ambulances, and when the siege commenced, such was the anxiety to obtain a *blessé*, that when a sortie took place, those who brought them in were offered bribes to take them to the house over which the flag of Geneva waved. A man with a broken leg or arm was worth thirty francs to his kind preservers. The largest ambulance is the International. Its headquarters are at the Grand Hotel. It seems to me over-manned, for the number of the healthy who receive pay and rations from its funds exceeds the number of the wounded. Many, too, of the former are young unmarried men, who ought to be serving either in the ranks of the army, or at least of the Garde Nationale. The following story I take from an organ of public opinion of to-day's date :—A lady went to her Mairie to ask to be given a wounded soldier to look after. She was offered a swarthy Zouave. "No," she said, "I wish for a blonde, being a brunette myself"—nothing like a contrast.

CHAPTER XII.

November 30*th*.

FROM morning to evening cannon were rolling and troops were marching through the streets. Since Saturday night the gates of the town had been rigidly closed to all civilians, and even those provided with passes from headquarters were refused egress. It was known that the grand effort which is to make or mar us was to be made the next morning, and it was hoped that the Prussians would be taken unawares. The plan, in its main details, was confided to me by half a dozen persons, and, therefore, I very much question whether it is a secret to the enemy. Most of those who take an interest in the war have, I presume, a map of Paris. If they consult it, they will see that the Marne from the east, and the Seine from the south, unite about a mile from the south-eastern corner of the enceinte. Two miles before the junction of the two rivers the Marne makes a loop to the south, in this way running parallel with the Seine for about three miles. On the north of the Marne towards Paris lies the wood of Vincennes, and beyond the loop there are the villages of Joinville, Nogent, and Brie. The line is defended by the forts of Vincennes and Nogent and the redoubt of La Faisanderie. To the south, between the loop and the Seine, is the fort of Charenton; a little farther on the village of Créteil; beyond it, just outside the loop, is Montmesly, where the Prussians have heavy batteries. On the north side of the loop is the village of Champigny, which is situated on a plateau that extends from there to Brie. On the south of Paris, between the Seine and Meudon, are first a line of forts, then a line of redoubts, except where Châtillon cuts in close by the Fort of Vanves. Beyond this line of redoubts is a plain, which slopes down towards the villages of L'Hay, Chevilly, Thiais, and Choisy-le-Roi, which is situated on the Seine about five miles from Paris. By Monday evening about 100,000 men and 400 cannon were massed under General Ducrot in the Bois de Vincennes and in the adjacent villages. About 15,000 men, under General Vinoy, were behind the southern line of redoubts close by the village of Villejuif. Troops were also placed near St. Denis and in the peninsula of Genevilliers to distract the attention of the enemy. It was arranged that early in the morning General Vinoy should push forward in the direction of L'Hay and Choisy, and then, when the Prussian reserves had been attracted to the south by this demonstration, Ducrot should throw bridges over the Marne and endeavour to force his way through the lines of investment by the old high road of Bâle. At one in the morning a tremendous cannonade from all the forts and redoubts round Paris commenced. It was so loud that I imagined that the Prussians were attempting an assault, and I went off to the southern ramparts to see what was happening. The sight there was a striking one. The heavy booming of the great guns, the bright flash each time they fired, and the shells with their lighted fusees rushing through the air, and bursting over the Prussian lines, realised what the French call a "feu d'enfer." At about three o'clock the firing slackened, and I went home, but at four it recommenced. At six o'clock General Vinoy's troops advanced in two columns, one against L'Hay, and the other against La Gare aux Bœufs, a fortified enclosure, about a mile above Choisy-le-Roi. The latter was speedily occupied, a body of sailors rushing into it, and carrying all before them, the Prussians falling back on Choisy. At L'Hay the attacking column met with a strenuous resistance. As soon as it had passed the barricade at the entrance of the village, a heavy fire was poured into it from the houses at both sides of the main street. A hand-to-hand encounter then took place with the Prussian Guard, which had been brought up as a reinforcement. While the fight was progressing an order arrived from General Trochu to retreat. The same order was sent to the Gare aux Bœufs, and by ten o'clock the troops to the south of Paris had fallen back to the positions they occupied the previous evening. General Vinoy, during the engagement, was with his staff on the bridge which crosses the Seine near Charenton. A battalion of National Guards were drawn up near him. A chance shell took off the legs of one of these heroes, his comrades fled in dismay—they were rallied and brought back with difficulty. A little later they were engaged in cooking their food, when some tin pans fell against each other. Thinking it was a bomb, they again scattered, and the General was obliged to ride along the line shouting "Courage, courage ; it is the soup, my children." In the meantime a terrible mishap had occurred on the north of the Marne. On Monday evening, General Trochu and General Ducrot slept at Vincennes. The latter had issued an address, in which he informed his troops that he meant either to conquer or die. During the night an exchange of shots had taken place across the river between the French and Prussian sharp-shooters. Towards morning the latter had withdrawn. At break of day the troops were drawn up ready to cross the river as soon as the engagement on the southern lines had diverted the attention of the enemy. The bridges were there ready to be thrown across, when it was discovered that the Marne had overflown its bed, and could not be crossed. Whether it be true or not that the

Prussians had cut a dam, or whether, as sometimes occurs with literary generals, the pontoons were too few in number, is not yet clear. Whatever the cause, the effect was to render it impossible to carry out to-day the plan which was to take General Ducrot and his troops down to Orleans, and at the present moment he and they are still at Vincennes, waiting for the river to go down. At twelve o'clock I managed to get through the gate of Vanves. Outside the walls everything was quiet. Troops were massed in all sheltered places to resist any attack which might be made from the plateau of Chatillon. None of the officers seemed to know what had occurred. Some thought that Choisy had been taken, others that Ducrot had got clear away. I was walking along the outposts in advance of Vanves, when a cantankerous officer, one of those beings overflowing with ill-regulated zeal, asked me what I was doing. I showed my pass. My zealous friend insisted that I had come in from the Prussian lines, and that I probably was a spy. I said I had left Paris an hour ago. He replied that this was impossible, as no civilian was allowed to pass through the gate. Things began to look uncomfortable. The zealot talked of shooting me, as a simple and expeditious mode of solving the question. To this I objected, and so at length it was agreed that I should be marched off to the fort of Vanves. We found the Commandant seated before his fort with a big stick in his hand, like a farmer before his farm yard. In vain the zealot endeavoured to excite his ire against me. The Commandant and I got into conversation and became excellent friends. He, too, knew nothing of what had occurred. He had been bombarding Chatillon, he said, and he supposed he should soon receive orders to recommence. What seemed to surprise him was that the Prussians during the whole night had not replied either from Chatillon, Sèvres, or Meudon to the French guns. From Vanves I went to Villejuif, where a temporary ambulance had been erected, and the surgeons were busy with the wounded. As soon as their wounds were dressed, they were taken in ambulance carts inside the town. The officers and soldiers, who had not yet learnt that General Ducrot had failed to cross the Marne, were in a very bad humour at having been ordered to withdraw at the very moment when they were carrying everything before them. They represented the Prussians as having fought like devils, and declared that they appeared to take a fiendish pleasure in killing even the wounded. Within the town the excitement to know what had passed is intense. The Government has posted up a notice saying that everything is happening as General Trochu wished it. Not a word is said about Ducrot's failure. The *Liberté*, which gives a guarded account of what really took place, has been torn to pieces on the Boulevards. I have just been talking with an officer on the headquarters staff. He tells me that Trochu is still outside, very much cast down, but determined to make a desperate effort to retrieve matters to-morrow.

We have received to-day some English newspapers, and you may imagine how far behind the age we are from the fact that we learn for the first time that Prince Gortschakoff has put his finger into the pie. Good heavens! I have invested my savings in Turkish Five per cents., and it gives me a cold shiver to think at what figure I shall find these Oriental securities quoted on the Stock Exchange when I emerge from my enforced seclusion and again find myself in communication with the outer world.

December 3rd.

For the last two days the public within the walls of Paris has been kept in profound ignorance of what has been passing outside. General Trochu has once or twice each day published a despatch saying that everything is happening as he anticipated, and the majority of those who read these oracular utterances religiously believe in them as though they had never been deceived. On the Boulevards there are crowds who question any soldier who is seen passing. "Tout va bien" is the only answer which they get; but they seem to be under the impression that the siege is already over, and that the Prussian lines have been forced. Along the road inside the ramparts, and at the gates, there are dense masses listening to the cannon, and on every mound from which a distant view of the smoke can be obtained men, women, and children are congregated. I managed to get both yesterday and to-day into the horse-shoe at the mouth of which the fighting was going on, and yesterday afternoon, when there was a semi-suspension of arms to bury the dead, I went with the ambulances on the debateable land between the two armies. The whole horse-shoe is full of artillery. The bombs and shells from the forts and batteries pass over them, and explode within the Prussian lines. A little behind, every house is filled with wounded, who are taken, as soon as their wounds are dressed, inside the town. One or two batteries occasionally open fire, and occasionally those of the Prussians respond. Trochu and Ducrot ride about, and, as far as I can see, the latter commands while the former make speeches. Yesterday afternoon we had lost ground at Champigny, and we had gained ground at Villiers. Before our lines a very large number of Prussian dead were lying. There were burying parties out on both sides, but they were getting on very slowly with their work, and were perpetually fired on. At 4 A.M. the Prussians had made a rush at our lines from Champigny to Brie, and the Mobiles and line, taken by surprise, hastily fell back. One or two regiments of Mobiles were literally charged by squadrons of gendarmerie, to force them back. Reinforcements came up, and by nine o'clock the positions had been regained—the Prussians being unable to withstand the fire of our forts, redoubts, and siege-guns. The battle then went on till about three o'clock, when it died out. Towards Villiers, I should say we had gained about three-quarters of a mile, and at Champigny we had lost about a third of the village. At about five o'clock I got back to my hotel, which is the headquarters of the Ambulance Internationale. Until eleven o'clock wounded were being brought in. It is quite full now. About 460 French, and 30 Germans—almost all Saxons. Many died during the night. In the room next to mine, Franchetti, the commander of the Eclaireurs of the Seine, is lying—a portion of his hip has been blown away by a shell, and the doctor has just told me that he fears that he will not recover, as the wound is too high up for an operation. In the room beyond him is a young lieutenant of Mobiles, who has had his leg amputated, and his right arm cut open to extract a portion of the bone, and who still has a ball in his shoulder. Most of the soldiers in here are wounded either in the leg or in the arm. There is a great dearth of doctors, and many wounded who were brought here last night had to wait until this morning before their turn came to be examined. The American Ambulance and several others are also, I hear, full. I go in occasionally to see the Germans, as I can talk their language, and it cheers them to hear it. I see in the newspapers that wounded Bavarians and Saxons are perpetually crying "Vive la France!" I can only say that those here do nothing of the kind. They do not seem to be particularly downcast at finding themselves in the hands of their enemies. They are treated precisely as the French are, and they are grateful for this.

This afternoon, when I got into the horse-shoe, I found the troops returning into Paris, and I was not able to get to the front. Some say that we have left 20,000 men at Villiers and Champigny; others that Champigny was lost last night. I hear, too, that early this morning the

Prussians attempted a surprise, but were driven back. The general idea seems to be, that to-morrow we are to try to get out either by Chatillon or Malmaison. A pigeon came in this morning from Bourbaki, with a despatch dated Nov. 30, stating that he is advancing, and among the soldiers this despatch has already become an official notice that he is at Meaux. All I know for certain is that the ambulances are ordered out for eight o'clock to-morrow morning, and that I am now going to bed, so as to be ready to start with them. I hear that there has been fighting both yesterday and to-day near Bondy; but not being able to be in two places at once, I cannot tell what really occurred. To my civilian judgment it appears that as our object was to force the line of heights on the south-east of Paris, which constitute the Prussian lines of investment in that direction, and as we have not done so, we can hardly be said to be in a better position than we were last Monday. At a heavy cost of life we have purchased the knowledge that our new artillery is better than was expected, and that Line and Mobiles will stand under fire with tolerable steadiness until their officers are bowled over, when they break. The National Guards were not engaged. General Trochu and General Pisani tried to get some of their battalions over the Marne, but found it impossible. After a long speech from Trochu, Pisani shouted, "Vive la France!" To this they responded; but when he added, "Vive Trochu!" they remained silent, and their commanders declared that this involved political considerations with regard to which they and their men "make certain reservations." They are, however, very proud of having been within two miles of a battle field, and Trochu congratulates them, in an order of the day, upon giving a "moral support" to the army. This is precisely what every one is willing to do. Moral support will not, however, get the Prussians away from Paris.

Food is becoming more scarce every day. Yesterday all our sausages were requisitioned. We have still got the cows to fall back on, but they are kept to the last for the sake of their milk. They are fed on oats, as hay is scarce. So you see the mother of a calf has many advantages over its uncle. All the animals in the Zoological Gardens have been killed except the monkeys; these are kept alive from a vague and Darwinian notion that they are our relatives, or at least the relatives of some of the members of the Government, to whom in the matter of beauty nature has not been bountiful. In the cellar of the English Embassy there are three sheep. Never did the rich man lust more after the poor man's ewe lamb than I lust after these sheep. I go and look at them frequently, much as a London Arab goes to have a smell at a cookshop. They console me for the absence of my ambassador. Some one has discovered that an excellent jelly can be made out of old bones, and we are called upon by the mayors to give up all our bones, in order that they may be submitted to the process. Mr. Powell is, I believe, a contractor in London. I do not know him; but yesterday I dined with a friend who produced from a tin some Australian mutton, which he had bought of Mr. Powell before the commencement of the siege. Better I never tasted, and out of gratitude I give the worthy Powell the benefit of a gratis advertisement. If we only had a stock of his meat here, we could defy the Prussians. As it is, I am very much afraid that in a very few weeks William will date his telegrams to Augusta from the Tuileries.

December 4th.

I wrote to you in a great hurry last night in order to catch a balloon which was to have gone this morning, but whose departure has been deferred as the wind was not favourable. I am now able to give some more accurate details respecting the affair of Friday, as I have had an opportunity of talking with several of the officers who were on the staffs of the different generals engaged. After the Prussians at 4 A.M. had surprised the whole of the French line from Brie to Champigny, they pushed forward a heavy column between the latter place and the Marne, thus outflanking their opponents. The column advanced about half-way up the horse-shoe formed by the bend in the river, and would have got as far as the bridges at Joinville, had not General Favé opened fire upon it from a small redoubt which he had built in advance of Joinville, and from forty field guns which he rapidly placed in position. Reinforcements were then brought up under General Blanchard, and the column was at length forced back, fighting hard to Champigny. Yesterday afternoon, most of the troops in the horse-shoe crossed over the river, and are now either in the wood of Vincennes or in other portions of the line between the forts and the enceinte. General Trochu has returned to the Louvre, and General Ducrot, I hear, yesterday evening expressed his regret that he had published that foolish manifesto, in which he declared that if he did not conquer he would die; for, not having done either, he felt the awkwardness of re-entering the city. Both Ducrot and Trochu freely exposed themselves; the latter received a slight wound in the back of the head from a piece of a shell which struck him. All the officers were obliged to keep well in advance of their soldiers in order to encourage them. The brunt of the fighting fell to the Line; the Mobiles, as a rule, only behaved tolerably well; the Vendeans, of whom much was expected, badly. The only battalion of the National Guards engaged was that from Belleville, and it very speedily fell back. I have always had my doubts about the valour of the Parisians. I found it difficult to believe in men who hunt for pretexts to avoid military service—who are so very fond of marching behind drums and vivandières inside a town, and who, in some way or other, manage either to avoid going out of it, or when forced out, avoid all danger.

The population is in profound ignorance of the real state of affairs outside. It still believes that the Prussian lines have been forced, and that the siege will be over in a few days. I presume that Trochu will make a second sortie in force. Unless, however, his operations are powerfully aided by the armies of the provinces, it is difficult to believe that the result will be anything beyond a useless sacrifice of life. On Friday, it is estimated that our loss amounted to 4,500 wounded, and 600 killed. That of the Prussians must have been very heavy, to judge from the number of dead bodies that were lying about in the fields and woods.

The ambulances were ordered out this morning, and at seven o'clock some 300 victims rendezvoused with the carriages on the Quai, near the Place de la Concorde. After freezing there for about two hours, it was suggested that a messenger should be sent to General Trochu, to ask him whether we were really wanted. The reply was that no attack would be made to-day, and consequently we went off home to thaw. If wars really must be made, I do hope that we shall fall back upon the old system of carrying on military operations in summer. When the thermometer is below zero, I feel like Bob Acres—all my valour oozing out at my fingers' ends. The doctors tell me that many slight wounds have gangrened owing to the cold. When a battle lasts until evening the mass of the wounded cannot be picked up until the next morning, and their sufferings during the night must be terrible. I saw several poor fellows picked up who appeared literally frozen.

The *Journal Officiel* of to-day contains a letter from Monseigneur Bauer, protesting against the Prussians having shot at him when he went forward with a flag of truce and a trompette. The fact is vouched for by, among others, a journalist who remained during the night of Friday outside the walls. I can easily believe it, for the Prussians are not a chivalrous enemy. They are perpetually firing on ambulances; and, when it suits their own purposes, raising the white flag. If, indeed, one-tenth part of the stories which I hear of their treacheries be true, they ought to be exterminated like wolves. This Monseigneur Bauer is a character. He began life as a German Jew, and he is now a Frenchman and a Christian Bishop. During the Empire he was chaplain to the court, and confessor of the Empress. He is now chaplain of the Ambulances de la Presse, and has under his orders 800 " Frères Chrétiens," who dress as priests, but are not in holy orders. Both he and they display the greatest courage. The Frères Chrétiens are the foremost in picking up the wounded; going forward long before the firing is over. The Bishop prances about on his horse, dressed in a soutane and long boots, the Grand Cross of the Legion of Honour on his breast, a golden crucifix hanging from his neck, and a huge episcopal ring on his finger, outside his gloves. Sometimes he appears in a red cloak, which, I presume, is a part of his sacerdotal gear. I am told by those who know him, that " Monseigneur" is a consummate humbug, but he is very popular with the soldiers, as he talks to them in their own language, and there certainly is no humbug about his pluck. He is as steady under fire as if he were in a pulpit. He was by the side of Ducrot when the general's horse was killed under him.

The events of the past week prove that General Trochu's sole available force for resisting the enemy consists of the Line and the Mobiles. As for the population of Paris, they are more than useless. They eat up the provisions; they are endowed with a mixture of obstinacy and conceit, which will very probably enable them to endure considerable hardships rather than surrender; fight, however, they will not, although I am convinced that, to the end of their lives, they will boast of their heroic valour, and in the legend which will pass muster as history of the siege of Paris, our grandchildren will be taught that in 1870, when the French troops were all prisoners of war, the citizens of the French capital "covered themselves with honour," and for nearly three months held their town against the furious onslaughts of the victorious German armies. The poor soldiers and the Mobiles, who do all the real fighting, will experience the eternal truth of Virgil's *Sic vos non vobis*. But there is no use being angry at what will happen in one hundred years, for what does it signify to any who are now alive either in Paris or out of Paris?

December 5th.

A proclamation has been issued by the Government, announcing that the troops have retired across the Marne, as the enemy has had time to collect such a force in front of Villiers and Champigny, that further efforts in this direction would be sterile. "The loss of the enemy during the glorious days of the 29th and 30th November, and December 2nd, has been so great that, struck down in its pride of power, it has allowed an army which it attacked the day before, to cross a river under its eyes, and in the light of day," continues this manifesto. Now, considering that the crossing took place at Joinville, and that the river at that point is under the fire of three forts and two redoubts, it appears to me that General Trochu might as well take credit to himself for crossing the Seine opposite the Place de la Concorde. I will say for the Government of to-day, that in any attempt to beat its predecessor in mendacity it had a hard task, but it has worked with a will, and completely succeeded. The military attachés who are still here, consider that the French loss during the three days cannot be less than 10,000 in killed and wounded. It is very unlikely that the Government will admit a loss of above 2,000 or 3,000. That of the Prussians is, we are told, far larger than ours. Without accepting this assertion as gospel, it must have been very heavy. A friend of mine himself counted 500 dead bodies in one wood. We have a certain number of prisoners. With respect to the wounded in our hands, I find that there are about 30 in my hotel, as against above 400 French. In the American ambulance, out of 130 only two are Germans: Colonel Claremont, who had put off his departure, witnessed the fight in the redoubt which General Favé had built opposite Joinville. He was nearly killed several times by bombs from La Faisanderie, which was behind him, bursting short.

The Parisians are somewhat taken aback at the victory resulting in a retreat. They appear, however, to be as ignorant of the environs of their own capital as they are of foreign countries, and they never condescend to consult a map. While some of them shake their heads in despair of success, the majority is under the impression that Villiers and Champigny are far beyond the range of the guns of our forts, and that as the ground near them is still occupied by our troops, something which will lead to the speedy retreat of the Prussians has been done. We are two millions, they say; we will all die rather than surrender: and they appear to be under the impression that if they only say this often enough, Paris never will be taken. The Ultra-Democrats in the clubs have a new theory to account for their refusal to fight. "We are," observed an orator, a few nights ago, "the children of Paris, she has need of us; can we leave her at such a moment?" Some of these heroes, indeed, assert that the best plan would be to allow the Prussians to enter and then convert them to the doctrines of Republicanism. I think it was St. Augustine who did not despair of the devil eventually turning over a new leaf; in the same way I heard an ardent patriot express the hope of being able to convert "William" himself to the creed of the Universal Republic. At the club where these fraternal sentiments were expressed there is a lady who sits on the platform. When anyone makes what she considers a good speech she embraces him on both cheeks. She is by no means ugly, and I had serious thoughts of making a few observations myself in view of the reward. That bashfulness, however, which has been my bane through life, prevented me. The lady occasionally speaks herself, and is fond of giving her own experiences. "I was on my way to this club," she said, "the other evening, when I observed a man following me. 'What dost thou want?' I asked, sternly eyeing him. 'I love you,' replied the vile aristocrat. 'I am the wife of a citizen,' I answered, 'and the mother of the Gracchi.' The wretch sneaked away, abashed to seek other prey. If he addresses himself to some princess or duchess he will probably find a victim." The loudest applause greeted this "experience," and several very unclean-looking patriots rushed forward to embrace the mother of the Gracchi, in order to show her how highly they appreciated her noble conduct.

The newspapers are already beginning to dread that possibly some doubts may be cast upon the heroism of everyone during the last week. The *Figaro* contains the following:—"No matter what certain correspondents—better known than they suppose—may say, and although they are preparing to infect foreign countries with their correspondence, our Bretons did not run away on Thursday. It is true that when they saw the Saxons emerging from their holes and shouting hurrah, our Bretons were a little troubled by this abrupt and savage joke, but"—then follows the statement of several of the heroes themselves that they fought like lions. The fact is, as I have already stated in my letter of yesterday, the Mobiles fought only tolerably well, and some of their battalions rather the reverse of well. The Line, for young troops, behaved very fairly; and the reckless courage of the officers, both of the Line and Mobile, was above all praise. It is, however, a military axiom that when an undue proportion of officers are killed in a battle their troops have hung back. Good soldiers cannot be made in two months, and it is absurd to expect that raw lads, who were taken from the plough a few weeks ago, would fight as well as trained and hardened warriors. This however, we are called upon, in defiance of facts, to believe, because " the soil of France produces soldiers."

It is difficult to guess what will happen now. The generals must be aware that unless one of the armies of the provinces take the Prussians in the rear, a fresh sortie will only result in a fresh butchery; but then, on the other hand, the Parisians will not be satisfied until all the Line and the Mobiles outside the walls have been killed, in order that it may be said that the resistance of Paris was heroic. If I were Trochu, I should organize a sortie exclusively of National Guards, in order to show these gentry what a very different thing real fighting is to parading about the streets of the capital and wearing a uniform.

The following is a list of the prices of "luxuries:"—Terrines of chicken, 16f.; of rabbit, 13f.; a fowl, 26f.; a rabbit, 18f.; a turkey, 60f.; a goose, 45f.; one cauliflower, 3f.; one cabbage, 4f.; dog is 2f. a lb.; a cat skinned costs 5f.; a rat, 1f., if fat from the drains, 1f. 50c. Almost all the animals in the Jardin des Plantes have been eaten. They have averaged about 7f. a lb. Kangaroo, however, has been sold for 12f. the lb. Yesterday I dined with the correspondent of a London paper. He had managed to get a large piece of mufflon, an animal which is, I believe, only found in Corsica. I can only describe it by saying that it tasted of mufflon, and nothing else. Without being absolutely bad, I do not think that I shall take up my residence in Corsica, in order habitually to feed upon it.

CHAPTER XIII.

December 6th.

I AM by no means certain that I should be a hero at the Equator, but I am fully convinced that I should be an abject coward at the North Pole. Three mornings ago I stood for two hours by the Ambulances de la Presse, and my teeth have not ceased to chatter ever since. I pity the unfortunate fellows who had to keep watch all night on the plateau of Villiers more than those who were put out of their misery the day before. When it is warm weather, one views with a comparative resignation the Prussian batteries, and one has a sort of fanatical belief that the bombs will not burst within striking distance; when the thermometer is below zero, one imagines that every cannon within four miles is pointed at one's head. I do not know how it may be with others, but on me cold has a most unheroic effect. My legs become as wilful as those of Mrs. Dombey's titled relative, and it is only by the strongest effort of mind over matter that I can prevent them carrying me beyond the reach of cannon-balls, bullets, and shells. I have a horrible vision of myself lying all night with a broken leg in a ditch, gradually freezing. On a warm summer's day I do not think very much of the courage of those who fight well; on a cold winter's day, however, any man who does not run away and take shelter by a fire deserves well of his country.

We are by no means a very happy family. General Ducrot and General Blanchard have "had words." The latter, in the course of the dispute, said to the former, "If your sword were as long as your tongue, you would be a wonderful warrior indeed." Ducrot and Trochu are the literary Generals; Vinoy and Blanchard the fighting Generals. It is reported also that General Favé is to be superseded, though why I cannot learn, as his redoubt may be said to have saved the army from a greater disaster. While, however, the military men differ among themselves, they are all agreed in abusing the National Guards, whom they irreverently call "Les Charcutiers"—the pork butchers. When La Gare aux Bœufs was carried by Admiral Polhuan and his sailors, two battalions of these heroes followed in the rear. The Admiral and the sailors were somewhat astonished to find that in the order of the day hardly anything was said of those who really did all the fighting, but that the "pork butchers" were lauded to the skies. General Trochu on this wrote a letter to the Admiral, informing him that it was necessary for political reasons to encourage the National Guard. Whilst the battle was going on at Villiers and Champigny, the marching battalions of the National Guard were drawn up almost out of shot. An order came to form them into line. Their commander, General Clément Thomas, replied that this would be impossible, as they would imagine that they were about to be taken into action. Notwithstanding this, General Trochu congratulates them upon the "moral support" which they afforded him. It is not surprising that the real soldiers should feel hurt at this system of humbug. They declare that at the next sortie they will force the Parisians to fight by putting them in front, and firing on them if they attempt to run away. It must be remembered that these fighting battalions consist of young unmarried men, and if Paris is to be defended, there is no reason why they should not be exposed to danger.

The inhabitants of this city seem to consider themselves a sacred race; they clamour for sorties, vow to die for their country, and then wish to do it by procuration. I am utterly disgusted with the difference between their words and their deeds. The Mobiles and the Line have as yet done all the fighting, and yet, to read the Paris newspapers, one would suppose that the National Guards, who have kept well out of all danger, have "covered themselves with glory." Since the siege commenced they have done nothing but swagger about in uniforms, and go in turns on the ramparts. They have learnt to knock a penny off a cork at a distance of ten yards, and they have carried on a very successful campaign against the sparrows.

A fresh order was issued yesterday, suppressing all passes until further notice. I have a pass *en règle* from General Vinoy; but even with this, the last time I went out of the town I was turned back at two gates before I got through at the third. A good deal of dissension has taken place among the foreign correspondents respecting the fairness of going out with an ambulance under guise of the Geneva flag. I see myself no objection to it, provided the correspondent really does make himself useful in picking up the wounded. In the Prussian camp a correspondent has a recognised position; here it is different, and he must use all legitimate means to obtain intelligence of what is passing. My pass, for instance, does not describe me as a correspondent, but as an Englishman accredited by the British Embassy. At the commencement of the siege I begged Mr. Wodehouse to give me a letter of introduction to M. Jules Ferry, one of the members of the Government. This I did not deliver, but at General Vinoy's headquarters I showed it to prove that I was not a Prussian spy, but that I was known by my natural guardian. An aide-de-camp then gave me a pass, and, not knowing precisely what to call me, described me as "accredited by the British

Embassy." I move about, therefore, as a mysterious being—perhaps an Ambassador, perhaps an Ambassador's valet. A friend of mine, who is an authority with the Ambulance de la Presse, and who owns a carriage, has promised to call for me when next the ambulances are sent for; but, as I have already said, all my energy oozes out of me when the thermometer is below zero; and unless the next battle is fought on a warm day, I shall not witness it. As a matter of fact, unless one is riding with the staff of the general who commands, one cannot form an idea of what is going on by hanging about, and it is a horrible sight to look with an opera-glass at men and horses being massacred. When knights charged each other with lances there was a certain chivalry in war; but there is nothing either noble or inspiriting in watching a quantity of unfortunate Breton peasants, who cannot even speak French, and an equal number of Berlin grocers, who probably ask for nothing better than to be back in their shops, destroying each other at a distance of two or three miles with balls of lead and iron, many of them filled with explosive materials. I confess that I pity the horses almost as much as the men. It seems a monstrous thing that in order that the Alsacians should be forced into becoming subjects of King William of Prussia, an omnibus horse, who has honestly done his work in the streets of Paris, should be taken outside the walls of the town to have his head blown off or to stump about on three legs until he dies of cold and hunger. Horses have a way when they are wounded of making desperate efforts to get up, and then letting their heads fall with a bang on the soil which is very horrible to witness.

Everybody in authority and out of it seems to have a different opinion as to when the siege will end. I cannot think that when a town with two million inhabitants is reduced to such expedients as this is now, it can hold out very long. The rations, consisting alternately of horse and salt fish, are still distributed, but they are hardly sufficient to keep body and soul together. Unless we make up our minds to kill our artillery horses, we shall soon come to the end of our supply. The rumour to-day is that the Prussians have evacuated Versailles, and that Frederick Charles has been beaten in a battle on the Loire, but I cannot say that I attach great credit to either story. No pigeon has arrived for the last three days, owing, it is supposed, to the cold; and until we know for certain what d'Aurelles de Paladine is doing, we are unable to form an accurate opinion of the chances of the siege being raised. All that can be said is that, left to ourselves, we shall not be able to break through the lines of investment, and that when we have eaten up all our food, we shall have to capitulate.

December 7th.

When this war commenced the Parisians believed in the bulletins which their own Government issued, because they thought it only natural that their arms should be successful, and they disbelieved in any foreign newspaper which ventured to contest their victories. At present they are incredulous alike of everything that comes from friend and foe. Nine-tenths of them are under the impression that Count Moltke, in announcing the defeat of the Army of the Loire, is guilty of a deliberate falsehood; the other tenth supposes that he has grossly exaggerated a slight mishap, and that the occupation of Orleans only proves that Orleans was not defended by a large body of troops. It takes about three days for any information which is not in accordance with the wishes of this extraordinary population to obtain credit, no matter what amount of evidence there may be to prove its truth. If really the Army of the Loire has been put *hors de combat*, sooner or later the fact will be admitted; then, although we shall still pin our faith on Kératry or Bourbaki, the disaster will no doubt tend to produce a certain degree of discouragement, more particularly as it is coupled with the retreat of Ducrot's forces from the south bank of the Marne. French politicians will insist upon dressing up their facts in order to meet the requirements of the moment, and they never seem to consider that so soon as the real state of things comes out there must be an inevitable reaction, which will be far more depressing than if the truth had been fairly told at once. I hear that when Count Moltke's letter arrived, two of the members of the Government of National Defence were inclined to accept his offer to verify what had occurred on the Loire, but that General Trochu stated that he intended to resist until the last, and that consequently, whether Orleans had fallen or not, was a matter of no importance. If Trochu really thinks that a further resistance and a further sacrifice of life will materially advance the interests of his country, of course he is right to hold out; but if, disregarding facts, he simply wishes to oblige the Prussians to continue the siege, for no purpose except to prove his own tenacity, he cannot be regarded either as a good patriot or a sensible man. When the vote on the Plébiscite was taken, his majority consisted of "Ouis" which were given because it was supposed that he was about to treat. Since then we have gone on from day to day vaguely hoping that either the Neutral Powers or the armies of the provinces would get us out of the mess in which we are, or, even if these failed us, that by a sortie the town would be revictualled. At present none believe in the intervention of the Neutrals; few in the success of a sortie; but all still cling, as drowning men do to a straw, to the armies of the provinces. To destroy this belief it will be necessary for the Prussians to obtain a substantial advantage not only at Orleans, but over the armies of Kératry and Bourbaki. When once we find that we are entirely left to our own resources, and that it is impossible for us to penetrate the lines of investment, I cannot help thinking that we shall yield to the force of circumstances. At present all the newspapers are for fighting on as long as we have a crust, regardless of the consequences; but then, as a rule, a besieged town is never so near surrendering as when it threatens to hang the first man who speaks of surrender. The majority would even now take a practical view of matters if they dared, but Trochu is their man, and Trochu, much to their secret sorrow, refuses to hear of a capitulation.

Some German officers who are prisoners on parole have been insulted in a restaurant, and for their own safety it has been found necessary to confine them in La Roquette. I am not surprised at this. French officers are, of course, incapable of this contemptible conduct, and it must be owned that the majority of the Parisians have not, under the trying circumstances in which they find themselves, lost that courtesy which is one of the peculiar attributes of the nation. But there is a scum, who lived from hand to mouth during the Empire, and who infest the restaurants and the public places. Some of them wear the uniform of the National Guard; others have attached themselves to the ambulances; and all take very good care not to risk their precious lives. I was peaceably dining last night in a restaurant; a friend with whom I had been talking English had left me, and I found myself alone with four of these worthies, who were dining at a table near me. For my especial benefit they informed each other that all strangers here were outlaws from their own country, and that the Americans and Italians who have established ambulances were in all probability Prussian spies. As I took no notice of these startling generalities, one of them turned to me and said, "You may look at me, sir, but I assert before you that Dr. Evans, the ex-dentist of the Emperor, was a spy." I quietly remarked, that not having the honour to know Dr. Evans, and being myself an Englishman, whilst the

Doctor is an American, I was not responsible for him. "You are a Greek," observed another; "I heard you talk Greek just now." I mildly suggested that his knowledge of foreign tongues was, perhaps, somewhat limited. "Well, if you are not a Greek," he said, "I saw you the other morning near the Ambulance of the Press, to which I belong, and so you must be a spy." "If you are an Englishman," cried his friend, "why do you not go back to your own country, and fight Russia?" I replied that the idea was an excellent one, but that it might, perhaps, be difficult to pass through the Prussian lines. "The English Ambassador is a friend of mine, and he will give you a pass at my request," answered the gentleman who had mistaken English for Greek. I thanked him, and assured him that I should esteem it a favour if he would obtain from his friend Lord Lyons this pass for me. He said he would do so, as it would be well to rid Paris of such vermin as myself and my countrymen. He has not yet, however, fulfilled his promise. Scenes such as these are of frequent occurrence at restaurants; bully and coward are generally synonymous terms; any scamp may insult a foreigner now with perfect impunity, for if the foreigner replies he has only to denounce him as a spy, when a crowd will assemble, and either set on him or bear him off to prison. While, as I have already said, nothing can be more courteous than the conduct of French officers, French gentlemen, and, unless they are excited, the French poorer classes, nothing can be more insolent than that of the third-class dandies who reserve their valour for the interior of the town, or who, if ever they venture outside of its fortifications, take care to skulk beneath the protection of the cross of Geneva.

The *Journal Officiel* contains a decree breaking up the battalion of Belleville. These warriors, says their own Commander, ran away in the presence of the enemy, refused the next day to go to the front, and commenced fighting with their neighbours from La Villette. M. Gustave Flourens, who is the hero of these men of war, and who, although exercising no official rank in the battalion, insisted upon their accepting him as their chief, is to be brought before a Council of War.

My next-door neighbour, Franchetti, died yesterday, and was buried to-day. He was a fine, handsome young man, well off, happily married, and, as the commander of the Eclaireurs of the Seine, has done good service during the siege. As he was an Israelite, he was followed to the grave by the Rothschilds and many other of his co-religionists.

December 8th.

M. de Sarcey, in the *Temps* of to-day, enters into a lengthy argument to prove that the Parisians are heroic. " Heroism is positive and negative," he says, " and we have, for the sake of our country, deprived ourselves during several months of the power to make money, and during this time we have existed without many of the comforts to which we are accustomed." Now, I by no means wish to undervalue the sacrifices of the Parisians, but heroism is not the word for them. So long as there are enough provisions in the town to enable every one to live without feeling the pangs of hunger, they have no opportunity to show negative heroism. So long as the town is not assaulted, and they do not take part in sorties, they cannot be said to be actively heroic. A blockade such as the Prussians have instituted round Paris, is no doubt most disagreeable to its inhabitants. In submitting to it, undoubtedly they show their patriotism and their power of passive endurance. Heroism is, however, something more than either patriotism or endurance—it is an exceptional quality which is rarely found in this world. If the Parisians possessed it, I should admire them; because they do not, no one has a right to blame them.

The newspapers have now proved to their own complete

satisfaction that Count Moltke's assertion respecting the defeat of the Army of the Loire can only refer to its rearguard, and although no news from without has been received for several days, they insist that the greater portion of this army has effected its junction with that of Bourbaki. A French journalist, even when he is not obliged to do so, generally invents his facts, and then reasons upon them with wonderful ingenuity. I do not know whether the Paris journals get to you through the Prussian lines; if they do not, you have little idea how much excellent advice you lose. One would think that just at present a Parisian would do well to keep his breath to cool his own porridge; such, however, is not his opinion. He thinks that he has a mission to guide and instruct the world, and this mission he manfully fulfils in defiance of Prussians and Prussian cannon. It is true that he knows rather less of foreign countries than an intelligent Japanese Daimio may be supposed to know of Tipperary, but by some curious law of nature, the less he knows of a subject the more strongly does he feel impelled to write about it. I read a very clever article this morning, pointing out that, if we are not on our guard, our empire in India will come to an end by a Russian fleet attacking it from the Caspian Sea; and when one thinks how very easy it would have been for the author not to write about the Caspian Sea, one is at once surprised and grateful to him for having called our attention to the danger which menaces us in that quarter of the globe.

M. Gustave Flourens has been arrested and is now in prison. The clubs of the Ultras are very indignant at the Government having accused the braves of Belleville of cowardice. They feel convinced that the "Jesuit" Trochu must have introduced some *mouchards* into the band of heroes, who received orders to run away, in order to discredit the whole battalion. I was in the "Club de la Délivrance" this evening. It holds its sittings in the

Salle Valentino—a species of Argyle Rooms in normal times. I held up my hand in favour of a resolution to call upon the Government to inscribe upon marble tablets the names of the National Guards who have died in the defence of Paris. The resolution was carried unanimously. No National Guard has, indeed, yet been good enough to die; but of course this fact was regarded as irrelevant. The next resolution was that the concubines of patriots should enjoy the same right to rations as legitimate wives. As the Club prides itself upon the stern severity of its morals, this resolution was not carried. An orator then proposed that all strangers should be banished from France. He was so exceedingly lengthy that I did not wait until the end of his speech; I am, therefore, unable to say whether his proposal was carried. The Club de la Délivrance is by far the most respectable public assembly in Paris. Those who take part in its proceedings are intensely respectable, and as intensely dull and prosy. The suppression of gas has been a heavy blow to the clubs. The Parisians like gas as much as lazzaroni like sunshine. The grandest bursts of patriotic eloquence find no response from an audience who listen to them beneath half-a-dozen petroleum lamps. It is somewhat singular, but it is not the less certain, that the effect of a speech depends very much upon the amount of light in the room in which it is delivered. I remember once I went down to assist a friend of mine in an electioneering campaign in a small borough. His opponent was a most worthy and estimable squire, who resided in the neighbourhood. It was, of course, my business to prove that he was a despicable knave and a drivelling idiot. This I was engaged in doing at a public meeting in the town-hall. The Philippics of Demosthenes were milk and water in comparison with my denunciations—when just at the critical moment—as I was carrying conviction into the breasts of the stolid Britons who were listening to me, the gas flickered and went out. Three candles were brought in. I recommenced my thunder; but it was of no use. The candles utterly destroyed its effect, and two days afterwards the squire became an M.P., and still is a silent ornament of St. Stephen's.

I trust that England never will be invaded. But if it is, we shall do well to profit by the experience of what is occurring here. There must be no English force, half citizen half soldier. All who take part in the national defence must submit to the strict discipline of soldiers. A vast amount of money has been laid out in equipping the National Guard. Their pay alone amounts to above 20,000fr. per diem, and, as far as the defence of Paris is concerned, they might as well have remained quietly by their own firesides. There are, no doubt, brave men among them, but as their battalions insist upon being regarded as citizens even when under arms, they have no discipline, and are little better than an armed mob. The following extract from an article in the last number of the *Revue des Deux Mondes* gives some interesting details respecting their habits when on duty behind that most useless of all works of defence, the line of the Paris fortifications:—" On the arrival of a battalion, the chief of the post arranges the hours during which each man is to be on active duty. After this, the men occupy themselves as they please. Some play at interminable games of *bouchon;* others, notwithstanding orders to the contrary, turn their attention to écarté and piquet; others gossip over the news of the day with the artillerymen, who are keeping guard by the side of their cannon. Some go away on leave, or disappear without leave; they make excursions beyond the ramparts, or shut themselves up in the billiard-room of some café. Many make during the course of the day frequent visits to the innumerable canteens, which succeed each other almost without interruption along the Rue des Ramparts. Here old women have lit a few sticks under a pot, and sell, for a penny the glass, a horrible brew called 'petit noir,' composed of sugar, eau de vie, and the grains of coffee, boiled up together. Behind there is a line of cook shops, the proprietors of which announce that they have been commissioned to provide food. These speculators offer for sale greasy soup, slices of horse, and every species of alcoholic drink. Each company has, too, its cantinière, and round her cart there is always a crowd. It seldom happens that more than one-half of the men of the battalion are sober. Fortunately, the cold of the night air sobers them. Between eight and nine in the evening there is a gathering in the tent. A circle is formed in it round a single candle, and whilst the flasks go round tale succeeds to song, and song to tale, until at length all fall asleep, and are only interrupted in their slumbers until morning by the corporal, who, once every hour, enters and calls out the names of those who are to go on the watch. The abuse of strong drink makes shameful ravages in our ranks, and is productive of serious disorder. Few nights pass without false alarms, without shots foolishly fired upon imaginary enemies, and without lamentable accidents. Every night there are disputes, which often degenerate into fights, and then in the morning, when explanations take place, these very explanations are an excuse for recommencing drinking. Rules, indeed, are not wanting to abate all this, but the misfortune is that they are never executed. The indiscipline of the National Guard contrasts strangely with the patriotism of their words. Most of the insubordination may be ascribed to drunkenness, but the *mauvais tenue* which is so apparent in too many battalions is due also to many other causes. The primary organisation of the National Guard was ill-conceived and ill-executed, and when the enrolments had been made, and the battalions formed, day after day a fresh series of orders were promulgated, so diffuse, so obscure, and so contradictory, that the officers, despairing to make head or tail of them, gave up any attempt to enforce them."

The attempt at the last hour to form marching battalions out of these citizen soldiers, by obliging each sedentary battalion to furnish 150 men, has not been a very successful one. The marching battalions, it is true, have been formed, but they have not yet been engaged with the enemy; and it certainly is the opinion of military men that it will be advisable, for the credit of French arms, to "keep them in reserve" during any future engagement which may take place. General Clément Thomas has issued a series of general orders, from the tenor of which it would appear that the system of substitutes has been largely practised in these battalions. I have myself no doubt of the fact. The fault, however, lies with the Government. When these battalions were formed, the respective categories of unmarried and married men between 25 and 35, and between 35 and 45, were only to be drawn upon in case a sufficient number of volunteers were not forthcoming. It became, consequently, the interest of the men in these categories to encourage volunteering, and this was done on a large and liberal scale. The Government, if it wanted men, should have called to arms all between 25 and 35, and have allowed no exemptions. These new levies should have been subjected to the same discipline as the Line and the Mobiles. They must now accept the consequences of not having ventured to take this step. For all operations beyond the enceinte General Trochu's force consists of the Line and the Mobiles. All that he can expect from the Parisians is a "moral support."

December 9th.

Nothing new. If the Government has received any news from without, it carefully conceals it. A peasant, the newspapers say, has made his way through the Prussian lines, and has brought the information that the armies of the Loire and of Bourbaki are close to Fontainebleau. The cry is still that we will resist to the last, and for the moment every one seems to have forgotten that in a few weeks our provisions will all have been consumed. If we wait to treat until our last crust has been eaten, the pinch will come after the capitulation; for with the railroads and the high roads broken up, and the surrounding country devastated, a fortnight at least must elapse before supplies, in any quantity, can be thrown into the town.

I hear that the Prussian officers who were (says the *Journal Officiel*) insulted in a café, have been exchanged. A friend of mine, an ex-French diplomatist, was present when the scene occurred, and he tells me that the officers, who were all young men, were, to say the least of it, exceedingly indiscreet. Instead of eating their dinner quietly, they indulged in a good deal of loud, and by no means wise conversation, and their remarks were calculated to offend those Frenchmen who heard them.

December 15th.

Still no news from the outer world. I trust that M. Jansen, who was dispatched the other day in a balloon to witness the eclipse of the sun, will be more fortunate in his endeavours to discover what is going on in that luminary, than we are in ours to learn what is happening within twenty miles of us. Search has been made to find the peasant who announced that he had seen a French army at Corbeil, but this remarkable agriculturist is not forthcoming. Persons at the outposts say that they heard cannon in the direction of Fontainebleau, when they put their ears to the ground, but none believe them. Four officers, who were taken prisoners on the 12th of the month near Orleans, have been sent in, as an exchange for the Prussian officers who were insulted at a restaurant, but they are so stupid that it has been impossible to glean anything from them except that their division was fighting when they were taken prisoners. A dead, apathetic torpor has settled over the town. Even the clubs are deserted. There are no groups of gossips in the streets. No one clamours for a sortie, and no one either blames or praises Trochu. The newspapers still every morning announce that victory is not far off. But their influence is gone. The belief that the evil day cannot be far off is gradually gaining ground, and those who are in a position to know more accurately the precise state of affairs, take a still more hopeless view of them than the masses. The programme of the Government seems to be this—to make a sortie in a few days, then to fall back beneath the forts; after this to hold out until the provisions are eaten up, and then, after having made a final sortie, to capitulate. Trochu is entirely in the hands of Ducrot, who, with the most enterprising of the officers, insists that the military honour of the French arms demands that there should be more fighting, even though success be not only improbable but impossible. The other day, in a council of war, Trochu began to speak of the armies of the provinces. "I do not care for your armies of the provinces," replied Ducrot. Poor Trochu, like many weak men, must rely upon some one. First it was the neutrals, then it was the armies of the provinces, and now it is Ducrot. As for his famous plan, that has entirely fallen through. It was based, I understand, upon some impossible manœuvres to the north of the Marne. The members of the Government of National Defence meddle little with the direction of affairs. M. Picard is openly in favour of treating at once. M. Jules Favre is very downcast; he too wishes to treat, but he cannot bring himself to consent to a cession of territory. Another member of the Government was talking yesterday to a friend of mine. He seemed to fear that when the people learn that the stock of provisions is drawing to a close, there will be riots. The Government dares not tell them the truth. Several members of the Government, I hear, intend to leave shortly in balloons, and Trochu, as military Governor of Paris, will be left to his own devices. He himself says that he never will sign a capitulation, and it is suggested that when there is no more food, the Prussians shall be allowed to enter without opposition, without any terms having been previously agreed to. The Parisians are now contending for their supremacy over the provinces, and they seem to think that if they only hold out until famine obliges them to give in, that supremacy will not hereafter be disputed.

It is impossible to give precise data respecting the store of provisions now in Paris, nor even were I able would it be fair to do so. As a matter of private opinion, however, I do not think that it will be possible to prolong the resistance beyond the first week in January at the latest. Last Sunday there were incipient bread-riots. By one o'clock all the bakers had closed their shops in the outer faubourg. There had been a run upon them, because a decree had been issued in the morning forbidding flour to be sold, and requisitioning all the biscuits in stock. Government immediately placarded a declaration that bread was not going to be requisitioned, and the explanation of the morning's decree is that flour and not corn has run short, but that new steam-mills are being erected to meet the difficulty. *La Vérité*, a newspaper usually well informed, says that for some days past the flour which had been stored in the town by M. Clement Duvernois has been exhausted, and that we are now living on the corn and meal which was introduced at the last moment from the neighbouring departments. It gives the following calculation of our resources—flour three weeks, corn three months, salt meat fifteen days, horse two months. The mistake of all these calculations seems to be that they do not take into account the fact that more bread or more corn will be eaten when they become the sole means of providing for the population. Thus the daily results of flour sold in Paris is about one-third above the average. The reason is simple, and yet it seems to occur to no one. French people, more particularly the poorer classes, can exist upon much less than Englishmen; but the prospect for any one blessed with a good appetite is by no means reassuring. In the Rue Blanche there is a butcher who sells dogs, cats, and rats. He has many customers, but it is amusing to see them sneak into the shop after carefully looking round to make sure that none of their acquaintances are near. A prejudice has arisen against rats, because the doctors say that their flesh is full of trichinæ. I own for my part I have a guilty feeling when I eat dog, the friend of man. I had a slice of a spaniel the other day, it was by no means bad, something like lamb, but I felt like a cannibal. Epicures in dog flesh tell me that poodle is by far the best, and recommend me to avoid bull dog, which is coarse and tasteless. I really think that dogs have some means of communicating with each other, and have discovered that their old friends want to devour them. The humblest of street curs growls when anyone looks at him. *Figaro* has a story that a man was followed for a mile by a party of dogs barking fiercely at his heels. He could not understand to what their attentions were due, until he remembered that he had eaten a rat for his breakfast. The friend of another journalist, who ate a dog called Fox, says that whenever anyone calls out "Fox" he feels an irresistible impulse which forces him to jump up. As every Christmas a number of books are published containing stories about dogs as remarkable as they are stale, I recommend to their authors these two veracious tales. Their veracity is guaranteed by Parisian journalists. Can better evidence be required?

We are already discussing who will be sent to Germany. We suppose that the army and the Mobiles, and perhaps the officers of the National Guard will have to make the journey. One thing, I do hope that the Prussians will convey across the Rhine all the Parisian journalists, and keep them there until they are able to pass an elementary examination in the literature, the politics, the geography, and the domestic economy of Germany. A little foreign travel would do these blind leaders of the blind a world of good, and on their return they would perhaps have cleared their minds of their favourite delusion that civilization is co-terminous with the frontiers of France.

How M. Picard provides for the financial requirements of his colleagues is a mystery. The cost of the siege amounts in hard cash to about £20,000,000. To meet the daily draw on the exchequer no public loan has been negotiated, and nothing is raised by taxation. The monthly instalments which have been paid on the September loan cannot altogether amount to very much, consequently the greater portion of this large sum can only have been obtained by a loan from the bank and by *bons de trésor* (exchequer bills). What the proportion between the bank loan and the *bons de trésor* in circulation is I am unable to ascertain. M. Picard, like all finance ministers, groans daily over the cost of the prolongation of the siege, and it certainly appears a very doubtful question whether France will really benefit by Paris being at its expense for another month.

Military matters remain *in statu quo*. The army is camped in the wood of Vincennes. The forts occasionally fire. The Prussians seem to be of opinion that our next sortie will be in the plain of Genevilliers, as they are working hard on their fortifications along their lines between St. Denis and St. Cloud, and they have replaced the levies of the smaller States by what we call here "real" Prussians. Our engineer officers consider that the Prussians have three lines of investment, the first comparatively weak, the second composed of strategical lines, by which a force of

40,000 men can be brought on any point within two hours; the third consisting of redoubts, which would prevent artillery getting by them. To invest a large town, say our officers, is not so difficult a task as it would appear at first sight. Artillery can only move along roads, and consequently all that is necessary is to occupy the roads solidly. General Blanchard has been removed from his command, and is to be employed in the Third Army under Vinoy. His dispute with Ducrot arose from a remark which the latter made respecting officers who did not remain with their men after a battle; as Blanchard had been in Paris the day before he took this general stricture to himself. Personalities of a very strong nature were exchanged between the two warriors, and it was thought well that henceforward they should, as much as possible, be kept apart. General Favé also, who commanded the redoubt near Joinville, which arrested the advance of the Prussians on the second battle of Villiers, has "had words." It appears that he declined to obey an order which was forwarded to him, on the ground of its absurdity, saying that he was responsible to his conscience. Indiscipline has been the curse of the French army since the commencement of the war, and it will continue to be so to the end. During the siege there have been many individual traits of heroism, but the armed force has been little better than a mob, and Trochu has not had the moral courage to enforce his will on his generals. Ducrot says that he is determined to take the war battalions of the National Guards under fire at the next sortie, but whether he will succeed remains to be seen. In these marching battalions there are undoubtedly many brave men, but both officers and soldiers are inexperienced, and when they see men falling before them, struck down by an invisible enemy, they lose all presence of mind.

I do not think, as far as regards the Parisians, Count Bismarck is right in his opinion that the French will for many years to come attempt to reverse the verdict of the present war. The Parisian bourgeois is fond of saving money. As long as war meant a military promenade of the army across the Rhine, followed by a triumphal entry into Paris, he was by no means averse to it, for he considered that a French victory reflected itself on him, and made him a hero in the eyes of the world. Now, however, that he has discovered that there is a reverse to this picture, and that it may very possibly mean ruin to himself, he will be very cautious before he again risks the hazard of the die. Should the disasters of France result in the emancipation of the provinces from the rule of Paris, they will be a positive benefit to the nation. If the thirty-eight million Frenchmen outside Paris are such fools as to allow themselves to be ruled by the two million amiable, ignorant, bragging humbugs who are within it, France will most deservedly cease to be a power of Europe. If this country is to recover from the ruin in which it is overwhelmed it is absolutely essential that Paris should cease to be its political capital, and that the Parisians should not have a greater share in moulding its future policy than they are numerically entitled to.

CHAPTER XIV.

December 18*th.*

PRISONERS have before now endeavoured to while away their long hours of captivity by watching spiders making their webs. I can understand this. In the dreary monotony of this dreariest of sieges a spider would be an event. But alas, the spider is outside, and we are the fly caught in his toils. Never did time hang so heavily on human beings as it hangs on us. Every day seems to have twice the usual number of hours. I have ceased to wind up my watch for many a week. I got tired of looking at it; and whether it is ten in the morning or two in the afternoon is much the same to me; almost everyone has ceased to shave; they say that a razor so near their throats would be too great a temptation. Some have married to avoid active service, others to pass the time. "When I knew that there was an army between my wife and myself," observed a cynic to me yesterday, "I rejoiced, but even the society of my wife would be better than this." There is a hideous old woman, like unto one of Macbeth's witches, who makes my bed. I had a horrible feeling that some day or other I should marry her, and I have been considerably relieved by discovering that she has a husband and several olive branches. Here is my day. In the morning the boots comes to call me. He announces the number of deaths which have taken place in the hotel during the night. If there are many he is pleased, as he considers it creditable to the establishment. He then relieves his feelings by shaking his fist in the direction of Versailles, and exit growling "Canaille de Bismarck." I get up. I have breakfast—horse, *café au lait*—the *lait* chalk and water. The portion of horse about two square inches of the noble quadruped; then I buy a dozen newspapers, and after having read them, discover that they contain nothing new. This brings me to about eleven o'clock. Friends drop in, or I drop in on friends. We discuss how long it is to last—if friends are French we agree that we are sublime. At one o'clock get into the circular railroad, and go to one or other of the city gates. After a discussion with the National Guards on duty, pass through. Potter about for a couple of hours at the outposts; try with glass to make out Prussians; look at bombs bursting; creep along the trenches; and wade knee deep in mud through the fields. The Prussians, who have grown of late malevolent even toward civilians, occasionally send a ball far over one's head. They always fire too high. French soldiers are generally cooking food. They are anxious for news, and know nothing about what is going on. As a rule they relate the episode of some *combat d'avantposte* which took place the day before. The episodes never vary. 5 P.M.—Get back home; talk to doctors about interesting surgical operations; then drop in upon some official to interview him about what is doing. Official usually first mysterious, then communicative, not to say loquacious, and abuses most people except himself. 7 P.M.—Dinner at a restaurant; conversation general; almost everyone in uniform. Still the old subjects—How long will it last? Why does not Gambetta write more clearly? How sublime we are; what a fool everyone else is. Food scanty, but peculiar. At Voisins to-day the bill of fare was ass, horse, and English wolf from the Zoological Garden. A Scotchman informed me that this latter was a fox of his native land, and patriotically gorged himself with it. I tried it, and not being a Scotchman, found it horrible, and fell back upon the patient ass. After dinner, potter on the Boulevards under the dispiriting gloom of petroleum; go home and read a book. 12 P.M.— Bed. They nail up the coffins in the room just over mine every night, and the tap, tap, tap, as they drive in the nails, is the pleasing music which lulls me to sleep. Now, I ask, after having endured this sort of thing day after day for three months, can I be expected to admire Geist, Germany, or Mr. Matthew Arnold? I sigh for a revolution, for a bombardment, for an assault, for anything which would give us a day's excitement.

I enclose you Gambetta's latest pigeon despatch. His style is so grandiloquently vague that we can make neither head nor tail of it. We cannot imagine what has become of Aurelle de Paladine and of the army of Kératry. The optimists say that it means that Bourbaki and Chanzy have surrounded Frederick Charles; the pessimists say that Frederick Charles has got between them. The general feeling seems to be that the provinces are doing more than was expected of them, but that they will fail to succour us. Here some of the newspapers urge Trochu to make a sortie, in order to prevent reinforcements being sent to Frederick Charles, others deprecate it as a useless waste of life. General Clément Thomas, who succeeded Tamisier about a month ago in the command of the National Guards, seems to be the right man in the right place. He is making great efforts to convert these citizens into soldiers, and stands no nonsense. Not a day passes without some patriotic captain being tried by court-martial for drunkenness or disobedience. If a battalion misbehaves itself, it is immediately gibbeted in the order of the day. The newspapers cry out against this. They say that Clément Thomas forgets that the National Guards are his children, and that dirty linen ought to be washed at home. "If this goes on, posterity," they complain, "will say that we were little more than a mob of undisciplined drunkards." I am afraid that Clément Thomas will not have time to carry out his reforms; had they been commenced earlier, there is no reason why Paris should not have had on foot 100,000 good troops.

Mr. Herbert tells me that there are now above 1,000 persons on the English fund, and that every week there are about 30 new applications. Unknown and mysterious English emerge from holes and corners every day. Mr. Herbert thinks that there cannot be less than 3,000 of them still in Paris, almost all destitute. The French Government sold him a short time ago 30,000 lbs. of rice, and this, with the chocolate and Liebig which he has in hand will last him for about three weeks. If the siege goes on longer it is difficult to know how all these poor people will live. Funds are not absolutely wanting, but it is doubtful whether even with money it will be possible to buy anything beyond bread, if that. Mr. Herbert thinks that it would be most desirable to send, if possible, a provision of portable food, such as Liebig's extract of meat, as near to Paris as possible; so that, whenever the siege ceases, it may at once be brought into the town, as otherwise it is very probable that many of these English will die of starvation before food can reach them. It does seem to me perfectly monstrous that for years we should have, in addition to an Embassy, kept a Consul here, and that he should have been allowed to go off on leave to some watering place at the very moment at which his services were most required. When the Embassy left, a sort of deputy-consul remained here; but with a perfect ingenuity of stupidity, the Foreign-office officials ordered this gentleman to withdraw with Mr. Wodehouse, the secretary. Heine said of his fellow-countrymen, "they are born stupid, and a bureaucratic education makes them wicked." Had he been an Englishman instead of a Prussian he would have said the same, and with even more truth, of certain persons who, not for worlds would I name, but who do not reside 100 miles from Downing-street.

December 21st.

When the Fenians in the United States meditate a raid upon Canada, they usually take very great care to allow their intentions to be known. Our sorties are much like these Hibernian surprises. If the Prussians do not know when we are about to attack, they cannot complain that it is our fault. The "Après vous, Messieurs les Anglais," still forms the chivalrous but somewhat naïf tactics of the Gauls. On Sunday, as a first step to military operations, the gates of the city were closed to all unprovided with passes. On Monday a grand council of generals and admirals took place at the Palais Royal. Yesterday and all last night drums were beating, trumpets were blowing, and troops were marching through the streets. The war battalions of the National Guard, in their new uniforms, spick and span, were greeted with shouts, to which they replied by singing a song, the chorus of which is "Vive la guerre, Piff-Paff," and which has replaced the "Marseillaise." As the ambulances had been ordered to be ready to start at six in the morning, I presumed that business would commence at an early hour, and I ordered myself to be called at 5.30. I was called, and got out of my bed, but, alas for noble resolutions! having done so, I got back again into it and remained between the sheets quietly enjoying that sleep which is derived from the possession of a good conscience, and a still better digestion, until the clock struck nine.

It was not until past eleven o'clock that I found myself on the outside of the gate of La Villette, advancing, as Grouchy should have done at Waterloo, in the direction of the sound of the cannon. From the gate a straight road runs to Le Bourget, having the Fort of Aubervilliers on the right, and St. Denis on the left. Between the fort and the gate there were several hundred ambulance waggons, and above a thousand "brancardiers," stamping their feet and blowing on their fingers to keep themselves warm. In the fields on each side of the road there were numerous regiments of Mobiles drawn up ready to advance if required. Le Bourget, everyone said, had been taken in the morning, our artillery was on ahead, and we were carrying everything before us, so towards Le Bourget I advanced. About a mile from Le Bourget, there is a cross-road running to St. Denis through Courneuve. Here I found the barricade which had formed our most advanced post removed. Le Bourget seemed to be on fire. Shells were falling into it from the Prussian batteries, and, as well as I could make out, our forts were shelling it too. Our artillery was on a slight rise to the right of Le Bourget, in advance of Drancy; and in the fields between Drancy and this rise, heavy masses of troops were drawn up in support. Officers assured me that Le Bourget was still in our possession, and that if I felt inclined to go there, there was nothing to prevent me. I confess I am not one of those persons who snuff up the battle from afar, and feel an irresistible desire to rush into the middle of it. To be knocked on the head by a shell, merely to gratify one's curiosity, appears to me to be the utmost height of absurdity. Those who put themselves between the hammer and the anvil, come off generally second best, and I determined to defer my visit to the interesting village before me until the question whether it was to belong to Gaul or Teuton had been definitely decided. So I turned off to the left and went to St. Denis.

Here everybody was in the streets, asking everybody else for news. The forts all round it were firing heavily. On the Place before the Cathedral there was a great crowd of men, women, and children. The sailors, who are quartered here in great numbers, said that they had carried Le Bourget early in the morning, but that they had been obliged to fall back, with the loss of about a third of their number. Most of them had hatchets by their sides, and they attack a position much as if they were boarding a ship. About 100 prisoners had been brought into the town in the morning, as well as two Frères Chrétiens, who had been wounded, and for whom the greatest sympathy was expressed. Little seemed to be known of what was passing. "The Prussians will be here in an hour," shouted one man; "The Prussians are being exterminated," shouted another. "What is this?" cried the crowd, as Monseigneur Bauer, the bishop *in partibus infidelium* of some place or other, now came riding along with his staff. He held up his two fingers, and turned his hand right and left. His pastoral blessing was, however, but a half success. The women crossed themselves, and the men muttered "farceur." The war which is now raging has produced many oddities, but none to my mind equal to this bishop. His great object is to see and be seen, and most thoroughly does he succeed in his object. He is a short, stout man, dressed in a cassock, a pair of jack-boots with large spurs, and a hat such as you would only see at the opera. On his breast he wears a huge star. Round his neck is a chain, with a great golden cross attached to it; and on his fingers, over his gloves, he wears gorgeous rings. The trappings of his horse are thickly sprinkled with Geneva crosses. By his side rides a standard-bearer, bearing aloft a flag with a red cross. Eight aides-de-camp, arrayed in a sort of purple and gold fancy uniform, follow him, and the *cortége* is closed by two grooms in unimpeachable tops. In this guise, and followed by this état major, he is a conspicuous figure upon a field of battle, and produces much the same effect as the head of a circus riding into a town on a piebald horse, surrounded by clowns and pets of the ballet. He was the confessor of the Empress, and is now the aumônier of the Press; but why he wears jack-boots, why he capers about on a fiery horse, why he has a staff of aides-de-camp, and why he has two grooms, are things which no one seems to know. He patronises generals and admirals, doctors and commissariat officers, and they submit to be patronised by him. Half-priest, half-buffoon, something of a Friar Tuck and something of a Louis XV. abbé, he is a sort of privileged person, who by the mere force of impudence has made his way in the world. Most English girls in their teens fall in love with a curate and a cavalry officer. Monseigneur Bauer, who combines in himself the unctuous curate and the dashing dragoon, is adored by the fair sex in Paris. He knows how to adapt his conversation to the most opposite kind of persons, and I should not be surprised if he becomes a Cardinal before he dies.

The arrival of Dr. Ricord was the next event. He was in a basket pony-chaise, driving two ponies not much larger than rats. A pole about twelve feet high, bearing the flag of the Geneva Cross, was stuck beside him, and it was knocking against the telegraph wires which ran along the street. The eminent surgeon was arrayed in a long coat buttoned up to his chin and coming down to his feet. On his head was a kepi which was far too large for him. He looked like one of those wooden figures of Noah, when that patriarch with his family is lodged in a child's ark. Having inspected the bishop and the doctor with respectful admiration, and instituted a search for some bread and wine, I thought it was time to see what was going on outside. On emerging from St. Denis everything except the guns of the forts appeared quiet. I had not, however, gone far in the direction of Le Bourget, which was still burning, when I was stopped by a regiment marching towards St. Denis, some of the officers of which told me that the village had been retaken by the Prussians—the artillery, too, which I had left on the rise before Drancy, had disappeared. At a farmyard close by Drancy I saw Ducrot and his staff. The General had his hood drawn over his head, and both he and his aide-de-camp looked so glum, that I thought it just as well not to congratulate him upon the operations of the day. In and behind Drancy there were a large number of troops, who I heard were to camp there during the night. None seemed exactly to know what had happened. The officers and soldiers were not in good spirits. On my return into Paris, however, I found the following proclamation of the Government posted on the walls:—" 2 p.m.—The attack commenced this morning by a great deployment from Mont Valérien to Nogent, the combat has commenced and continues everywhere, with favourable chances for us. —Schmitz." The people on the Boulevards seem to imagine that a great victory has been gained. When one asks them where? They answer "everywhere." I can only answer myself for what occurred at Le Bourget. I hear that Vinoy has occupied Nogent, on the north of the Marne; the resistance he encountered could not, however, have been very great, as only seven wounded have been brought into this hotel, and only one to the American ambulance. General Trochu announced this morning that 100 battalions of the National Guards are outside the walls, and I shall be curious to learn how they conduct themselves under fire. Far be it from me to say that they will not fight like lions. If they do, however, it will surprise most of the military men with whom I have spoken on the subject. As yet all they have done has been to make frequent " pacts with death," to perform unauthorised strategical movements to the rear whenever they have been sent to the front, to consume much liquor, to pillage houses, and—to put it poetically—toy with Amaryllis in the trench, or with the tangles of Nereus' hair. Their General, Clément Thomas, is doing his best to knock them into shape, but I am afraid that it is too late. There are cases in which, in defiance of the proverb, it is too late to mend.

Officers in a position to know, assure me that no really serious sortie will be made, but that after two or three days of the sham fights, such as took place to-day, the troops will quietly return into Paris. The object of General Trochu is, they say, to amuse the Parisians, and if he can by hook or by crook get the National Guard under the mildest of fires, to celebrate their heroism, in order that they may return the compliment. I cannot, however, believe that no attempt will be made to fight a battle; the troops are now massed from St. Denis to the Marne; within two hours they can all be brought to any point along this line, and I should imagine that either to-morrow or the next day, something will be done in the direction of the Forest of Bondy. Trochu, it is daily felt more strongly, even by calm temperate men, is not the right man in the right place. He is a respectable literary man, utterly unfit to cope with the situation. His great aim seems now to be to curry favour with the Parisian population by praising in all his proclamations the National Guards, and ascribing to them a courage of which as yet they have given no proof. This, of course, injures him with the Line and the Mobiles, who naturally object to their being called upon to do all the fighting, whilst others are lauded for it. The officers all swear by Vinoy, and hold the military capacity both of Trochu and Ducrot very cheap. In the desperate strait to which Paris is reduced, something more than a man estimable for his private virtues, and his literary attainments is required. Trochu, as we are frequently told, gave up his brougham in order to adopt his nephews. Richard III. killed his; but these are domestic questions, only interesting to nephews, and it by no means follows that Richard III. would not have been a better defender of Paris than Trochu has proved himself to be. His political aspirations and his military combinations are in perpetual conflict. He is ever sacrificing the one to the other, and, consequently, he fails both as a general and as a statesman.

In order to form an opinion with regard to the condition of the poorer classes, I went yesterday into some of the back slums in the neighbourhood of the Boulevard de Clichy. The distress is terrible. Women and children, half starved, were seated at their doorsteps, with hardly clothes to cover them decently. They said that, as they had neither firewood nor coke, they were warmer out-of-doors than in-doors. Many of the National Guards, instead of bringing their money home to their families, spent it in drink; and there are many families, composed entirely of women and children, who, in this land of bureaucracy, are apparently left to starve whilst it is decided to what category they belong. The Citizen Mottu, the Ultra-Democratic Mayor, announced that in his arrondissement all left-handed marriages are to be regarded as valid, and the left-handed spouses of the National Guards are to receive the allowance which is granted to the legitimate wives of these warriors. But a new difficulty has arisen. Left-handed polygamy prevails to a great extent among the Citizen Mottu's admirers. Is a lady who has five husbands entitled to five rations, and is a lady who only owns the fifth of a National Guard to have only one-fifth of a ration? These are questions which the Citizen Mottu is now attempting to solve. As for the future, he has solved the matrimonial question by declining to celebrate marriages, because, he says, this bond is an insult upon those who prefer to ignore it. As regards marriage, consequently—and that alone—his arrondissement resembles the kingdom of heaven. I went to see, yesterday, what was going on in the house of a friend of mine in the Avenue de l'Impératrice, who has left Paris. The servant who was in charge told me that up there they had been unable to obtain bread for three days, and that the last time that he had presented his ration ticket he had been given about half an inch of cheese. "How do you live, then?" I asked. After looking mysteriously round to see that no one was watching us, he took me down into the cellar, and pointed to some meat in barrel. "It is half a horse," he said, in the tone of a man who is showing some one the corpse of his murdered victim. "A neighbouring coachman killed him, and we salted him down and divided it." Then he opened a closet in which sat a huge cat. "I am fattening her up for Christmas-day, we mean to serve her up surrounded with mice, like sausages," he observed. Many Englishmen regard it as a religious duty to eat turkey at Christmas, but fancy fulfilling this duty by devouring cat. It is like an Arab in the desert, who cannot wash his hands when he addresses his evening prayer, and makes shift with sand. This reminds me that some antiquarian has discovered that in eating horse we are only reverting to the habits of the ancient Gauls. Before the Christian religion was introduced into the country, the Druids used to sacrifice horses, which were afterwards eaten. Christianity put an end to these sacrifices, and horseflesh then went out of fashion.

La France thus speaks of the last despatch of Gambetta:—"At length we have received official news from Tours. We read the despatch feverishly, then we read it a second time with respect, with admiration, with enthusiasm. We are asked our opinion respecting it. Before answering, we feel an irresistible impulse to take off our hat and to cry 'Vive la France.'" The *Electeur Libre* is still more enraptured with the situation. It particularly admires the petroleum lamp, so different, it says, to those orgies of light, which under the tyrant, in the form of gas, gave a fictitious vitality to Paris. The *Combat* points out that no fires have broken out since September 4—a coincidence which is ascribed to the existence since that date of a Republican form of government. I recommend this curious phenomenon to insurance companies. The newspapers, one and all, are furious, because they hear that the Prussians contest our two victories at Villiers. "How singular," observes the *Figaro*, with plaintive morality, "is this rage, this necessity for lying." It is notorious that, having gained two glorious victories, we returned into Paris to repose on our laurels, and I must beg the Prussians not to be so mean as to contest the fact.

December 23rd.

Since Wednesday the troops—Line, Mobiles, and marching battalions of the National Guard—have remained outside the enceinte. There has been a certain amount of spade work at Drancy, but beyond this absolutely nothing. The cold is very severe. This afternoon I was outside in the direction of Le Bourget. The soldiers had lit large fires to warm themselves. Some of them were lodged in empty houses, but most of them had only their little *tentes d'abri* to shelter them. The sentinels were stamping their feet in the almost vain endeavour to keep their blood in circulation. There have been numerous frost-bitten cases. When it is considered that almost all of these troops might, without either danger to the defence, or without compromising the offensive operations, have been marched back into Paris, and quartered in the barracks which have been erected along the outer line of Boulevards, it seems monstrous cruelty to keep them freezing outside. The operations, however, on Wednesday are regarded as very far short of a success. General Trochu does not venture, in the state of public opinion, to bring the troops back into Paris, and thus confess a failure. The ambulances are ordered out to-morrow morning; but I cannot help thinking that the series of operations which were with great beating of drums announced to have commenced on Wednesday, will be allowed gradually to die out, without anything further taking place. The National Guards are camped in the neighbourhood of Bondy and Rosny. They have again, greatly to the disgust of the Mobiles and Line, been congratulated in a general order upon their valorous bearing. As a matter of fact, there was a panic among these braves which nearly degenerated into a rout. Several battalions turned tail, under the impression that the Prussians were going to attack them. One battalion did not stop until it had found shelter within the walls of the town. General Trochu's attempt, for political ends, to force greatness upon these heroes, is losing him the goodwill of the army. On Wednesday and Thursday several regiments of the Line and of the Mobiles bitterly complained that they should always be ordered to the front to protect not only Paris but the National Guards. The marching battalions are composed of unmarried men between twenty-five and thirty-five, and why they should not be called upon to incur the same risks, and submit to the same discipline as the Mobiles, it is difficult to understand. We may learn from the experience of this siege that in war, armed citizens who decline to submit to the discipline of soldiers are worse than useless. The lesson, however, has not profited the Parisians. The following letter appears in the *Combat*, signed by the "adjoint" of the 13th arrondissement. The defence on the part of this municipal functionary of a marching battalion, which, at the outposts, broke into a church, and there parodied the celebration of the mass, is a gem in its way :—

"The marching companies of this battalion left Paris on the morning of the 16th to go to the outposts at Issy. The departure was what all departures of marching battalions must fatally be—copious and multiplied libations between parting friends, paternal handshakings in cabarets, patriotic and bacchic songs, loose and indecent choruses—in a word, the picturesque exhibition of all that arsenal of gaiety and courage which is the appanage of an ancient Gallic race. The old troopers, who pretend to govern us by the sword, do not approve of this joyous mode of regarding death; and all the writers whose pens are dipped in the ink of reaction and Jesuitism are eager to discover any eccentricity in which soldiers who are going under fire for the first time permit themselves to indulge. The Intendance, with that intelligence which characterises our military administrations, had put off the departure of the battalion for several hours. What were the men to do whilst they were kept waiting, except drink? This is what these brave fellows did. Mars, tired of Venus, sung at the companionship of Bacchus. If the God of Wine too well seconded the God of War, it is only water drinkers who can complain; it is not for us, Republicans of the past and of the future, to throw stones at good citizens in order to conceal the misconduct of the old Bonapartist Administration which still is charged with the care of our armies."

General Blaise has been killed at Villa Evrard. These buildings, which go by this name, were occupied on Wednesday by General Vinoy's troops. In the night a number of Prussians, who had concealed themselves in the cellars, emerged, and a hand-to-hand fight took place. Some of the Prussians in the confusion got away, and some were killed. Several French officers who ran away and rushed in a panic into the presence of General Vinoy, who was at Fort Rosney, announcing that all was lost, are to be tried by Court Martial. The troops when they heard this were very indignant; but old Vinoy rode along the line, and told them that they might think what they pleased, but that he would have no cowards serving under him. Pity that he is not General-in-Chief.

A curious new industry has sprung up in Paris. Letters supposed to be found in the pockets of dead Germans are in great request. There are letters from mothers, from sisters, and from the Gretchens who are, in the popular mind, supposed to adore warriors. Unless every corpse has half a dozen mothers, and was loved when in the flesh by a dozen sweethearts, many of these letters must be fabricated. They vary in their style very little. The German mothers give little domestic details about the life at home, and express the greatest dread lest their sons should fall victims to the valour of the Parisians, which is filling the Fatherland with terror and admiration. The Gretchens are all sentimental; they talk of their inner feelings like the heroines of third-rate novels, send the object of their affections cigars and stockings knitted by their own fair hands, and implore him to be faithful, and not forget, in the toils of some French syren, poor Gretchen. But what is more strange is that in the pocket of each corpse a reply is found which he has forgotten to post. In this reply the warrior tells a fearful tale of his own sufferings, and says that victory is impossible, because the National Guards are such an invincible band.

The number of the wounded in my hotel has considerably diminished owing to the deaths among them. For the Société Internationale to have made it their central ambulance was a great mistake. Owing to the want of ventilation the simplest operations are usually fatal. Four out of five of those who have an arm or a leg amputated die of pyæmia. Now, as in the American tents four out of five recover; and as French surgeons are as skilful as American surgeons, the average mortality in the two ambulances is a crucial proof of the advantage of the American tent system. Under their tents there is perfect ventilation, and yet the air is not cold. If their plan were universally adopted in hospitals, it is probable that many lives which are now sacrificed to the gases which are generated from operations, and which find no exit from buildings of stone or brick, would be saved. " Our war," said an American surgeon to me the other day, " taught us that a large number of cubic inches of air is not enough for a sick man, but that the air must be perpetually renewed by ventilation."

December 24th.

The papers publish extracts from German newspapers which have been found in the pockets of the prisoners who were taken on Wednesday. The news from the provinces is not considered encouraging. Great stress is laid upon a proclamation addressed by King William to his troops on December 6, in which it is considered that there is evidence that the Prussians are getting tired of the war. We hear now, for the first time, that Prussia has " denounced " the Luxemburg Treaty of '67, and forgetting that the guarantee of neutrality with respect to these lotus-eaters was collective, and not joint and several, we anxiously ask whether England will not regard this as a *casus belli.* "As soon as Parliament assembles," says *La Vérité,* " that great statesman Disraeli will turn out Mr. Gladstone, and then our old ally will be restored to us." The *Gaulois* observes that "the English journalists residing at Paris keep up the illusion that Paris must fall by sending to their journals false news, which is reproduced in the organs of Prussia." "These journalists," adds the *Gaulois,* " who are our guests, fail in those duties which circumstances impose upon them." Every correspondent residing abroad must be the guest, in a certain sense, of the country from which he is writing; but that this position should oblige him to square his facts to suit the wishes of his hosts appears to me a strange theory. Had I been M. Jules Favre, I confess that I should have turned out all foreign journalists at the commencement of the siege. He, however, expressed a wish that they should remain in Paris, and his fellow-citizens must not now complain that they decline to endorse the legend which, very probably, will be handed down to future generations of Frenchmen as the history of the siege of Paris. The Prussians will not raise the siege for anything either French or English journalists say. The Parisians themselves must perceive that the attempt to frighten their enemies away by drum-beating and trumpet-blowing has signally failed. Times have altered since Jericho. It is telling the Prussians nothing new to inform them that the National Guard are poor troops. For my part, nothing would give me greater pleasure than to learn some morning that the German armies round Paris had met with the fate which overwhelmed Sennacherib and his hosts. I should be delighted to be able to hope that the town will not eventually be forced to capitulate; but I cannot conceal from myself the truth that, if no succour comes from without, it must eventually fall. I blame the French journalists for perpetually drawing upon their imagination for their facts, and in their boasts of what France will do, not keeping within the bounds of probability; but I do not blame them for hoping against hope that their armies will be successful. I am ready to admit that the Parisians have shown a most stubborn tenacity, and that they have disappointed their enemies in not cutting each other's throats; but this is no reason why I should assert that they are sublime. After all, what is patriotism? The idea entertained by each nation that it is braver and better and wiser than the rest of the world. Does not every Englishman feel this to be true of his own countrymen? It is consequently not absurd that Frenchmen should think the same of themselves. The French are intensely patriotic—country with them is no abstraction. They moan over its ruin as though it were a human being, and far then be it from me to laugh at them for doing so. When, however, I find persons dressing themselves up in all the paraphernalia of war, visiting tombs and statues in order to register with due solemnity that they intend to die rather than yield, and when, after all this nonsense, these same persons decline to take their share in the common danger on the score that they have a mother, or a sister, or a wife, or a child, dependent upon them, and when month after month they drum and strut up and down the Boulevards, I consider that they are ridiculous, and I say so. When a man does a silly thing it is his own fault—not that of the person who chronicles it. Was it wise, for instance, of General Ducrot to announce a fortnight ago that he was about to lead his soldiers against the enemy, and that he himself intended either to conquer or die? Was it wise of General Trochu six weeks ago to issue a proclamation pledging himself to force the Prussians to raise the siege of Paris. The Prussians will have read these manifestoes, and they will form their own estimate respecting them. That I call them foolish does not "keep up illusions in Germany." The other day the members of an Ultra club, in the midst of a discussion respecting the existence of a divinity, determined to decide the question by a general scrimmage. I think that these patriots might have been better employed. It does not follow, however, that I do not regret that they were not better employed. The siege of Paris is in the hands of General Moltke, and the *Gaulois* may depend upon it that this wary strategist is not at all likely to give up the task by any number of journalists informing him that he is certain to fail.

I have got a cold, so I have not been out this morning. I hear that some of the troops have come in from Aubervilliers, and several regiments have marched by my windows. At Neuilly-sur-Marne and Bondy, it is said, earthworks are being thrown up; and it is supposed that Chelles will, as the Americans say, be the objective point of any movement which may take place in that direction.

The *Patrie* has been suspended for three days for alluding to military operations. It did more than allude, it ventured to doubt the wisdom of our generals. As many other journals have done the same I do not understand why the *Patrie* should have been singled out for vengeance.

CHAPTER XV.

December 25th.

REAL Christmas weather—that is to say, the earth is as hard as a brickbat, and the wind freezes one to the very marrow. To the rich man, with a good coal fire in his grate, turkey, roast beef, plum pudding, and mince pies on his table, and his family gorging themselves on the solid eatables, a frost at Christmas is very pleasant. Poor people cowering in their rags before the door of a union, cold, hungry, and forlorn, or munching their dry bread in some cheerless garret, may not perhaps so fully appreciate its advantages; but then we all know that poor people never are contented, and seldom understand the fitness of things. Here in Paris, the numbed soldiers out in the open fields, and the women and children, who have no fires and hardly any food, bitterly complain of the "seasonable" weather. With plenty of money, with warm clothes, and a good house, a hard frost has its charms, without them it is not quite so agreeable. For my part I confess that I never have seen a paterfamilias with his coat tails raised, basking himself before his fire, and prating about the delights of winter, and the healthy glow which is caused by a sharp frost, without feeling an irresistible desire to transplant him stark naked on the highest peak of Mont Blanc, in order to teach by experience what winter means to thousands of his fellow-creatures. We are not having a " merry Christmas," and we are not likely to have a happy new year. Christmas is not here the great holiday of the year, as it is in England. Still, everyone in ordinary times tries to have a better dinner than usual, and usually where there are children in a family some attempt is made to amuse them. Among the bourgeoisie they are told to put their shoes in the grate on Christmas-eve, and the next morning some present is found in them, which is supposed to have been left during the night by the Infant Jesus. Since the Empire introduced English ways here, plum-pudding and mincepies have been eaten, and even Christmas-trees have flourished. This year these festive shrubs, as an invention of the detested foe, have been rigidly tabooed. Plum-puddings and mincepies, too, will appear on few tables. In order to comfort the children, the girls are to be given soup tickets to distribute to beggars, and the boys are to have their choice between French and German wooden soldiers. The former will be treasured up, the latter will be subjected to fearful tortures. Even the midnight mass, which is usually celebrated on Christmas-eve, took place in very few churches last night. We have, indeed, too much on our hands to attend either to fasts or festivals, although in the opinion of the *Univers*, the last sortie would have been far more successful had it taken place on the 7th of the month, the anniversary of the promulgation of the Immaculate Conception. Among fine people New Year's-day is more of a fête than Christmas. Its approach is regarded with dark misgivings by many, for every gentleman is expected to make a call upon all the ladies of his acquaintance, and to leave them a box of sugarplums. This is a heavy tax upon those who have more friends than money—300fr. is not considered an extraordinary sum to spend upon these bonbonnières. A friend of mine, indeed, assured me that he yearly spent 1000fr., but then he was a notorious liar, so very possibly he was not telling the truth. "Thank Heaven," says the men, "at least we shall get off the sugarplum tax this year." But the ladies are not to be done out of their rights this way, and they throw out very strong hints that if sugarplums are out of season, anything solid is very much in season. A dandy who is known to have a stock of sausages, is overwhelmed with compliments by his fair friends. A good leg of mutton would, I am sure, win the heart of the proudest beauty, and by the gift of half-a-dozen potatoes you might make a friend for life. The English here are making feeble attempts to celebrate Christmas correctly. In an English restaurant two turkeys had been treasured up for the important occasion, but unfortunately a few days ago they anticipated their fate, and most ill-naturedly insisted upon dying. One fortunate Briton has got ten pounds of camel, and has invited about twenty of his countrymen to aid him in devouring this singular substitute for turkey. Another gives himself airs because he has some potted turkey, which is solemnly to be consumed to-day spread on bread. I am myself going to dine with the correspondent of one of your contémporaries. On the same floor as himself lives a family who left Paris before the commencement of the siege. Necessity knows no law; so the other day he opened their door with a certain amount of gentle violence, and after a diligent search, discovered in the larder two onions, some potatoes, and a ham. These, with a fowl, which I believe has been procured honestly, are to constitute our Christmas dinner.

It is very strange what opposite opinions one hears about the condition of the poor. Some persons say that there is no distress, others that it cannot be greater. The fact is, the men were never better off, the women and children never so badly off. Every man can have enough to eat and too much to drink by dawdling about with a gun. As his home is cold and cheerless, when he is not on duty he lives at a pot-house. He brings no money to his wife and children, who consequently only just keep body and soul together by going to the national cantines, where they get soup, and to the Mairies, where they occasionally get an order for bread. Almost all their clothes are in pawn, so how it is they do not positively die of cold I cannot understand. As for fuel even the wealthy find it difficult to procure it. The Government talks of cutting down all the trees and of giving up all the clothes in pawn ; but, with its usual procrastination, it puts off both these measures from day to day. This morning all the firewood was requisitioned. At a meeting of the Mayors of Paris two days ago, it was stated that above 400,000 persons are in receipt of parish relief.

The troops outside Paris are gradually being brought back inside. A trench has been dug almost continuously from Drancy to Aubervilliers, and an attempt has been made to approach Le Bourget by flying sap. The ground, is, however, so hard, that it is much like attempting to cut through a rock. To my mind the whole thing is merely undertaken in order to persuade the Parisians that something is being done. For the moment they are satisfied. " The Prussians," they say, "have besieged us ; we are besieging the Prussians now." What they will say when they find that even these operations are suspended, I do not know. The troops have suffered terribly from the cold during these last few days. Twelve degrees of frost "centigrade" is no joke. I was talking to some officers of Zouaves who had been twenty hours at the outposts. They said that during all this time they had not ventured to light a fire, and that this morning their wine and bread were both frozen. In the tents there are small stoves, but they give out little warmth. Even inside the deserted houses it is almost as cold as outside. The windows and the doors have been converted into firewood, and the wind whistles through them. The ambulance waggons of the

Press alone have brought in nearly 500 men frost-bitten, or taken suddenly ill. From the batteries at Bondy and Avron there has been some sharp firing, the object of which has been to oblige the Prussians to keep inside the Forest of Bondy, and to disquiet them whenever they take to digging anywhere outside it. The plain of Avron is a very important position as it commands the whole country round. The end of Le Bourget, towards Paris appears entirely deserted. An ambulance cart went up to a barricade this morning which crosses the main street, when a Prussian sentinel emerged and ordered it to go back immediately. Behind Le Bourget, a little to the right, is a heavy Prussian battery at Le Blanc Mesnel which entirely commands it. The Line and the Mobiles bitterly complain that they, and not the marching battalions, are exposed to every danger. The soldiers, and particularly those of the Mobiles, say that if they are to go on fighting for Paris, the Parisians must take their fair share in the battles.' As for the marching battalions, they are, as soldiers, worth absolutely nothing. The idea of their assaulting, with any prospect of success, any positions held by artillery, is simply ludicrous. The system of dividing an army into different categories, is subjected to a different discipline, is fatal for any united offensive operations. It is to be hoped that Trochu will at last perceive this, and limit his efforts to keeping the Prussians out of Paris, and harassing them by frequent and partial sorties. I hear that General Ducrot wanted to attempt a second assault of Le Bourget, but this was overruled at a council of war which was held on Thursday.

December 26th.

The *Journal Officiel* announces that military operations are over for the present, owing to the cold, and that the army is to be brought inside Paris, leaving outside only those necessary for the defence. This is a wise measure, although somewhat tardily taken. The Parisians will no doubt be very indignant; but if they do not like fighting themselves, they insist that the Line and the Mobiles should have no repose.

M. Felix Pyat gives the following account of Christmas in England:—"Christmas is the great English fête—the Protestant Carnival—an Anglo-Saxon gala—a gross, pagan, monstrous orgie—a Roman feast, in which the vomitorium is not wanting. And the eaters of 'bif' laugh at us for eating frogs! Singular nation! the most Biblical and the most material of Europe—the best Christians and the greatest gluttons. They cannot celebrate a religious fête without eating. On Holy Friday they eat buns, and for this reason they call it Good Friday. Good, indeed, for them, if not for God. They pronounce messe mass, and boudin pudding. Their pudding is made of suet, sugar, currants, and tea. The mess is boiled for fifteen days, sometimes for six months; then it is considered delicious. No pudding, no Christmas. The repast is sacred, and the English meditate over it for six months in advance—they are the only people who put money in a savings'-bank for a dinner. Poor families economise for months, and take a shilling to a publican every Saturday of the year, in return for which on Christmas Day they gorge themselves, and are sick for a week after. This is their religion—thus they adore their God." M. Pyat goes on to describe the butchers' shops before Christmas; one of them, he says, is kept by a butcher clergyman, and over his door is a text.

The *Gaulois* gives an extract of a letter of mine from a German paper, in which I venture to assert that the Parisians do not know that Champigny is within the range of the guns of their forts, and accompanies it with the following note:—"The journal which has fallen into our hands has been torn, and consequently we are unable to give the remainder of this letter. What we have given is sufficient to prove that our Government is tolerating within our walls correspondents who furnish the enemy with daily information. What they say is absurd, perhaps, but it ought not to be allowed." Does the *Gaulois* really imagine that the German generals would have raised the siege in despair had they not learnt that, as a rule, the Parisians do not study the map of the environs of the city?

Old Vinoy has issued an order of the day denouncing the conduct of the soldiers and officers who ran away when the Prussians issued from the cellars at Villa Evrard. It requires a great deal of courage just now to praise the Line, and to find fault with the National Guard. But General Vinoy is a thorough soldier, and stands no nonsense. If anything happens to Trochu, and he assumes the command-in-chief, I suspect the waverers of the National Guard will have to choose between fighting and taking off their uniforms. The General is above seventy—a hale and hearty old man; sticks to his profession, and utterly ignores politics. He has a most unsurrendering face, but I do not think that he would either hold out vain hopes to the Parisians, or flatter their vanity. He would tell them the truth, and with perfect indifference as to the consequences. He is a favourite both with the soldiers and the officers, and hardly conceals his contempt for the military capacity of Trochu, or the military qualities of Trochu's civic heroes.

December 28*th.*

The proverbial obstinacy of the donkey has been introduced into our systems, owing to the number of these long-eared quadrupeds which we have eaten. We "don't care" for anything. We don't care if the armies of the provinces have been beaten, we don't care if we have been forced to suspend offensive operations, we don't care if the Prussians bombard us, we don't care if eventually we have to capitulate. We have ceased to reason or to calculate. We are in the don't-care mood. How long this will last with so impulsive a people it is impossible to say. Our stomachs have become omnivorous; they digest anything now; and even if in the end they will be called upon to digest the leek, as we shall not be called upon to eat this vegetable either to-morrow or the next day, we don't care. The cold is terrible, and the absence of firewood causes great suffering. The Government is cutting down trees as fast as possible, and by the time it thaws there will be an abundance of fuel. In the meantime it denounces in the *Official Journal* the bands of marauders who issue forth and cut down trees, park benches, and garden palings. I must say that I don't blame them. When the thermometer is as low as it is now, and when there is no fire in the grate, the sanctity of property as regards fuel becomes a mere abstraction. Yesterday the Prussians unmasked several batteries, and opened fire against the plateau of Avron and the eastern forts. They fired above 3000 shells, but little damage was done. We had only thirty-eight killed and wounded. One shell fell into a house where eight people were dining and killed six of them. The firing is going on to-day, but not so heavily. The newspapers seem to be under the impression that we ought to rejoice greatly over this cannonade. Some say that it proves that the Prussians have given up in despair the idea of reducing us by famine; others that it is a clear evidence that Prince Frederick Charles has been beaten by General Chanzy. On Monday, Admiral La Roncière received a letter from a general whose name could not be deciphered about an exchange of prisoners. In this letter there was an allusion to a defeat which our troops in the North had sustained. But this we consider a mere wile of our insidious foe.

The *Gaulois* continues its crusade against the English Correspondents in Paris. They are all, it says, animated by a hostile feeling towards France. "We give them warning, and we hope that they will profit by it." Now, we know pretty well what French journalists term a hostile feeling towards their country. We were told at the commencement of the war that the English press was sold to Prussia, because it declined to believe in the Imperial bulletins of victories. That a correspondent should simply tell the truth, without fear or favour, never enters into the mind of a Gaul. For my part, I confess that my sympathies are with France; and I am glad to hear, on so good authority, that these sympathies have not biassed my recital of events. Notwithstanding the denunciations of the *Gaulois*, I have not the remotest intention to describe the National Guards as a force of any real value for offensive operations. If, as the *Gaulois* insists, they are more numerous and better armed than the Prussians, and if the French artillery is superior to the Prussians, they will be able to raise the siege; and then I will acknowledge that I have been wrong in my estimate of them. As yet they have only blown their own trumpets, as though this would cause the Prussian redoubts, like the walls of Jericho, to fall down. I make no imputation on their individual courage; but I say that this siege proves once more the truth of the fact, that unless citizen soldiers consent to merge for a time the citizen in the soldier, and to submit to discipline, as troops they are worthless. The *Gaulois* wishes to anticipate the historical romance which will, perhaps, be handed down to future generations. Posterity may, if it pleases, believe that the Parisians were Spartans, and that they fought with desperate valour outside their walls. I, who happen to see myself what goes on, know that all the fighting is done by the Line and the Mobiles, and that the Parisians are not Spartans. They are showing great tenacity, and suffering for the sake of the cause of their country many hardships. That General Trochu should pander to their vanity, by telling them that they are able to cope outside with the Prussians, is his affair. I do not blame him. He best knows how to deal with his fellow-countrymen. I am not, however, under the necessity of following his example.

The usual stalls which appear at this season of the year have been erected on the Boulevards. They are filled with toys and New Year's gifts. But a woolly sheep is a bitter mockery, and a "complete farmyard" in green and blue wood only reminds one painfully of what one would prefer to see in the flesh. The customers are few and far between. I was looking to-day at a fine church in chalk, with real windows, price 6fr., and was thinking that one must be a Mark Tapley to buy it, and walk home with it under one's arm under present circumstances. Many of the stall-keepers have in despair deserted the toy business, and gone in for comforters, kepis, and list soles.

Until the weather set in so bitterly cold, elderly sportsmen, who did not care to stalk the human game outside, were to be seen from morning to night pursuing the exciting sport of gudgeon-fishing along the banks of the Seine. Each one was always surrounded by a crowd deeply interested in the chase. Whenever a fish was hooked, there was as much excitement as when a whale is harpooned in more northern latitudes. The fisherman would play it for some five minutes, and then, in the midst of the solemn silence of the lookers-on, the precious capture would be landed. Once safe on the bank, the happy possessor would be patted on the back, and there would be cries of "Bravo!" The times being out of joint for fishing in the Seine, the disciples of Isaac Walton have fallen back on the sewers. The *Paris Journal* gives them the following directions how to pursue their new game:—"Take a long, strong line, and a large hook, bait with tallow, and gently agitate the rod. In a few minutes a rat will come and smell the savoury morsel. It will be some time before he decides to swallow it, for his nature is cunning. When he does, leave him five minutes to meditate over it; then pull strongly and steadily. He will make convulsive jumps; but be calm, and do not let his excitement gain on you, draw him up, *et voilà votre dîner.*"

December 29th.

So we have withdrawn from the plateau of Avron. Our artillery, says the *Journal Officiel*, could not cope with the Krupp cannons, and, therefore, it was thought wise to withdraw them. The fire which the Prussians have rained for the last two days upon this position has not been very destructive of human life. It is calculated that every man killed has cost the Prussians 24,000lbs. of iron. We are still speculating upon the reasons which induced the Prussians at last to become the assailants. That they wished to drive us from this plateau, which overlooks many of their positions, is far too simple an explanation to meet with favour. The *Vérité* of this morning contains an announcement that a Christmas Session of the House of Commons has turned out Mr. Gladstone by a hostile vote, and that he has been succeeded by a "War Minister." We are inclined to think that the Prussians, being aware of this, have been attempting to terrify us, in order that we may surrender before Sir B. Disraeli and Milord J. Pakington come to our rescue. The Parisians, intelligent and clever as they are, are absolutely wanting in plain common sense. I am convinced that if 500 of them were boiled down, it would be impossible to extract from the stew as much of this homely, but useful quality, as there is in the skull of the dullest tallow-chandler's apprentice in London.

The vital question of food is now rarely alluded to in the journals. The Government is, however, called to task for not showing greater energy, and the feeling against the unfortunate Trochu is growing stronger. He is held responsible for everything—the frost, the dearth of food, the ill-success of our sorties, and the defeats of the armies of succour. I am sorry for him, for he is a well-meaning man, although unfitted for such troubled waters. But to a great extent he has himself to thank for what is occurring. He has risked his all upon the success of his plan, and he has encouraged the notion that he could force the Prussians to raise the siege. In the meantime no one broaches the question as to what is to be done when our provisions fail. The members of the Government still keep up the theory that a capitulation is an impossible contingency. The nearer the fatal moment approaches the less anyone speaks of it, just as a man, when he is growing old, avoids the subject of death. Frenchmen have far more physical than civic courage. They prefer to shut their eyes to what is unpleasant than to grapple with it. How long our stores of flour will last it is difficult to say, but if our rulers wait to treat until they are exhausted, they will perforce be obliged to accept any terms; and, for no satisfactory object, they will be the cause that many will starve before the town can be revictualled. They call this, here, sublime. I call it folly. Its sublimity is beyond me. As is the case with a sick man given over by the physicians, the quacks are ready with their nostrums. The Ultra journals recommend that the Government should be handed over to a commune. The Ultra clubs demand that all generals and colonels should be cashiered, and others elected in their place. One club has subscribed 1,600frs. for Greek fire; another club suggests blowing up the Hôtel de Ville; another sending a deputation clothed in white to offer the King of Prussia the presidency of the Universal Republic; another—and this comes home to me—passed a vote yesterday evening demanding the immediate arrest of all English correspondents.

I am looking forward with horrible misgivings to the moment when I shall have no more money, so that perhaps I shall be thankful for being lodged and fed at the public expense. My banker has withdrawn from Paris, and his representative declines to look at my bill, although I offer ruinous interest. As for friends, they are all in a like condition, for no one expected the siege to last so long. At my hotel, need I observe that I do not pay my bill, but in hotels the guests may ring in vain now for food. I sleep on credit in a gorgeous bed, a pauper. The room is large. I wish it were smaller, for the firewood comes from trees just cut down, and it takes an hour to get the logs to light, and then they only smoulder, and emit no heat. The thermometer in my grand room, with its silken curtains, is usually at freezing point. Then my clothes—I am seedy, very seedy. When I call upon a friend, the porter eyes me distrustfully. In the streets the beggars never ask me for alms; on the contrary, they eye me suspiciously when I approach them, as a possible competitor. The other day I had some newspapers in my hand, an old gentleman took one from me and paid me for it. I had read it, so I pocketed the halfpence. My wardrobe is scanty, like the sage *omnia mea mecum porto*. I had been absent from Paris before the siege, and I returned with a small bag. It is difficult to find a tailor who will work, and even if he did I could not send him my one suit to mend, for what should I wear in the meantime? Decency forbids it. My pea jacket is torn and threadbare, my trousers are frayed at the bottom, and of many colours—like Joseph's coat. As for my linen, I will only say that the washerwomen have struck work, as they have no fuel. I believe my shirt was once white, but I am not sure. I invested a few weeks ago in a pair of cheap boots. They are my torment. They have split in various places, and I wear a pair of gaiters—purple, like those of a respectable ecclesiastic, to cover the rents. I bought them on the Boulevard, and at the same stall I bought a bright blue handkerchief which was going cheap; this I wear round my neck. My upper man resembles that of a dog-stealer, my lower man that of a bishop. My buttons are turning my hair grey. When I had more than one change of raiment these appendages remained in their places, now they drop off as though I were a moulting fowl. I have to pin myself together elaborately, and whenever I want to get anything out of my pocket I have elaborately to unpin myself, with the dread of falling to pieces before my eyes. For my food, I allowance myself, in order to eke out as long as possible my resources. I dine and breakfast at a second-class restaurant. Cat, dog, rat, and horse are very well as novelties, but taken habitually, they do not assimilate with my inner man. Horse, doctors say, is heating; I only wish it would heat me. I give this description of my existence, as it is that of many others. Those who have means, and those who have none, unless these means are in Paris, row in the same boat.

The society at my second-class restaurant is varied. Many are regular customers, and we all know each other. There are officers who come there whenever they get leave from outside—hardy, well-set fellows, who take matters philosophically and professionally. They make the most of their holiday, and enjoy themselves without much thought of the morrow. Then there are tradesmen who wear kepis, as they belong to the National Guard. They are not in such good spirits. Their fortunes are ebbing away, and in their hearts I think they would, although their cry is still "no surrender," be glad if all were over. They talk in low tones, and pocket a lump of the sugar which they are given with their coffee. Occasionally an ex-dandy comes in. I see him look anxiously around to make sure that no other dandy sees him in so unfashionable a resort. The dandy keeps to himself, and eyes us haughtily, for we are too common folk for the like of him. Traviatas, too, are not wanting in the second-class restaurant. Sitting by me yesterday was a girl who in times gone by I had often seen driving in a splendid carriage in the Bois. Her silks and satins, her jewellery and her carriage, had vanished. There are no more Russian Princes, no more Boyards, no more Milords to minister to her extravagances. She was eating her horse as though she had been "poor but honest" all her life; and as I watched her washing the noble steed down with a pint of vin ordinaire, I realized the alteration which this siege was effecting in the condition of all classes. But the strangest *habitués* of the restaurant are certain stalwart, middle-aged men, who seem to consider that their function in life is to grieve over their country, and to do nothing else for it. They walk in as though they were the soldiers of Leonidas on the high road to Thermopylæ—they sit down as though their stools were curule chairs—they scowl at anyone who ventures to smile, as though he were guilty of a crime—and they talk to each other in accents of gloomy resolve. When anyone ventures to hint at a capitulation, they bound in their seats, and cry, *On verra*. Sorrow does not seem to have disturbed their appetites, and, as far as I can discover, they have managed to escape all military duty. No human being can be so unhappy, however, as they look. They remind me of the heir at the funeral of a rich relative. Speaking of funerals reminds me that the newspapers propose that the undertakers, like the butchers, should be tariffed. They are making too good a thing out of the siege. They have raised their prices so exorbitantly that the poor complain that it is becoming impossible for them even to die.

A letter found, or supposed to be found, in the pocket of a dead German from his Gretchen is published to-day. "If you should happen to pillage a jeweller's shop," says this practical young lady, "don't forget me, but get me a pretty pair of earrings." The family of this warrior appears to be inclined to look after the main chance; for the letter goes on to say that his mother had knitted him a jacket, but having done so, has worn it herself ever since instead of sending it to him. Gretchen will never get her earrings, and the mother may wear her jacket now without feeling that she is depriving her son of it, for the poor fellow lies under three feet of soil near Le Bourget.

December 30th.

I hear that a story respecting a council which was held a few days ago, at which Trochu was requested to resign, is perfectly true. Picard and Jules Favre said that if he did resign they should do so also, and the discussion was closed by the General himself saying, " I feel myself equal to the situation, and I shall remain." Yesterday evening there were groups everywhere, discussing the withdrawal of the troops from Avron. It was so bitterly cold, however, that they soon broke up. This morning the newspapers, one and all, abuse Trochu. Somehow or other, they say, he always fails in everything he undertakes. I hear from military men that the feeling in the army is very strong against him. While the bombardment was going on at Avron he exposed himself freely to the fire, but instead of superintending the operations he attitudinized and made speeches. General Ducrot, who was there, and between whom and Trochu a certain coldness has sprung up, declared that he had always been opposed to any attempt to retain this position. The behaviour of Vinoy was that of a soldier. He was everywhere encouraging his men. What I cannot understand is why, if Avron was to be held, it was not fortified. It must have been known that the Prussians could, if they pleased, bring a heavy concentric fire from heavy siege guns to bear upon it. Casemates and strong earthworks might have been made—but nothing was done. 1 was up there the other day, and I then asked an engineer officer why due precautions were not being taken; but he only shrugged his shoulders in reply. General Vinoy, who was in the Crimea, says that all that the French, English, and Russians did there was child's play in comparison with the Prussian artillery. From the size of the unburst shells which have been picked up, their cannon must be enormous. The question now is, whether the forts will be able to hold out against them. The following account of what has taken place from the *Vérité* is by far the best which has been published :—

"Notwithstanding that the fire of the enemy slackened on the 26th, the Prussians were not losing their time. Thanks to the hardness of the soil, and to the fog, they had got their guns into position in all their batteries from Ville-nomble to Montfermeil. The injury done to the park of Drancy by the precision of the aim of our artillery at Fort Nogent was repaired; cannon were brought to the trenches which the day before we had occupied at Ville Evrart; and, as well as it was possible, twelve new batteries, armed with cannon of long range, were unmasked. All through the 28th the fire continued; shells fell thickly on our batteries, and in the village of Rosny. The roof of the station was knocked in, and several Mobiles were killed in the main street. The evacuation of the church, which had been converted into an ambulance, was thought advisable. All this, however, was nothing in comparison with the fire which was poured in during the night. The plateau of Avron was literally inundated with shells, many of them of far larger size than had previously been fired. The range of the guns was too great, and it was evident that the Prussians had rectified their aim. Their projectiles no longer fell wide in the field; they almost all burst close to the trenches. Two guns in battery No. 2 were struck; the same thing soon occurred in battery No. 3. Every moment the wheels of some ammunition waggon were struck, or one of the horses killed. Several men were wounded in the trenches, which were so shallow as to afford little protection. Two shells bursting at the same moment killed a naval officer and three men at one of the guns. All who were so imprudent as to venture to attempt to cross the plateau were struck down. It was a sad and terrible spectacle to see these sailors coolly endeavouring to point their guns, undisturbed by the rain of fire; while their officers, who were encouraging them, were falling every moment, covering those round them with their blood. The infantry and the Mobiles were, too, without shelter; for the Krupp guns swept the portion of the plateau on which they were drawn up within supporting distance. Most of them made the best of it, and laughed when they heard the shells whistling above their heads and bursting near them. Many, however, were so terrified, that they fell back, and spread abroad in their rear disquieting reports, which the terrified air of the narrators rendered still more alarming. The National Guard were drawn up on the heights in advance of the village of Rosny; a few shells reached their ranks. An officer and a soldier of the 114th were slightly wounded; but they remained firm. Every hour the Prussian cannonade became heavier. On our side our fire slackened; then ceased entirely. An *estafette* came with an order to evacuate the plateau, and to save the artillery. No time was lost. Fortunately, at this moment the enemy's fire also slackened; and the preparations for a retreat were hurriedly made. The guns were taken from their carriages, the baggage was laden on the carts, and the munition on the waggons. The soldiers strapped on their knapsacks, struck their tents, and harnessed the horses. All this was not accomplished without difficulty, for it had to be done noiselessly and in the dark, for all the fires had been put out. General Trochu, seated on a horse, issued his directions, and every moment received information of what was taking place. Notwithstanding the expostulations of his staff, the General refused to withdraw from this exposed point. 'No, gentlemen,' he said, 'I shall not withdraw from here until the cannon are in safety.' At two in the morning all was ready; the long train began to move; the cannon of 7 and the mitrailleuses of Commandant Pothier took the lead. Then followed the heavy naval guns, then the munition and baggage waggons; the troops of the Line, the Marines, and the National Guard were ordered to cover the retreat. It was no easy matter to descend from the plateau to Rosny. The frost had made the road a literal ice-hill. The drivers walked by the side of their animals, holding the reins and pulling them up when they stumbled. Until four o'clock, however, everything went well. The march slowly continued, and the Prussian batteries were comparatively calm. Their shells fell still occasionally where our guns had been. The noise of the wheels, however, and the absence of all cannonade on our parts, at length awakened the suspicions of the enemy. Their fire was now directed on the fort of Rosny, and the road from the plateau leading to it. At this moment the line of guns and waggons was passing through the village, and only carts with baggage were still on the plateau. At first the shells fell wide; then they killed some horses; some of the drivers were hit; a certain confusion took place. That portion of our line of march which was in Rosny was in imminent danger. Fortunately, our chiefs did not lose their heads. The guns whose horses were untouched passed those which were obliged to stop. Some of them took to the fields; the men pushed the wheels, and, thanks to their efforts, our artillery was saved. As soon as the guns had been dragged up the hill opposite the plateau, the horses started off at a gallop, and did not stop until they were out of the range of the enemy's fire. The guns were soon in safety at Vincennes and Montreuil. The troops held good, the men lying down on their stomachs, the officers standing up and smoking their cigars until the last waggon had passed. Day had broken when they received orders to withdraw. The National Guard went back into Paris, and the Line, after a short halt at Montreuil, camped in the barracks of St. Maur. At eight o'clock, the evacuation of the plateau was complete; but the Prussian shells still fell upon the deserted houses and some of the gun-carriages which had been abandoned. The enemy then turned their attention to the forts of Rosny and Noisy. It hailed shot on these two forts, and had they not been solidly built they would not have withstood it. The noise of this cannonade was so loud that it could be heard in the centre of Paris. Around the Fort of Noisy the projectiles sank into the frozen ground to a depth of two and a half metres, and raised blocks of earth weighing 30lbs. Shells fell as far as Romainville. In the Rue de Pantin a drummer had his head carried off; his comrades buried him on the spot. In the court of Fort Noisy three men, hearing the hissing of a shell, threw themselves on the ground. It was a bad inspiration; the shell fell on the one in the middle, and killed all three. These were the only casualties in the fort, and at ten o'clock the enemy's batteries ceased firing on it. All their efforts were then directed against the Fort of Rosny. The shells swept the open court, broke in the roof of the barracks, and tore down the peach-trees whose fruit is so dear to the Parisians. From eleven o'clock, it was impossible to pass along the road to Montreuil in safety. In that village, the few persons who are still left sought shelter in their cellars. At three o'clock the sun came out, and I passed along the strategical road to Noisy. I met several regiments—Zouaves, Infantry, and Marines—coming from Noisy and Bondy. I could distinctly see the enemy's batteries. Their centre is in Rancy, and the guns seem to be in the houses. The destruction in Bondy commenced by the French artillery has been completed by the Prussians. From three batteries in the park of Rancy they have destroyed the wall of the cemetery, behind which one battery was posted and an earthwork. What remained of the church has been literally reduced to dust. Except sentinels hid in the interior of the houses, all our troops had been withdrawn. Some few persons, out of curiosity, had adjourned to the Grande Place; their curiosity nearly cost them dear, and they had to creep away. At three o'clock the enemy's fire had redoubled; some of our Mobiles, in relieving guard, were killed; and from that hour no one ventured into the streets. 9 P.M. The moon has risen, and shines brightly—the ground is covered with snow, and it is almost like daylight. The Prussian positions can distinctly be seen. The cannon cannot be distinguished, but all along the line between Villenomble and Gagny tongues of fire appear, followed by long columns of smoke. The fire on Rosny is increasing in violence; the village of Noisy is being bombarded."

CHAPTER XVI.

PARIS, *January 1st*, 1871.

OUR forts still, like breakwaters before a coast, keep back the storm which the Prussians are directing against us. I went out yesterday by the Vincennes gate to see how matters were looking. In the Bois de Vincennes there were troops of every description, and a large number of guns. The usual scenes of camp life were going on, although, owing to the cold, everyone seemed gloomy and depressed. I confess that if I were called upon to camp out in this weather under a *tente d'abri*, and only given some very smoky green wood to keep me warm, I should not be quite so valorous as I should wish to be. Passing through the Bois, which is rapidly becoming a treeless waste, I went forward in the direction of Fontenay. As the Prussian bombs, however, were falling thickly into the village, I executed a strategical movement to the left, and fell back by a cross road into Montreuil. In this village several regiments were installed. It is just behind Fort Rosny, and on the upper portion, towards the fort, the Prussian shells fell. It is very singular what little real danger there is to life and limb from a bombardment. Shells make a hissing noise as they come through the air. Directly this warning hiss is heard, down everyone throws himself on the ground. The shell passes over and falls somewhere near, it sinks about two feet into the hard ground, and then bursts, throwing up great clouds of earth, like a small mine. The Prussians are unmasking fresh batteries every day, and approaching nearer and nearer to the forts. Their fire now extends from behind Le Bourget to the Marne, and at some points reaches to within a mile of the ramparts. Bondy is little more than a heap of ruins. As for the forts, we are told that, with the exception of their barracks having been made untenable, no harm has been done. Standing behind and looking at the shells falling into them, they certainly do not give one the idea of places in which anyone would wish to be, unless he were obliged; and they seemed yesterday to be replying but feebly to the fire of the enemy. I suppose that the Prussians know their own business, and that they really intend wholly to destroy Fort Rosny. Before you get this letter the duel between earth and iron will be decided, so it is useless my speculating on the result. If Rosny or Nogent fall, there will be nothing to protect Belleville from a bombardment. Many military sages imagine that this bombardment is only a prelude to an attack upon Mont Valérien. About 3,500 metres from that fort there is a very awkward plateau called La Bergerie. It is somewhat higher than the hill on which Valérien stands. The Prussians are known to have guns on it in position, and as Valérien is of granite, if bombarded, the value of granite as a material for fortifications will be tested.

Since the Prussians have opened fire, there have been numerous councils of war, and still more numerous proclamations. General Trochu has issued an appeal to the city to be calm, and not to believe that differences of opinion exist among the members of the Government. General Clement Thomas has issued an address to the National Guards, telling them that the country is going to demand great sacrifices of them. In fact, after the manner of the Gauls, everybody is addressing everybody. *Toujours des proclamations et rien que cela*, say the people, who are at last getting tired of this nonsense. Yesterday there was a great council of all the generals and commanders. General Trochu, it is said, was in favour of an attempt to pierce the Prussian lines; the majority being in favour of a number of small sorties. What will happen no one seems to know, and I doubt even if our rulers have themselves any very definite notion. The Ultra journals clamour for a sortie *en masse*, which of course would result in a stampede *en masse*. One and all the newspapers either abuse Trochu, or damn him with faint praise. It is so very much a matter of chance whether a man goes down to posterity as a sage or a fool, that it is by no means easy to form an opinion as to what will be the verdict of history on Trochu. If he simply wished to keep the Prussians out of Paris, and to keep order inside until the provisions were exhausted, he has succeeded. If he wished to force them to raise the siege he has failed. His military critics complain that, admitting he could not do the latter, he ought, by frequent sorties, to have endeavoured to prevent them sending troops to their covering armies. One thing is certain, that all his sorties have failed not only in the result, but in the conception. As a consequence of this, the French soldiers, who more than any other troops in the world require, in order to fight well, to have faith in their leader, have lost all confidence in him.

We have had no pigeon for the last eighteen days, and the anxiety to obtain news from without is very strong. A few days ago a messenger was reported to have got through the Prussian lines with news of a French victory. The next day a Saxon officer was said, with his last breath, to have confided to his doctor that Frederick Charles had been defeated. Yesterday Jules Favre told the mayor that there was a report that Chanzy had gained a victory. Everything now depends upon what Chanzy is doing, and, for all we know, he may have ceased to exist for the last week.

A census which has just been made of the population within the lines, makes the number, exclusive of the Line, Mobiles, and sailors, 2,000,500. No attempt has yet been made to ration the bread, but it is to be mixed with oats and rice. The mayor of this quarter says that in this arrondissement—the richest in Paris—he is certain that there is food for two months. Should very good news come from the provinces, and it appear that by holding out for two months more the necessity for a capitulation would be avoided, I think that we should hold on until the end of February, if we have to eat the soles of our boots. If bad news comes, we shall not take to this food; but we shall give in when everything except bread fails, and we shall then consider that our honour is saved if nothing else is. M. Louis Blanc to-day publishes a letter to Victor Hugo, in which he tells the Parisians that if they do capitulate they will gain nothing by it, for the Prussians will neither allow them to quit Paris, nor, if the war continues, allow food to enter it.

As yet there are no signs of a real outbreak; and if a successful one does occur, it will be owing to the weakness of the Government, which has ample means to repress it. The Parisian press is always adjuring the working men not to cut either each others' or their neighbours' throats, and congratulating them on their noble conduct in not having done so. This sort of praise seems to me little better than an insult. I see no reason why the working men should be considered to be less patriotic than others. That they are not satisfied with Trochu, and that they entertain different political and social opinions to those of the bourgeoisie, is very possible. Opinions, however, are free, and they have shown as yet that they are willing to subordinate the expression of theirs to the exigencies of the national defence. I go a good deal among them, and while many of them wish for a general system of rationing, because they think that it will make the provisions last longer, they have no desire to pillage or to provoke a conflict with the Government. I regard them myself, in every quality which makes a good citizen, as infinitely superior to the journalists who lecture them, and who would do far better to shoulder a musket and to fall into the ranks, than to waste paper in reviling the Prussians and bragging of their own heroism. As soldiers, the fault of the working men is that they will not submit to discipline; but this is more the fault of the Government than of them. As citizens, no one can complain of them. To talk with one of them after reading the leading article of a newspaper is a relief. A French journalist robes himself in his toga, gets upon a pedestal, and talks unmeaning, unpractical claptrap. A French workman is, perhaps, too much inclined to regard every one except himself, and some particular idol which he has set up, as a fool; but he is by no means wanting in the power to take a plain practical view, both of his own interests, and those of his country. Since the commencement of the siege, forty-nine new journals have appeared. Many of them have already ceased to exist, but counting old and new newspapers, there must at least be sixty published every day. How they manage to find paper is to me a mystery. Some of them are printed upon sheets intended for books, others upon sheets which are so thick that I imagine they were designed to wrap up sugar and other groceries. Those which were the strongest in favour of the Empire, are now the strongest in favour of the Republic. Editors and writers whose dream it was a few months ago to obtain an invitation at the Tuileries or to the Palais Royal, or to merit by the basest of flatteries the

Legion of Honour, now have become perfect Catos, and denounce courts and courtiers, Bonapartists and Orleanists. War they regard as the most wicked of crimes, and they appear entirely to have forgotten that they welcomed with shouts of ecstacy in July last the commencement of the triumphal march to Berlin.

January 2nd.

Yesterday evening, notwithstanding the cold, there were groups on the Boulevards shouting "*à bas Trochu.*" It is understood that henceforward no military operation is to take place before it has been discussed by a Council of War, consisting of generals and admirals. As the moment approaches when we shall, unless relieved, be obliged to capitulate, everyone is attempting to shift from himself all responsibility. This is the consequence of the scapegoat system which has so long prevailed in France. Addresses are published from the commanders outside congratulating the National Guard who have been under their orders. The *Vérité*, in alluding to them, asks the following questions:—"Why are battalions which are accused by General Thomas, their direct superior, of chronic drunkenness, thus placed upon a pinnacle by real military men? Why do distinguished generals, unless forced by circumstances, declare the mere act of passing four or five cold nights in the trenches heroic? Why is so great a publicity given to such contradictory orders of the day?"

The *Journal Officiel* contains a long address to the Parisians. Beyond the statement that no news had been received since the 14th ult., this document contains nothing but empty words. Between the lines one may, perhaps, read a desire to bring before the population the terrible realities of the situation.

The deaths for the last week amount to 3,280, an increase on the previous week of 552. I am told that these bills of mortality do not include those who die in the public hospitals. Small-pox is on the increase—454 as against 388 the previous week.

Nothing new outside. The bombardment of the eastern forts still continues. It is, however, becoming more intermittent. Every now and then it almost ceases, then it breaks out with fresh fury. The Prussians are supposed to be at work at Chatillon. If they have heavy guns there, it will go hard with the Fort of Vanves. The rations are becoming in some of the arrondissements smaller by degrees and beautifully less. In the 18th (Montmartre) the inhabitants only receive two sous worth of horse-flesh per diem. The rations are different in each arrondissement, as the Mayor of each tries to get hold of all he can, and some are more successful than others. These differences cause great dissatisfaction. The feeling to-day seems to be that if Trochu wishes to avoid riots, he must make a sortie very shortly.

The *Gaulois* says :—

"How sad has been our New Year's-day! Among ourselves we may own it, although we have bravely supported it, like men of sense, determined to hold good against bad fortune, and to laugh in the face of misery. It is hard not to have had the baby brought to our bedside in the morning; not to have seen him clap his hands with pleasure on receiving some toy; not to have pressed the hands of those we love best, and not to have embraced them and been able to say—' The year which has passed has had its joys and its sorrows, sun and shadow—but what matters it? We have shared them together. The year which is commencing cannot bring with it any sorrows that by remaining united we shall not be able to support?' Most of us breakfasted this morning—the New Year's breakfast, usually so gay—alone and solitary; a few smoky logs our only companions. There are sorrows which no philosophy can console. On other days one may forget them, but on

New Year's-day our isolation comes home to us, and, do what we may, we are sad and silent. Where are they now? What are they doing now? is the thought which rises in every breast. The father's thoughts are with his children; he dimly sees before him their rosy faces, and their mother who is dressing them. How weary, too, must the long days be for her, separated from her husband. Last year she had taught the baby to repeat a fable, and she brought him all trembling to recite it to the father. She, too, trembles like a child. She follows him with her looks, she whispers to him a word when he hesitates, but so low that he reads it on her lips, and the father hears nothing. Poor man! Sorry indeed he would have been to have had it supposed that he had perceived the mother's trick. He was himself trembling, too, lest the child should not know his lesson. What a disappointment it would have been to the mother! For a fortnight before she had taken baby every night on her knees and said, 'Now begin your fable.' She had taught it him verse by verse with the patience of an angel, and she had encouraged him to learn it with many a sugar-plum. 'He is beginning to know his fable,' she said a hundred times to her husband. 'Really,' he answered, with an air of doubt. The honest fellow was as interested in it as his wife, and he only appeared to doubt it in order to make her triumph greater. He knew that baby would know the fable on New Year's morn. You Prussian beggars, you Prussian scoundrels, you bandits, and you Vandals, you have taken everything from us; you have ruined us; you are starving us; you are bombarding us; and we have a right to hate you with a royal hatred. Well, perhaps one day we might have forgiven you your rapine and your murders; our towns that you have sacked; your heavy yokes; your infamous treasons. The French race is so light of heart, so kindly, that we might perhaps in time have forgotten our resentments. What we never shall forget will be this New Year's Day, which we have been forced to pass without news from our families. You at least have had letters from your Gretchens, astounding letters, very likely, in which the melancholy blends with blue eyes, make a wonderful literary salad, composed of sour-krout, Berlin wool, forget-me-nots, pillage, bombardment, pure love, and transcendental philosophy. But you like all this just as you like jam with your mutton. You have what pleases you. Your ugly faces receive kisses by the post. But you kill our pigeons, you intercept our letters, you shoot at our balloons with your absurd *fusils de rempart*, and you burst out into a heavy German grin when you get hold of one of our bags, which are carrying to those we love our vows, our hopes, our remembrance, our regrets, and our hearts. It is a merry farce, is it not? Ah, if ever we can render you half the sufferings which we are enduring, you will see *des grises*. Perhaps you don't know what the word means, and, like one of Gavarni's children, you will say, 'What! *des grises?*' You will, I trust, one of these days learn what is the signification of the term at your own cost. One of your absurd pretensions is to be the only people in the world who understand how to love, or who care for domestic ties. You will see, by the hatred which we shall ever bear to you, that we too know how to love—our time will come some day, be assured. This January 1 of the year 1871 inaugurates a terrible era of bloody revenge. Poor philosophers of universal peace, you see now the value of your grand phrases and of your humanitarian dreams! Vainly you imagined that the world was entering into a period of everlasting peace and progress. A wonderful progress, indeed, has 1870 brought us! You never calculated on the existence of these Huns. We are back again now in the midst of all the miseries of the 13th and 14th centuries. The memory of to-day will be written on the hearts of our children.

'It was the year,' they will say, 'when we received no presents, when we did not kiss our father, because of the Prussians. They shall pay for it!' Let us hope that the payment will commence this very day. But if we are still to be vanquished, we will leave to our children the memory of our wrongs, and the care to avenge them."

The following article is from the *Vérité*:—

"What troubles would not have been spared to our unhappy country if only it had been told the truth. If only anyone had been courageous enough to tell us what were our resources when Grammont made his famous declaration from the tribune, the war would not have taken place. On the 4th of September, many members of the new Government were under no delusions, but as it was necessary to say that we were strong, in order to be popular, they did not hesitate to proclaim that the Republic would save France. To-day the situation has not changed. On the faith of the assertions of their rulers, the population of Paris imagines that ultimate victory is certain, and that our provisions can never be exhausted. They have no idea that if we are not succoured we must eventually succumb. What a surprise—and perhaps what a catastrophe—it will be when they learn that there is no more bread, and no chance of victory. The people will complain that they have been deceived, and they will be right. They will shout 'treason,' and seek for vengeance. Will they be entirely in the wrong? If the Government defends itself, what future awaits us! If it does not defend itself, through what scenes shall we pass before falling into the hands of the Prussians! The Republic, like the Empire, has made mendacity the great system of government. The Press has chosen to follow the same course. Great efforts are being made to destroy the reciprocal sentiments of union and confidence, to which we owe it that Paris still resists, after 100 days of siege. The enemy, despairing to deliver over Paris to Germany, as it had solemnly promised, on Christmas, adds now the bombardment of our advanced posts and our forts to the other means of intimidation by which it has endeavoured to enervate the defence. Use is being made, before public opinion, of the deceptions which an extraordinary winter and infinite sufferings and fatigues are causing us. It is said, indeed, that the members of the Government are divided in their views respecting the great interests the direction of which has been confided to them. The army has suffered great trials, and it required a short repose, which the enemy endeavours to dispute by a bombardment more violent than any troops were ever exposed to. The army is preparing for action with the aid of the National Guards, and all together we shall do our duty. I declare that there are no differences in the councils of the Government, and that we are all closely united in the presence of the agonies and the perils of the country, and in the thought and the hope of its deliverance."

La Patrie, of Jan. 2, says :—

"Perhaps Bourbaki has gone to meet General von Werder. If he is victorious, the road to Paris by the valley of the Seine will be open to him, or the road to Southern Germany by Besançon and Belfort, and the bridge of Bâle, the neutrality of which we are not obliged to respect any more than that of Belgium, since Europe has allowed Bismarck to violate that of Luxemburg. Ah! if Bourbaki were a Tortensen, a Wrangel, or a Turenne—perhaps he is—what a grand campaign we might have in a few weeks on the Danube, the Lech, and the Saar."

The *Liberté*, of Jan. 2, says :—

"A great manifestation is being organised against the Government. The object is to substitute in its place the college of Mayors of Paris and their adjuncts. The manifestation, if it occurs, will not get further than the Boulevards. General Trochu is in no fear from Mayor

Mothe, but he must understand that the moment for action has arrived. His proclamation has only imperfectly replied to the apprehensions of Paris. A capitulation, the very idea of which the Government recoils from, and which would only become possible when cold, hunger, and a bombardment have made further resistance impossible, besieges the minds of all, and presses all the hearts which beat for a resistance à outrance in a vice of steel. Trochu should reply to these agonies no longer by proclamations, but by acts."

January 4th.

It is said, I know not with what truth, that there always are, on an average, 5000 families who are in destitute circumstances, because their chiefs never would play out their trumps at whist until it became too late to use them effectively. If Trochu really was under the impression that he had trumps in his hand good enough to enable him to win the game he is playing against the Prussians, he has kept them back so long that they are worthless. If he could not break through the Prussian lines a month ago, *à fortiori*, he will not be able to do so now. They are stronger, and he is weaker; for the inaction of the last few weeks, and the surrender of Avron, would have been enough to damp the ardour of far more veteran troops than those which he has under his command. The outcry against this excellent but vain man grows stronger every day, and sorry, indeed, must he be that he "rushed in where others feared to tread." "Action, speedy action," shout the newspapers, much as the Americans did before Bull's Run, or as M. Felix Pyat always calls it, Run Bull. The generals well know that if they yield to the cry, there will most assuredly be a French edition of that battle. In fact, the situation may be summed up in a very few words. The generals have no faith in their troops, and the troops have no faith in their generals. Go outside the walls and talk to the officers and the soldiers who are doing the real fighting, and who pass the day dodging shells, and the night freezing in their tents. They tell you that they are prepared to do their duty, but that they are doubtful of ultimate success. Come inside, and talk to some hero who has never yet got beyond the ramparts, Cato at Utica is a joke to him, Palafox at Saragossa a whining coward. Since the forts have been bombarded, he has persuaded himself that he is eating, drinking, and sleeping under the fire of the enemy. "Human nature is a rum 'un," said Mr. Richard Swiveller; and most assuredly this is true of French nature. That real civil courage and spirit of self-sacrifice which the Parisians have shown, in submitting to hardship and ruin rather than consent to the dismemberment of their country, they regard as no title to respect. Nothing which does not strike the imagination has any value in their eyes. A uniform does not make a soldier; and although they have all arrayed themselves in uniform, they are far worse soldiers than the peasantry who have been enrolled in the Mobiles. To tell them this, however, would make them highly indignant. Military glory is their passion, and it is an unfortunate one. To admire the pomp and pride of glorious war no more makes a warrior than to admire poetry makes a poet. The Parisian is not a coward; but his individuality is so strongly developed that he objects to that individuality being destroyed by some stray shot. To die with thousands looking on is one thing; to die obscurely is another. French courage is not the same as that of the many branches of the great Saxon family. A Saxon has a dogged stubbornness which gives him an every-day and every-hour courage. That of the Frenchman is more dependent upon external circumstances. He must have confidence in his leader, he must have been encouraged by success, and he must be treated with severity tempered with judicious flattery. Give him a sword, and let him prance about on a horse like a circus rider, and, provided there are a sufficient number of spectators, he will do wonders, but he will not consent to perish obscurely for the sake of anything or anyone. Trochu has utterly failed in exciting enthusiasm in those under his command; he issues many proclamations, but they fail to strike the right chord. Instead of keeping up discipline by judicious severity, he endeavours to do so by lecturing like a schoolmaster. And then, since the commencement of the siege he has been unsuccessful in all his offensive movements. I am not a military man, but although I can understand the reasons against a sortie *en masse*, it does appear to me strange that the Prussians are not more frequently disquieted by attacks which at least would oblige them to make many a weary march round the outer circle, and would prevent them from detaching troops for service elsewhere.

Not an hour passes without some new rumour respecting the armies of the Provinces being put in circulation. A letter in which General Chanzy is said to be playing with Frederick Charles as a cat plays with a mouse, and which is attributed to Mr. Odo Russell, English Under-Secretary of State, and Correspondent of the *Times*, has been read by some one, and this morning all the newspapers are jubilant over it. A copy of the *Moniteur de Versailles* of the 1st has found its way in; there is nothing in it about Frederick Charles, but this we consider evidence that he has sustained a defeat. Then somebody has found a bottle in the Seine with a letter in it; this letter alludes to a great French victory. Mr. Washburne has the English papers up to the 22nd, but he keeps grim guard over them, and allows no one to have a glimpse of them; since our worthy friend Otto von Bismarck sent in to him an extract from a letter of mine, in which I alluded to the contents of some of them which had reached us. He passes his existence, however, staving off insidious questions. His very looks are commented on. "We saw him to-day," says an evening paper I have just bought; "he smiled! Good sign! Our victory must have been overwhelming if John Bull is obliged to confess it." Another newspaper asks him whether, considering the circumstances, he does not consider it a duty to violate his promise to Count Bismarck, and to hand over his newspapers to the Government. In this way, thinks this tempter, the debt which America owes to France for aiding her during her revolution will be repaid. "We gave you Lafayette and Rochambeau, in return we only ask for one copy of an English paper." The anxiety for news is weighing heavier on the population than the absence of provisions or the cold. Every day, and all day, there are crowds standing upon the elevated points in the city, peering through glasses, in the wild hope of witnessing the advent of Chanzy, who is apparently expected to prick in with Faidherbe by his side, upon two gorgeously caparisoned steeds, like the heroes in the romances of the late Mr. G. P. R. James. Many pretend to distinguish, above the noise of the cannon of our forts and the Prussian batteries, the echoes of distant artillery, and rush off to announce to their friends that the army of succour has fallen on the besiegers from the rear. In the meantime the bombardment of the forts and villages to the east of the city is continuing, and with that passion for system in everything which distinguishes the Germans, it is being methodized. A fixed number of shells are fired off every minute, and at certain hours in the day there are long pauses. What is happening in the forts is, of course, kept very secret. The official bulletins say that no damage in them has yet been done. As for the villages round them, they are, I presume, shelled merely in order to make them untenable.

The Government appears now as anxious to find others to share responsibility with it as heretofore it has been averse to any division of power. The Mayors of the city are to meet with their deputies once a week at the Hôtel de Ville to express their opinions respecting municipal matters, and once a week at the Ministry of the Interior to discuss the political situation. As there are twenty mayors and forty adjuncts, they, when together, are almost numerous enough to form a species of Parliament. The all important food question remains *in statu quo*. It is, however, beginning to be hinted in semi-official organs, that perhaps the bread will have to be rationed; I may be wrong, but I am inclined to think that the population will not submit to this. Government makes no statement with respect to the amount of corn in store. Some say that there is not enough for two weeks, others that there is enough for two months' consumption; M. Douait assured a friend of mine yesterday that, to the best of his belief, there is enough to carry us into March. Landlords and tenants are as much at loggerheads here as they are in Ireland; the Government has issued three decrees to regulate the question. By the first is suspended all judicial proceedings on the part of landlords for their rent; by the second, it granted a delay of three months to all persons unable to pay the October term; by the third, it required all those who wished to profit by the second to make a declaration of inability to pay before a magistrate. To-day a fourth decree has been issued, again suspending the October term, and making the three previous decrees applicable to the January term, but giving to landlords a right to dispute the truth of the allegation of poverty on the part of their tenants; the question is a very serious one, for on the payment of rent depends directly or indirectly the means of livelihood of half the nation. Thus the landlords say that if the tenants do not pay them they cannot pay the interest of the mortgages on their properties. If this interest be not paid, however, the shareholders of the Crédit Foncier and other great mortgage banks get nothing.

Paris, under the fostering care of the Emperor, had become, next to St. Petersburgh, the dearest capital in Europe. Its property was artificial, and was dependent upon a long chain of connecting links remaining unbroken. In the industrial quarters money was made by the manufacture of *Articles de Paris*, and for these, as soon as the communications are reopened, there will be the same market as heretofore. As a city of pleasure, however, its prosperity must depend, like a huge watering-place, upon its being able to attract strangers. If they do not return, a reduction in prices will take place, which will ruin most of the shopkeepers, proprietors of houses, and hotel keepers; but this, although unpleasant to individuals, would be to the advantage of the world at large. Extravagance in Paris makes extravagance the fashion everywhere; under the Empire, to spend money was the readiest road to social distinction. The old *bourgeoisie* still retained the careful habits of the days of Louis Philippe, and made fortunes by cheeseparing. Imperial Paris was far above this. Families were obliged to spend 20 per cent. of their incomes in order to lodge themselves; shops in favoured quarters were let for fabulous prices, and charged fabulous prices for their wares. *Cocodettes* of the Court, *cocottes* of the Bois, wives of speculators, shoddy squaws from New York, Calmucs recently imported from their native steppes, doubtful Italian Princesses, gushing Polish Countesses, and foolish Englishwomen, merrily raced along the road to ruin. Good taste was lost in tinsel and glitter; what a thing cost was the only standard of its beauty. Great gingerbread palaces were everywhere run up, and let even before they were out of the builder's hands. It was deemed fashionable to drive about in a carriage with four horses, with perhaps a black man to drive, and an Arab sitting on the box by his side. Dresses by milliners in vogue gave a ready currency to their wearers. The Raphael of his trade gave himself all the airs of a distinguished artist; he received his clients with vulgar condescension, and they—no matter what their rank—submitted to his insolence in the hope that he would enable them to outshine their rivals. Ambassadors' wives and Court ladies used to go to take tea with the fellow, and dispute the honour of filling his cup or putting sugar into it. I once went into his shop—a sort of drawing-room hung round with dresses; I found him lolling on a chair, his legs crossed before the fire. Around him were a bevy of women, some pretty, some ugly, listening to his observations with the rapt attention of the disciples of a sage. He called them up before him like school girls, and after inspecting them, praised or blamed their dresses. Once, a pretty young girl, found favour in his eyes, and he told her that he must dream and meditate several days over her, in order to find the inspiration to make a gown worthy of her. "Why do you wear these ugly gloves?" he said to another, "never let me see you in gloves of that colour again." She was a very grand lady, but she slipped off her gloves, and put them in her pocket with a guilty look. When there was going to be a ball at Court, ladies used to go down on their knees to him to make them beautiful. For some time he declined to dress any longer the wife of a great Imperial dignitary who had not been sufficiently humble towards him; she came to him in tears, but he was obdurate, and he only consented at last to make a gown for her on condition that she would put it on for the first time in his shop. The Empress, who dealt with him, sent to tell him that if he did not abate his prices she would leave him. "You cannot," he replied, and in fact she could not, for she stood by him to the last. A morning dress by this artist, worth in reality about 4*l*., cost 30*l*.; an evening dress, tawdry with flounces, ribbons, and bad lace could not be had under 70*l*. There are about thirty shops in Paris where, as at this man-milliner's, the goods are not better than elsewhere, but where they cost about ten times their value. They are patronised by fools with more money than wits, and chiefly by foreign fools. The proprietor of one of these establishments was complaining to me the other day of what he was losing by the siege; I told him that I sympathised with him about as much as I should with a Greek brigand, bewailing a falling off of wealthy strangers in the district where he was in the habit of carrying on his commercial operations. Whenever the communications are again open to Paris, and English return to it, I would give them this piece of advice—never deal where *ici on parle Anglais* is written up; it means *ici on vole les Anglais*. The only tradesmen in Paris who are making a good thing out of their country's misfortunes are the liquor sellers and the grocers; their stores seem inexhaustible, but they are sold at famine prices. "I who speak to you, I owe myself to my country. There is no sacrifice I would not make rather than capitulate to those Huns, those Vandals," said a grocer to me, with a most sand-the-sugar face, this morning, as he pocketed about ten times the value of a trifle—candles, in fact, which have risen twenty-five per cent. in the last two days—and folding his arms, scowled from under his képi into futurity, with stern but vacuous resolution.

January 6th.

I have just returned from Point-du-Jour, where I went with Mr. Frank Lawley in order to see myself what truth there was in the announcement that we were being bombarded. Point-du-Jour is the point where the Seine issues from Paris. The circular, railroad passes over the river here on a high brick viaduct, which forms a species of fortification. The hills outside the city form a sort of amphitheatre, in which are situated the towns of Sèvres and Meudon. To the right of the river is Mont Valérien and the batteries in the Bois de Boulogne; to the left the

x

Fort of Issy. The noise of the cannonade was very loud; but very little could be seen, owing to the sun shining on the hills outside. Speculators, however, with telescopes, were offering to show the Prussian artillerymen for one sou —one of them offered to let me see a general for two sous. When I got within about half a mile of the ramparts I began to hear the whistling of the shells. Here the sightseers were not so numerous. Whenever a shell was heard, there was a rush behind walls and houses. Some people threw themselves down, others seemed to imagine that the smallest tree would protect them, and congregated behind the thinnest saplings. Boys were running about picking up pieces of shells, and offering them for sale. Women were standing at their doors, and peeping their heads out: "Brigands, bandits, they dare to bombard us; wait till tomorrow, we will make them rue it." This, and expressions of a similar nature, was the tone of the small talk. My own impression is, that the Prussians were firing at the ramparts, and that, as often occurs, their projectiles overshot the mark. I did not see anyone either killed or wounded, and it seems to me that the most astonishing thing in a bombardment is the little damage it does to life and limb. I saw a bit of iron cut away a branch from one of the trees, and one shell I saw burst on the road by the river. In 15 minutes we counted 11 shells whizzing through the air, over our heads, which fell I presume somewhere behind us. The newspaper which I have just bought, I see, says that two shells have fallen close by the Invalides, and that they have been coming in pretty thickly all along the zone near the southern ramparts. This may or may not be the case. Like Herodotus in Egypt, I make a distinction between what I am told and what I see, and only guarantee the authenticity of the latter. The only house which as far as I could perceive had been struck was a small one. A chimney-stack had been knocked over; an old lady who inhabited it pointed this out to me. She seemed to be under the impression that this was the result of design, and plaintively asked me what she had done to "William" and to Bismarck that they should knock over her chimney. On the ramparts no damage seemed to have been done. The National Guard on duty were in the casemates. The noise, however, was tremendous. Issy, Valérien, the guns of the bastions and those of the cannon-boats were firing as hard as they could, and the Prussian batteries were returning their fire with a will. After the sun went down the dark hills opposite were lit up with the flashes of light which issued every second from the batteries.

The Government has issued a proclamation; in it is announced that we are to be relieved by the Army of the North. Another proclamation has been posted, purporting to proceed from the "delegates of the twenty arrondissements," calling upon the population to turn out Trochu. It has attracted little notice. Several mayors, too, it is reported, have threatened to resign unless more energetic counsels prevail in high places. Frenchmen, however, as one of their statesmen said, cannot grasp two ideas at a time, and for to-day at least the bombardment is the all-absorbing idea. Whether Frederick Charles has been really defeated I do not know, but we are all assured that he has been. Paris journals state that he has been wounded, and that 45,000 of his army have surrendered. It is asserted, too, that the prisoners who were taken yesterday admit that one of their armies has had a very serious reverse. The bombardment of the forts still continues, and it has extended to the southern ones. With respect to its effect, I will say nothing, lest I be accused of giving aid and comfort to the enemy. *La Vérité* of yesterday already calls upon the Government to open and either suppress or expurgate the letters of English correspondents.

The vin ordinaire is giving out. It has already risen

nearly 60 per cent. in price. This is a very serious thing for the poor, who not only drink it, but warm it and make with bread a soup out of it. Yesterday, I had a slice of Pollux for dinner. Pollux and his brother Castor are two elephants, which have been killed. It was tough, coarse, and oily, and I do not recommend English families to eat elephant as long as they can get beef or mutton. Many of the restaurants are closed owing to want of fuel. They are recommended to use lamps; but although French cooks can do wonders with very poor materials, when they are called upon to cook an elephant with a spirit lamp the thing is almost beyond their ingenuity. Castor and Pollux's trunks sold for 45fr. a lb.; the other parts of the interesting twins fetched about 10fr. a lb. It is a good deal warmer to-day, and has been thawing in the sun; if the cold and the siege had continued much longer, the Prussians would have found us all in bed. It is a far easier thing to cut down a tree than to make it burn. Proverbs are not always true; and I have found to my bitter experience of late that the proverb that "there is no smoke without a fire" is untrue. The Tupper who made it never tried to burn green wood.

CHAPTER XVII.

January 7th.

THE attempt of the "Ultras" to force Trochu to resign has been a failure. On Friday bands issuing from the outer Faubourgs marched through the streets shouting "No capitulation!" A manifesto was posted on the walls, signed by the delegates of the 20 arrondissements, calling on the people to rise. At the weekly meeting of the Mayors M. Delescluze, the Mayor of the 19th arrondissement, proposed that Trochu and Le Flô should be called upon to resign, and that a supreme council should be established in which the "civil element should not be subordinated to the military element." M. Gustave Flourens published a letter from his prison suggesting that the people should choose as their leader a young energetic Democrat—that is to say himself. M. Félix Pyat, on the other hand, explained that generals are tyrants, and that the best thing would be to carry on the operations of the siege without one. The "bombardment" is, however, still the absorbing question of the day; and all these incipient attempts at revolution have failed. Trochu issued a proclamation, in which he said, "The Governor of Paris will never capitulate." M. Delescluze has resigned, and several arrests have been made. The Government, however, owes its triumph, not so much to its own inherent merits, as to the demerits of those who wished to supplant it. Everyone complains of Trochu's strange inaction, and distrusts his colleagues, who seem to be playing fast-and-loose with the Commune, and to be anxious by a little gentle violence to be restored to private life. The cry still is, "We will not capitulate!" and the nearer the moment approaches that the provisions must fail, the louder is it shouted. Notwithstanding the bitter experience which the Parisians have had of the vanity of mere words to conjure disaster, they still seem to suppose that if they only cry out loud enough that the Prussians cannot, will not, shall not, enter Paris, their men of war will be convinced that the task is beyond their powers, and go home in despair. We are like a tribe of Africans beating tomtoms and howling in order to avert a threatening storm. Yesterday a great council of war was held, at which not only the generals of division and admirals, but even generals of brigade, were present. Although it is a military dictum that "councils of war never fight," I think that in a few days we shall have a sortie, as that anonymous general "public opinion" insists upon it.

We are still without news from the provinces. The General Order to-day publishes an extract from a German paper which hardly seems to bear out the assertion of the Government that the Army of the North is advancing to our succour. As evidence that our affairs are looking up in the provinces *La France* contains the following: " A foreigner who knows exactly the situation of our departments said yesterday, 'These damned French, in spite of their asinine qualities, are getting the better of the Prussians.'" We are forced to live to-day upon this crumb of comfort which has fallen from the lips of a great unknown. Hope is the last feeling which dies out in the human breast, and rightly or wrongly nine persons out of ten believe that Chanzy will shortly force the Prussians to raise the siege. The bombardment is supposed to mask their having been obliged to send heavy reinforcements to Frederick Charles, who regularly every morning is either killed, wounded, or taken prisoner.

It is almost needless to say that the newspapers are filled with wondrous tales respecting the bombardment; with denunciations against the Prussians for their sacrilege in venturing upon it; and with congratulations to the population on their heroism in supporting it. The number of persons who have been all but hit by shells is enormous. I went to the left bank of the Seine in order to see myself the state of affairs. At Point du Jour there is a hot corner sparsely inhabited. The Prussians are evidently here firing at the viaduct which crosses the river. From here I followed the ramparts as close as I could as far as Montrouge. I heard of many shells which had fallen, but except at Point-du-Jour I did not myself either see any fall, or hear any whiz through the air. I then went to the Observatory, where according to the *Soir* the shells were falling very freely. A citizen who was sweeping before the gate told me that he knew nothing about them. In the Rue d'Enfer, just behind, there was a house which had been struck during the night, and close by there was a cantinière, on her way to be buried, who had been killed by one. At the garden of the Luxembourg and at the artesian well near the Invalides I heard of shells, but could not find out where they had struck. As far as I can make out, the Prussians aim at the bastions, and occasionally, but rarely, at some public building. Probably about 50 shells have been sent with malice prepense inside the town. Just behind a bastion it is a little dangerous; but in Grenelle, Vaugirard, and Montrouge, the risk to each individual is not so great as it would be to go over a crowded crossing in London. In these quarters I saw a few people moving away with their goods and chattels; but the population generally seemed rather pleased than otherwise with what was going on. Except close in by the ramparts, there was no excitement.

Almost the whole of the portion of the town on the left bank of the Seine is now under fire; but even should it be seriously bombarded, I doubt if the effect will be at all commensurate with the expense of powder and projectiles. When shells fall over a very large area, the odds against each separate person being hit by them are so large that no one thinks that—happen what may to others—he will be wounded.

January 11th.

The spy mania, which raged with such intensity at the commencement of the siege, has again broken out. Every day persons are arrested because they are supposed, by lighted candles and other mysterious devices, to be in communication with the enemy. Sergeant Hoff, who used to kill his couple of brace of Germans every day, and who disappeared after Champigny, it is now said was a spy; and instead of mourning over his wife, who had been slain by the Prussians, kept a mistress in splendour, like a fine gentleman. Foreigners are looked upon suspiciously in the streets. Very black looks are cast upon the Americans who have established and kept up the best ambulance there is in Paris at their own cost. Even the French ambulances are suspected, since some of their members, during a suspension of arms, broke bread with the Prussians; for it is held that any one who does not hate a German must be in the pay of Bismarck. But this is not all: the newspapers hint that there are spies at head-quarters. General Schmitz has a valet who has a wife, and this wife is a German. What more clear than that General Schmitz confides what passes at councils of war to his valet—generals usually do; that the valet confides it to his wife, who, in some mysterious manner, confides it to Bismarck. Then General Trochu has an aide-de-camp, a Prince Bibesco. He is a Wallachian, and a son of an ex-Hospodar—I never yet heard of a Wallachian who was not more or less. Can a doubt exist in the mind of any reasonable being that this young gentleman, a harmless lad, who had passed the greater part of his existence dancing cotillons at Paris, is in direct communication with the Prussians outside? A day or two ago two National Guards were exchanging their strategical views in a café, when they observed a stranger write down something. He was immediately arrested, as he evidently intended to transmit the opinions of these two military sages to General Moltke. I was myself down at Montrouge yesterday, when I was requested by two National Guards to accompany them to the nearest commissary. I asked why, and was told that a woman had heard me speak German. I replied that I was English. "Zat ve sall soon zee," said one of my captors. "I spek Anglish like an Anglishman, address to me the vord in Anglish." I replied that the gentleman spoke English with so perfect an accent that I thought he must be a fellow-countryman. The worthy fellow was disarmed by the compliment, and told a crowd which had collected round us to do prompt justice on the spy, that I not only was an Englishman, but *un Cockné*; that is to say, he explained, an inhabitant of London. He shook me by the hand; his friend shook me by the hand; and several ladies and gentlemen also shook me by the hand; and then we parted. Yesterday evening on the Boulevards there were groups discussing "the traitors." Some said that General Schmitz had been arrested; others that he ought to be arrested. A patriot observed to me that all foreigners in Paris ought, as a precautionary measure, to be extirpated. "Parbleu," I replied, and you may depend upon it I rolled my eyes and shrugged my shoulders in true Gallic fashion. This morning General Trochu has published a proclamation, denouncing all attacks upon his staff, and making himself responsible for its members. It is an honest, manly protest, and by far the best document which this prolific writer has issued for some time. Another complaint is made against the generals who damp the popular enthusiasm by throwing doubts upon ultimate victory. In fact, we have got to such a condition that a military man dares not venture to express his real opinion upon military matters for fear of being denounced. We are, indeed, still in a most unsurrendering mood. I was talking to-day to a banker—a friend who would do anything for me except cash my bill. In business he is a clear-headed, sensible man. I asked him what would occur if our provisions gave out before the armies of the provinces arrived to our succour. He replied that the Government would announce the fact, and call upon all able-bodied men to make a dash at the Prussian lines; that 300,000 at least would respond to that call, and would either be killed or force their way out. This will give you an idea of the present tone of the population. Nine men out of ten believe that we have enough provisions to last at least until the end of February. The only official utterance respecting the provisions is contained in a paragraph in the *Journal Officiel* to-day, in which we are informed that there are 15,000 oxen and 40,000 sheep in Bordeaux waiting for marching orders to Paris. This is much like telling a starving man in the Strand that figs are plentiful in Palestine, and only waiting to be picked.

The bombardment has diminished in intensity. The Government has put the Prussian prisoners in the ambulances on the left bank of the Seine. It appears to me that it would have been wiser to have moved the ambulances to the right bank. By day few shells fall into the town beyond the immediate vicinity of the ramparts. At night they are more plentiful, and seem to be aimed promiscuously. I suppose about ten people are hit every twenty-four hours. Now as above fifty people die every day in Paris of bronchitis, there is far more danger from the latter than from the batteries of the disciples of Geist outside. It is not worse to die by a bomb than of a cold. Indeed I am by no means sure that of two evils the latter is not the least; yet a person being suddenly struck down in the streets of a capital by a piece of iron from a cannon will always produce a more startling effect upon the mind than a ·rise in the bills of mortality from natural causes. Those who are out of the reach of the Prussian guns are becoming accustomed to the bombardment. "You naughty child," I heard a woman who was walking before me say to her daughter, "if you do not behave better I will not take you to see the bombardment." "It is better than a vaudeville," said a girl near me on the Trocadero, and she clapped her hands. A man at Point-du-Jour showed me two great holes which had been made in his garden the night before by two bombs close by his front door. He, his wife, and his children seemed to be rather proud of them. I asked him why he did not move into the interior of the town, and he said that he could not afford it. In a German paper which recently found its way in, it was stated that the bombardment of Paris would commence when the psychological moment had arrived. We are intensely indignant at this term; we consider it so cold-blooded. It is like a doctor standing by a man on the rack, and feeling his pulse to see how many more turns of the screw he can bear. All the forts outside are still holding their own against the Prussian batteries. Issy has had as yet the greatest amount of attention paid to it by the besiegers. There is a battery at Meudon which seems never to tire of throwing shells into it. It is said, however, that the enemy is endeavouring to establish breaching guns at a closer range, in order to make his balls strike the ground and then bound into the fort—a mode of firing which was very successful at Strasburg.

The sensation news of to-day is that Faidherbe has

driven Manteuffel across the Belgian frontier, and that Frederick Charles, who always seems to come to life after being killed, has been recalled from Orleans to Paris. The funds rose to-day one per cent. upon these rumours. Our chief confidence, however, just now is in Bourbaki; we think that he has joined Garibaldi, and that these two will force the Prussians to raise the siege by throwing themselves on their communications. I only hope they may.

Mr. Washburne has not been allowed to send out his weekly bag. I presume, however, that this embargo will not be kept up. The Government has not yet announced its intention with respect to M. Jules Favre proceeding to London to represent France in the conferences on the Eastern Question. Most of the newspapers seem to be of opinion that until the Republic has been officially recognised, it is not consistent with her dignity to take part in any European Conference. The diplomatists, who have been a little thrown in the background of late, by wars and generals, must be delighted to find their old friend, the "Eastern Question," cropping up. The settlement of the Schleswig-Holstein question was a heavy blow to them; but for many a year they will have an opportunity to prose and protocol over Turkey. An Austrian wit—indeed the only wit that Austria ever produced—used to say that Englishmen could only talk about the weather, and that if by some dispensation of Providence there ever should be no such thing as weather, the whole English nation would become dumb. What the weather is to Englishmen the Eastern Question is to diplomatists. For their sakes, let us hope that it never will be satisfactorily settled. Diplomatists, like many other apparently useless beings, must live.

January 15th.

Yesterday we were made comparatively happy by a report that the Prussian funds had fallen 3 per cent. at Berlin. To-day we are told that Bourbaki has gained a great victory, raised the siege of Belfort, and is about to enter Germany. German newspapers up to the 7th have been seized at the advanced posts, but whatever in them tells against us we put down to a general conspiracy on the part of Europe to deceive us. It is somewhat curious to watch the transmutations of the names of English statesmen after they have passed through a German and a French translation. Thus the latest news from London is that Mr. Hackington is made Irish Secretary, and that Mr. Floresko is Minister of Commerce.

The diplomatists and consuls still at Paris have sent a collective note to Count Bismarck, complaining that the notice of the bombardment was not given, and asking him to afford them the means to place the persons and the property of their respective countrymen out of danger. The minnows sign with the whales. Mr. Washburne's name is inserted between that of the representative of Monaco and that of the Chargé d'Affaires of Honduras.

The bombardment still continues. The cannon now make one continuous noise. Each particular discharge cannot be distinguished. The shells fall on the left bank to a distance of about a mile from the ramparts. A return of the *Official Journal* gives 138 wounded and 51 killed up to the 13th. Among the killed are 18 children and 12 women; among the wounded, 21 children and 45 women. Waggons and hand-carts packed with household goods are streaming in from the left to the right bank. In the bombarded quarters many shops are closed. Some householders have made a sort of casemate reaching to the first story of their houses; others sleep in their cellars. The streets are, however, full of people, even in the most exposed districts; and all the heights from which a view is to be had of the Prussian batteries are crowded with sightseers. Every now and then one comes across some house through which a shell has passed. The public buildings have, as yet, suffered very slightly. The dome of the Pantheon, which we presume is used as a mark for the aim of the Prussian artillerymen, has been hit once. The shell has made a round hole in the dome, and it burst inside the church. In the Jardin des Plantes all the glass of the conservatories has been shattered by the concussion of the air, and the orchids and other tropical plants are dying. Although war and its horrors are thus brought home to our very doors, it is even still difficult to realise that great events are passing around us which history will celebrate in its most solemn and dignified style. Distance in battles lends grandeur to the view. Had the charge of Balaclava taken place on Clapham Common, or had our gallant swordsmen replaced the donkeys on Hampstead Heath, even Tennyson would have been unable to poetise their exploits. When one sees stuck up in an omnibus-office that omnibuses "will have to make a circuit from *cause de bombardement;*" when shells burst in restaurants and maim the waiters; when the trenches are in tea-gardens; and when one is invited for a sou to look through a telescope at the enemy firing off their guns, there is a homely domestic air about the whole thing which is quite inconsistent with "the pomp and pride of glorious war."

On Friday night there was an abortive sortie at Clamart. Some of the newspapers say that the troops engaged in it were kept too long waiting, and that they warmed their feet by stamping, and made so much noise that the Prussians caught wind of the gathering. Be this as it may, as soon as they got into Clamart they were received with volleys of musketry, and withdrew. I am told that the marching battalions of the National Guard, now in the trenches, are doing their work better than was expected. The generals in command are satisfied with them, but whether they will be of any great use for offensive operations, is a question yet to be solved. The clubs still keep up their outcry for "La Commune," which they imagine will prove a panacea for every evil. In the club of the Rue Arras last night, a speaker went a step still further, and demanded "the establishment of anarchy as the ruling power." Trochu is still either attacked, or feebly defended, in the newspapers. The French are so accustomed to the State doing everything for them, that their ruler is made responsible for everything which goes wrong. The demand for a sortie *en masse* is not so strong. Every one is anxious not to surrender, and no one precisely knows how a surrender is to be avoided. Successes on paper have so long done duty for successes in the field, that no one, even yet, can believe that this paper currency has been so depreciated that bankruptcy must ensue. Is it possible, each man asks, that 500,000 armed Frenchmen will have to surrender to half the number of Germans? And as they reply that it is impossible, they come to the conclusion that treason must be at work, and look round for the traitor. Trochu, who is as honest and upright as a man as he is incompetent as a general, will probably share the fate of the "Man of Sedan" and the "Man of Metz," as they are called. "He is a Laocoon," says M. Felix Pyat in his newspaper, with some confusion of metaphor, "who will strangle the Republic."

We hear now that Government is undertaking an inquiry to discover precisely how long our stock of provisions will last. Matters are managed so carelessly, that I doubt whether the Minister of Commerce himself knows to within ten days the precise date when we shall be starved out. The rations of meat now amount to 1-27th of a pound per diem for each adult. At the fashionable restaurants the supply is unlimited, and the price as unlimited. Two cutlets of donkey cost 18 francs, and everything else in the way of animal food is in proportion. The real vital question, however, is how long the bread will last. In some arron dissements the supply fails after 8 o'clock in the morning; at others, each resident receives 1 lb. upon production of a *carte de subsistance*. The distribution has been thrown into disorder by the people from the bombarded quarters flocking into the central ones, and wanting to be fed. The bread itself is poor stuff. Only one kind is allowed to be manufactured; it is dark in colour, heavy, pasty, and gritty. There is as little corn in it as there is malt in London beer when barley is dear. The misery among the poorer classes is every day on the increase. Most of the men manage to get on with their 1fr. 50c. a day. In the morning they go to exercise, and afterwards loll about until night in cafés and pot-houses, making up with liquids for the absence of solids. As for doing regular work, they scoff at the idea. Master tailors and others tell me that it is almost impossible to get hands to do the few orders which are now given. They are warmly clad in uniforms by the State, and except those belonging to the marching battalions really doing duty outside, I do not pity them. With the women and children the case is different. The latter, owing to bad nourishment and exposure, are dying off like rotten sheep; the former have but just enough food to keep body and soul together, and to obtain even this they have to stand for hours before the doors of the butchers and bakers, waiting for their turn to be served. And yet they make no complaints, but patiently suffer, buoyed up, poor people, by the conviction that by so doing they will prevent the Prussians from entering the town. If one of them ventures to hint at a capitulation, she is set on by her neighbours. Self-assertion, however, carries the day. Jules and Jaques will hereafter quaff many a petit verre to their own heroism; and many a story will they inflict upon their long-suffering friends redounding to their own special glory. Their wives will be told that they ought to be proud to have such men for husbands. But

Jules and Jacques are in reality but arrant humbugs. Whilst they boozed, their wives starved; whilst they were warmly clad, their wives were in rags; whilst they were drinking confusion to their enemies in some snug room, their wives were freezing at the baker's door for their ration of bread. In Paris the women—I speak of those of the poorer classes—are of more sterling stuff than the men. They suffer far more, and they repine much less. I admire the crowd of silent, patient women, huddling together for warmth every morning, as they wait until their pittance is doled out to them, far more than the martial heroes who foot it behind a drum and a trumpet to crown a statue, to visit a tomb, and to take their turn on the ramparts; or the heroes of the pen, who day after day, from some cosy office, issue a manifesto announcing that victory is certain, because they have made a pact with death.

January 16th.

If I am to believe the Paris papers, the Fort of Issy is gradually extinguishing the guns of the Prussian batteries which bear on it. If I am to believe my eyes, the Fort of Issy is not replying at all to these said guns; and if I am to believe competent military authorities, in about eighteen days from now at the latest the Fort of Issy will cease to be a fort. The batteries at Meudon appeared to-day to be of opinion that the guns were effectually silenced, and shells fell thick and fast on the bastions at Point-du-Jour; so well aimed were they, that between the bastions a looker-on was in comparative safety. The noise, however, of the duel between the bastions and the batteries was so deafening, that it was literally impossible for two persons to hear each other speak at a few feet distance; the shells, too, which were passing to the right and left, seemed to give the whole air a tremulous motion. At the bastions the artillery-men were working their guns, but the National Guards on duty were under cover. The houses, on both sides of the

Seine, within the city, for about half a mile from the viaduct are deserted; not above a dozen of them, I should imagine, are still inhabited. Outside, in the villages of Vanvres and Issy, several fires have broken out, but they have been promptly extinguished, and there has been no general conflagration. The most dangerous spot in this direction is a road which runs behind the Forts of Vanvres and Montrouge; as troops are frequently marching along it the Prussians direct their guns from Clamart and Châtillon on it. In the trenches the danger is not great, and there are but few casualties; the shells pass over them. If anyone, however, exposes himself, a ball about the size of an egg, from a *canon de rampart*, whizzes by him, as a gentle reminder to keep under cover. The area of the bombardment is slightly extending, and will, I presume, very soon reach the right bank. More people are killed in the daytime than at night, because they will stand in groups, notwithstanding every warning, and stare at any house which has been damaged.

The bill of mortality for the week ending January 13th, gives an increase on the previous week of 302; the number of deaths registered is 3982. This is at the rate of above twenty per cent. per annum, and it must be remembered that in this return those who die in the public hospitals, or of the direct effect of the war, are not included. Small-pox is about stationary, bronchitis and pneumonia largely on the increase.

Bourbaki, we are told to-day, is at Freiburg, in the Grand Duchy of Baden. The latest German papers announce that Mézières has fallen, and it seems to occur to no one that Gambetta's last pigeon despatch informed us that the siege of this place had been raised. *La Liberté* thus sums up the situation :—" Nancy menaced; Belfort freed; Baden invaded; Hamburg about to be bombarded. This is the reply of France to the bombardment of Paris. The hour has arrived; the Prussians brought to bay, hope to find refuge in Paris. This is their last hope; their last resource."

In order to encourage us to put up with our short commons, we are now perpetually being told that the Government has in reserve vast stores of potted meats, cheese, butter, and other luxuries, of which we have almost forgotten the very taste; and that when things come to the worst we shall turn the corner, and enter into a period of universal abundance. These stores seem to me much like the mirage which lures on the traveller of the desert, and which perpetually recedes as he advances. But the great difficulty of the moment is to procure fuel. I am ready, as some one said, to eat the soles of my boots for the sake of my country; but then they must be cooked. All the mills are on the Marne, and cannot be approached. Steam mills have been put up, but they work slowly; and whatever may be the amount of corn yet in store, it is almost impossible to grind enough of it to meet the daily requirements.

A good deal of dissension is going on as to the time which it will take to revictual Paris; it is thought that it can be done in seven days, but I do not myself see how it is to be done in anything like this time. One of the principal English bankers here has, I understand, sent an agent by balloon to buy boats of small draught in England, in order to bring provisions up the Seine. As a speculation, I should imagine that the best plan would be to amass them on the Belgian or Luxemburg frontier. About two-thirds of the population will be without means to buy food, even if the food were at their doors. Trade and industry will not revive for some time; they will consequently be entirely dependent upon the State for their means of subsistence. Even if work is offered to them, many of them will not be able at once to reassume their habits of daily industry; the Bohemian life which they have led for the last four months, and which they are still leading, is against it. A siege is so abnormal a condition of things, that the State has been obliged to pay them for doing practically nothing, as otherwise they would have fallen into the hands of the anarchists; but this pottering about from day to day with a gun, doing nothing except play at billiards and drink, has been very demoralising, and it will be long before its effect ceases to be felt.

The newspapers are somewhat irreverent over the diplomatic protest against the bombardment. They say that while Paris is deserted by the Great European Powers, it is a source of pleasure to think that the Principality of Monaco and the Republics of San Marino and Honduras still stand by her. They suggest that M. Jules Favre should go to Andorre to endeavour to induce that republic also to reason with the Prussians upon the bombardment. I am told that the "proud young porter," who now the sheep is dead, represents alone the Majesty of England at the British Embassy is indignant at not having been invited to add his signature to the protest. He considers—and justly I think —that he is a far more important personage than the Plenipotentiary of his Highness of Monaco; a despot who exercises sway over about 20 acres of orange trees, 60 houses, and two roulette tables. The diplomatists are not, however, alone in their protest. Everybody has protested, and is still protesting. If it is a necessity of war to throw shells into a densely populated town like this; it is—to say the least—a barbarous necessity; but it seems to me that it is but waste of time and paper to register protests against it; and if it be thought desirable to do so, it would be far more reasonable to protest against human beings—women and children—being exposed to its effects, than to indite plaintive elegies about the possibility of the Venus de Milo being damaged, or the orchids in the hot-houses being killed. I know that, for my part, I would rather that every statue and every plant in the world were smashed to atoms by shells, than that I were. This, in an æsthetical point of view, is selfish; but it is none the less true. *Chacun pour soi.* The Panthéon was struck yesterday. What desecration! everyone cries; and I am very sorry for the Panthéon, but very glad that it was the Panthéon, and not me. The world at large very likely would lose more by the destruction of the Panthéon than of any particular individual; but each particular individual prefers his own humble self to all the edifices that architects have raised on the face of the globe.

I have been endeavouring to discover, whether in the councils of our rulers, the question as to what is to be done in the possible contingency of a capitulation becoming necessary, has been raised. As far as I can hear, the contingency is not yet officially recognised as within the realms of possibility, and it has never been alluded to. General Trochu has officially announced "that the Governor of Paris will never capitulate." His colleagues have periodically said much the same thing. The most practical of them, M. Ernest Picard, has, I believe, once or twice endeavoured to lead up to the subject, but he has failed in the attempt. Newspaper articles and Government proclamations tell the population every day that they only have to persevere in order ultimately to triumph. If the end must come, it is difficult to see how it will come. I have asked many intelligent persons what they think will happen, but no one seems to have a very distinct notion respecting it. Some think the Government will issue some day a notice to say that there are only provisions for a week longer; and that at the end of this time the gates of the city will be opened, and the Prussians told that, if they insist upon entering, there will be nothing to prevent them. Others think that the Government will resign their power into the hands of the mayors, as the direct representatives of Paris. Trochu rides about a good deal outside, and says to the soldiers, "Courage, my children, the moment is coming." But to what moment he alludes no one is aware. No word is more abused in the French language than "sublime." To call a folly a sublime folly is considered a justification of any species of absurdity. We call this refusal to anticipate a contingency which certainly is possible, if not probable, sublime. We are proud of it, and sleep on in our fool's paradise as though it were to last for ever.

CHAPTER XVII.

January 17th.

THE papers publish reports of the meetings of the clubs. The following is from the *Débats* of to-day :—

"At the extremity of the Rue Faubourg St. Antoine is a dark passage, and in a room which opens into this passage is the Club de la Revendication. The audience is small, and consists mainly of women, who come there to keep warm. The club is peaceable—hardly revolutionary—for Rome is Rome no more, and the Faubourg St. Antoine, formerly so turbulent, has resigned in favour of Belleville and La Villette. Yesterday evening the Club de la Revendication was occupied, as usual, in discussing the misery of the situation, and the necessity of electing a Commune. An orator, whose patriotic enthusiasm attained almost to frenzy, declared that as for himself he scorned hams and sausages in plenty, and that he preferred to live on the air of liberty. (The women sigh). Another speaker is of opinion that if there were a Commune there would also be hams and sausages in plenty. We still pay, he says, the budget of the clergy, as though Bonaparte were still on the throne, instead of having rationed the large appetites and forced every one to live on 1fr. 50c. a day. In order to make his meaning clear the orator uses the following comparison. Suppose, he says, that I am a peasant, and that I have fattened a chicken. (Excitement.) Were I obliged to give the wings to the clergy, the legs to the military, and the carcass to civil functionaries, there would be nothing of my chicken left for me. Well, this is our case. We fatten chickens; others eat them. It would be far wiser for us to keep them for ourselves. (Yes, yes.) A Pole, the Citizen Strassnowski, undertakes to defend the Government. He obtains a hearing, but not without difficulty. You complain that the Government, he says, has not cast more cannon. Where were the artillerymen? (Ourselves.) But three months ago you were citizens, you were not soldiers. In making you march and counter-march in the streets and on the ramparts you have been converted into soldiers. The Government was right therefore to wait. (Murmurs.) The orator is not angry with the German nation; he is angry only with the potentates who force the people to kill each other; and he hopes that the day will come when the European nations will shake hands over the Pyrenées, the Alps, the Balkan, and the mountains of Carpathia. (Feeble applause and murmurs.) A citizen begs the audience to have patience with the Citizen Strassnowski, who is a worthy man and a volunteer; but the citizen then reproaches the worthy man for having attempted to defend a Government whose incapacity is a matter of notoriety. Come now, Citizen Strassnowski, he says, what has the Government done to merit your praise? It has armed us and exercised us; but why? To deliver us over with our guns and our cannons to the Prussians after we have all caught cold on the ramparts. Has it tried to utilise us? No, it has passively looked on whilst the Prussians surrounded Paris with a triple circle of citadels. We are told every day that the armies of the provinces will deliver us. We do not see them. We are not even secure in Paris. Every kind of story is afloat. Yesterday it was reported that General Schmitz had betrayed us; to-day it is an actress who has arrested a spy whose cook was on intimate terms with a cook of the member of the Government. Why these reports? Because the Government has no moral support, and no one feels confidence in it. In the meantime the food gets less and less, and this morning at eight o'clock all the bakers in this arrondissement had closed their shops. (True, true; we waited five hours at the closed doors.) When we get the bread, it is more like plaster than bread. In the third arrondissement, on the other hand, it is good and plentiful. So much for the organising spirit of the Government. We have to wait hours for bread, hours for wood, and hours for meat; and frequently we do not get either bread, meat, or wood. Things cannot last long like this, my worthy Strassnowski. The speaker concludes by urging the people to take the direction of their affairs into their own hands. (Cries of "Vive la Commune.") The President urges his hearers to subscribe towards a society, the object of which is civic instruction. The club breaks up, the President is applauded."

Here is another description of a club meeting from the same journal:—

"The laurels of Belleville prevented La Villette from sleeping. La Villette, therefore, determined to have, like her rival, a central democratic and social club, and yesterday she inaugurated in the Salle Marseillaise an opposition to the "Rue Fae." In some respects the Marseillaise club is even more democratic than her parent. The Salle is a sort of barn, and the *sans culottes* themselves, notwithstanding their horror of all luxury, hardly found its comforts sufficient for them. The Club Faire, with its paintings on the walls and its lustres, has a most aristocratic air in comparison with this new hall of democracy. To judge by its first séance, the Club Marseillaise promises well. Last night enough treasons were unveiled to make the fortune of most other clubs for a week at least. From the commencement of the war we have been in the meshes of a vast network of treason; and these meshes can only be broken through by the Commune and the Republic. The conspiracy was hatched long ago between the Emperors and the Kings, and the other enemies of the people. The war had been arranged amongst them, and it is an error to suppose that we were beaten at Rhichshofen or Sédan. "No," cried an orator, with conviction, "we have never been defeated; but we have been betrayed." ("True.") Applause. "We are still betrayed.") The men of the Hôtel de Ville imitate Bonaparte, and, like him, they have an understanding with the Prussians, to enslave the people, after having betrayed the country. To whom then must we turn to save the country? To the Legitimists? To the Orleanists?" (No, no.) The orator does not hesitate to avow that he would turn to them if they could save France. (Impossible.) Yes, it is impossible for them. The orator admits it; and all the more because Legitimists and Orleanists are enrolled in the conspiracy against the nation. The people can be the only saviours of the people, by the establishment of the commune; and this is why the men of the Hôtel de Ville and the Reactionists are opposed to its establishment. A second speaker abandons the question of the Commune and of the conspiracy, in order to call attention to the resignation of Citizen Delescluze, late mayor of the nineteenth arrondissement. While this orator thinks that it would be unjust to accuse the patriot Delescluze of treason, he ought not the less to be blamed for having abandoned a post to which he had been called by his fellow citizens. The people elected him, and he had no right to put his resignation in the hands of the men of the Hôtel de Ville in the critical circumstances in which we find ourselves—at a moment when the tide of misery is mounting—when the mayors have a great mission to fulfil. What has been the consequence of this act of weakness?

The men of the Hôtel de Ville have named a commission to administer the nineteenth arrondissement exactly as was done under Bonaparte. This is what we citizens of Belleville have gained by the desertion of Delescluze. (Applause.) A citizen pushes his way to the tribune to justify the mayor. He admits that at first sight it is difficult to approve of a magistrate who has been elected by the people resigning his office at the very moment when the people have the greatest need of him, but—and again we get into the dark mystery of the conspiracy—if he gave in his resignation, it was because he would not be an accomplice of treason. In a meeting presided over by Jules Favre, what do you suppose the mayors were asked to do? (Here the orator pauses a moment to take breath. The curiosity of the audience is intense.) They were asked to take part in the capitulation. (Violent murmurs—Infamous.) Well yes—Delescluze would have nothing to do with this infamy, and he withdrew. Besides, there was another reason. In the division of the succour afforded to necessitous citizens the nineteenth arrondissement was only supposed to have 4000 indigent persons, whilst in reality the number is 50,000, and by this means it was hoped that the popularity of this pure Republican would suffer, and perhaps riots break out which would be put down—(the divulgation of this plot against the mayor of the nineteenth arrondissement is received in different ways. A person near us observes—"All the same, he ought not to have resigned.") This incident over, the discussion goes back to the treasons of the Hôtel de Ville. It is well known, says a speaker, that a sortie had been determined on in a Council composed of four generals, presided over by Trochu, and that the next morning the Prussians were informed of it. Who told them, who betrayed us. Was it Schmitz, or another general. (A voice: "It was the man who eats pheasants." Indignation.) In any case, Trochu is responsible, even if he was not the traitor himself. ("Yes, yes; it was Trochu!") Another citizen, not personally known to the audience, but who announces that he lives in the Rue Chasson, says that he has received by accident a confidential communication which, perhaps, may throw some light on the affair. This citizen has some friends who are the friends of Ledru Rollin and of the citizen Tibaldi; and one of these friends heard a friend say that either Ledru Rollin or Tibaldi had heard Trochu say that it was impossible to save Paris; but that he would have 30,000 men killed, and then capitulate. (Murmurs of indignation.) The citizen of the Rue Chasson has received a second confidential communication, which corroborates the first. He has been told by one of his neighbours that everything is ready for a capitulation, and he thinks that he will soon be enabled to communicate something still more important on this subject; but in the meanwhile he entreats the energetic citizens of Belleville— (indignation "This is not Belleville")—pardon, of La Villette and of the other Republican faubourgs, to keep their eyes on the Government. They must have no confidence in the *quartiers* inside the town. The Rue Chasson, in which he lives, is utterly demoralised. La Villette, with Belleville and Montmartre, must save Paris. (Applause.) Another citizen says that he has of late frequently heard the odious word capitulation. How can it be otherwise? Everything is being done to make it necessary. We, the National Guard, who receive 1fr. 50c. a-day, are called the indigent. What do the robbers and the beggars who thus insult us do? They indulge in orgies in the fashionable restaurants. The Zoological Gardens have been shut. Why? Because the elephants, the tigers, and other rare animals have been sold in order to enable wretches who laugh at the public misery to gorge themselves. What can we, the indigent, as they call us, do with 30 sous, when a few potatoes cost 30fr., and a piece of celery 2fr. And they talk now of capitulating, because they have grown rich on the war. Every one knows that it was made in order that speculators should make fortunes. As long as they had goods to sell at ten times their value they were for resistance to the death. Now that they have nothing more to sell, they talk of capitulating. Ah! when one thinks of these scandals one is almost inclined to blow one's brains out. (Laughter and applause.) A fourth citizen takes up the same theme with the same energy and conviction. He knows, he says, a restaurant which is frequented by bank clerks, and where last week there were eaten two cows and a calf, whilst the ambulance opposite was without fresh meat. (Violent murmurs.) This is a part of the system of Trochu and his colleagues. They starve us and they betray us. Trochu, it is true, has said that he would not capitulate, but we know what that means. When we are worn out and demoralised he will demand a fresh plébiscite on the question of a capitulation, and then he will say that the people, and not he, capitulated. ("True, he is a Jesuit.") We must make an end of these speculators and traitors. ("Yes, yes, it is time.") We must have the Commune. We have not more than eighteen days of provisions, and we want fifteen of them to revictual. If the Commune is not proclaimed in three days we are lost. ("True. La Commune! La Commune!") The orator explains how the Commune will save Paris. It will establish domiciliary visits not only among the shopkeepers, but among private persons who have stores of provisions. Besides, he adds, when all the dogs are eaten we will eat the traitors. (Laughter and applause.) The Commune will organise at the same time a sortie *en masse*, the success of which is infallible. From statistics furnished by Gambetta it results that at this moment there are not above 75,000 Prussians round Paris. And shall our army of 500,000 men remain stationary before this handful of

Germans? Absurd. The Commune will burst through this pretended circle of iron. It will put an end to treason. It will place two commissaries by the side of each general. (The evening before, at the club in the Rue Blanche, one commissary with a revolver had been proposed. At the Marseillaise two were thought requisite. This evening, probably at the Club Faire, in order to beat La Villette, three will be the number. The position of a general of the Commune will not be an easy one.) These commissaries, continues the orator, will watch all the movements of the general. At the first sign he gives of yielding, they will blow his brains out. Inexorably placed between victory and death, he will choose the former. (General approbation.) The hour is getting late, but before concluding the sitting, the President announces that the moment is approaching when Republicans must stand shoulder to shoulder. Patriots are invited to give in their names and addresses, in order to be found when they are wanted. This proposal is adopted by acclamation. A certain number of citizens register their names, and then the meeting breaks up with a shout of " Vive la Commune de Paris ! "

January 19th.

All yesterday artillery was rolling and troops were marching through Paris on their way to the Porte de Neuilly. The soldiers of the line were worn and ragged; the marching battalions of the National Guards, spick and span in their new uniforms. All seemed in good spirits, the soldiers, after the wont of their countrymen, were making jokes with each other, and with everyone else—the National Guards were singing songs. In some instances they were accompanied by their wives and sweethearts, who carried their muskets or clung to their arms. Most of them looked strong, well-built men, and I have no doubt that in three or four months, under a good general, they would make excellent soldiers. In the Champs Elysées, there were large crowds to see them pass. "Pauvres garçons," I heard many girls say, "who knows how many will return!" And it was indeed a sad sight, these honest bourgeois, who ought to be in their shops or at their counters, ill-drilled, unused to war, marching forth with stout hearts, but with little hope of success, to do battle for their native city, against the iron legions which are beleaguering it. They went along the Avenue de la Grande Armée, crossed the bridge of Neuilly over the Seine, and bivouacked for the night in what is called the "Peninsule of Genevilliers." This peninsula is formed by a loop in the Seine. Maps of the environs of Paris must be plentiful in London, and a glance at one will make the topography of to-day's proceedings far clearer than any description. The opening of the loop is hilly, and the hills run along the St. Cloud side of the loop as far as Mont Valérien, and on the other side as far as Rueil. About half a mile from Mont Valérien following the river is St. Cloud; and between St. Cloud and the Park of the same name is Montretout, a redoubt which was commenced by the French, but which, since the siege began, has been held by the Prussians. The enemy's line extends across the loop from Montretout through Garches to La Malmaison. The latter lies just below Rueil, which is a species of neutral village. The troops passed the night in the upper part of the loop. In numbers they were about 90,000, as far as I can ascertain, and they had with them a formidable field artillery. The object of the sortie was a vague idea to push forward, if possible, to Versailles. Most of the generals were opposed to it, and thought that it would be wiser to make frequent sudden attacks on the enemy's lines; but General Public Opinion insisted upon a grand operation; and this anonymous but all powerful General, as usual, carried the day. The plan appears to have been this: one half the army was under General Vinoy, the other half under General Ducrot. The former was to attack Montretout and Garches, the latter was to push forward through Rueil and La Malmaison, carry the heights of La Jonchère, and then unite with Vinoy at Garches. General Trochu, from an observatory in Mont Valérien, commanded the whole movement. At 7 o'clock troops were pushed forward against Montretout. This redoubt was held by about 200 Poles from Posen; and they made so determined a resistance that the place was not taken until 9.30. No guns were found in the redoubt. At the same time General Bellemare, who commands one of Vinoy's divisions, advanced on Garches, and occupied the wood and park of Buzanval, driving in the Prussian outposts. Here several battalions of the National Guards were engaged. Although their further advance was arrested by a stone wall, from behind which the Prussians fired, they maintained themselves in the wood and the park. The Prussians now opened a heavy fire along the line. At Montretout it was impossible to get a single gun into position. This went on until a little after three o'clock. By this time reinforcements had come up from Versailles, and were pushed forward against the centre of the Feenel line. At the same time shells fell upon the reserves, which consisted of National Guards, and which were drawn up upon the incline of the heights looking towards Paris. They were young troops, and for young troops nothing is so trying as being shelled without being allowed to move. They broke and fell back. Their companions who were in advance, and who held the crest of the heights, saw themselves deserted, and at the same time saw the attacking column coming forward, and they too fell back. The centre of the position was thus lost. A hurried consultation was held, and Montretout and Buyenval were evacuated. As night closed the French troops were falling back to their bivouacs of the previous night, and the Prussians were recrossing the trench which formed their advanced posts in the morning. The day was misty, the mud was so deep that walking was difficult, and I could not follow very clearly the movements of the troops from the house in which I had ensconced myself. What became of General Ducrot no one seemed to know. I have since learnt that he advanced with little resistance through Rueil and La Malmaison, and that he then fought during the day at La Jonchère, detaching a body of troops towards the Park of Buzanval. He appears, however, to have failed in taking La Celle St. Cloud, and from thence flanking La Bergerie, and marching on Garches. Everything is consequently very much where it was this morning before the engagement took place. It has been the old story. The Prussians did not defend their first line, but fell back on their fixed batteries, there keeping up a heavy fire until reinforcements had had time to be brought up. More troops are ordered out for to-morrow; so I presume that the battle is to be renewed. If it ends in a defeat, the consequences will be serious, for the artillery can only be brought back to Paris by one bridge. The wounded are numerous. In the American ambulance, which is close by in the Champs Elysées, there are about seventy. In the Grand Hotel they are arriving every moment. The National Guard at Buzanval behaved very fairly under fire. Many of them had not been above a few days in uniform. Their officers were in many cases as inexperienced as the men. During the fight companies of them were wandering about looking for their battalions, and men for their companies. As citizen soldiers they did their best, and individually they were made of good stuff; but the moral is—do not employ citizen soldiers for offensive operations. When I returned into the town at about 5 o'clock this afternoon, the peninsula of Gennevilliers resembled the course at Epsom on a wet Derby Day. To my civilian eyes, cavalry, artillery, and infantry, seemed to be in inextricable confusion.

This morning the bread was rationed all over the city. No one is to have more than 300 grammes per diem; children only 150. I recommend anyone who has lived too high to try this regime for a week. It will do him good. No costermonger's donkey is so overloaded as the stomachs of most rich people. The Government on December 12 solemnly announced that the bread never would be rationed. This measure, therefore, looks to me very much like the beginning of the end. A perquisition is also being made in search of provisions in the apartments of all those who have quitted Paris. Another sign of the end. But it is impossible to know on how little a Frenchman can live until the question has been tested. I went yesterday into the house of a friend of mine, in the Avenue de l'Impératrice, which is left in charge of a servant, and found three families, driven out of their homes by the bombardment, installed in it—one family, consisting of a father, a mother, and three children, were boiling a piece of horse meat, about four inches square, in a bucket full of water. This exceedingly thin soup was to last them for three days. The day before they had each had a carrot. The trouble of the bread is that the supply ceases before the demand in most quarters, so that those who come last get none. My friend's servant was giving a dinner to the English coachman. The sole dish was a cat with mice round it. I tasted one of the latter, crunching the bones as if it had been a lark. I can recommend mice, when nothing more substantial is to be obtained.

I hear that a pigeon has arrived this evening. Its despatch has not yet been published. The "traitor-mania" still rages. Last night at the Belleville Club an orator announced an awful discovery—the bread was being poisoned by traitors. The Correspondent of one of your contempo-

,raries, having heard that he had been accused of being a Prussian spy, went to-day to the Prefect of the Police. This august being told him that he did not suspect him, and then showed him a file of papers duly docketed relating to each London paper which is represented here. For my part, although I have not failed to blame what I thought blameable, and although I have not gone into ecstacies over the bombastic nonsense which is the legacy of the vile despotism to which the French were foolish enough to submit for twenty years, and which has vitiated the national character, I have endeavoured in my correspondence to be, as far as was consistent with truth, "to all their virtues very kind, to all their faults a little blind."

January 20th.

This morning several fresh regiments of National Guards were ordered to march out to the Isthmus of Gennevilliers. I accompanied one of them; but when we got into Neuilly a counter-order came, and they were marched back. Every house in Neuilly and Courbevoie was full of troops, and regiments were camping out in the fields, where they had passed the night without tents. Many of the men had been so tired that they had thrown themselves down in the mud, which was almost knee-deep, and thus fallen asleep with their muskets by their sides. Bitter were the complaints of the commissariat. Bread and *eau de vie* were at a high premium. Many of the men had thrown away their knapsacks, with their loaves strapped to them, during the action, and these were now the property of the Prussians. It is impossible to imagine a more forlorn and dreary scene. Some of the regiments—chiefly those which had not been in the action—kept well together; but there were a vast number of stragglers wandering about looking for their battalions and their companies. At about twelve o'clock it became known that the troops were to re-enter Paris, and that the battle was not to be renewed; and at about one the march through the gate of Neuilly commenced, colours flying and music playing, as though a victory had been won. I remained there some time watching the crowd that had congregated at each side of the road. Most of the lookers on appeared to be in a condition of blank despair. They had believed so fully that the grand sortie must end in a grand victory, that they could hardly believe their eyes when they saw their heroes returning into Paris, instead of being already at Versailles. There were many women anxiously scanning the lines of soldiers as they passed by, and asking every moment whether some relative had been killed. As I came home down the Champs Elysées it was full of knots of three and four soldiers, who seemed to consider that it was a waste of time and energy to keep up with their regiments.

In the evening papers the despatch announcing the defeat of Chanzy has been published, and a request from Trochu to General Schmitz to apply at once for an armistice of two days to bury the dead. "The fog," he adds, "is very dense," and certainly this fog appears to have got into the worthy man's brain. Almost all the wounded have already been picked up by the French and the Prussian ambulances. Nearly all the dead are in what are now the Prussian lines, and will no doubt be buried by them. In the afternoon, as a suspension of arms for two hours was agreed to, our ambulances pushed forward, and brought back a few wounded, but not many. Most of those who had fallen in the Prussian lines had already been moved, their officers said, to St. Germain and St. Cloud, where they would be cared for. At three P.M. Jules Favre summoned the Mayors to a consultation, and General Trochu also came in to the Ministry of Foreign Affairs for half an hour, and then returned to Valérien. The feeling against him is very strong. It is said that he has offered to resign; and I think it very probable that he will be the Jonah thrown out to the whale. But will this sacrifice save the ship? All the Generals are roundly abused. Indeed, in France there is no medium between the Capitol and the Tarpeian Rock. A man who is not a victor must be a traitor. That undisciplined National Guards fresh from their shops, should be unable to carry by assault batteries held by German troops, is a thing which never can be admitted. If they fail to do this, it is the fault of their leaders. Among those who were killed yesterday is M. Regnault, the painter who obtained at the last salon, the gold medal for his picture of "Salome." He went into action with a card on his breast, on which he had written his name and the address of the young lady to whom he was engaged to be married. When the brancardiers picked him up, he had just strength to point to this address. Before they could carry him there he was dead. But the most painful scene during the battle was the sight of a French soldier who fell by French balls. He was a private in the 119th Battalion, and refused to advance. His commander remonstrated. The private shot him. General Bellemare, who was near, ordered the man to be killed at once. A file was drawn up and fired on him; he fell, and was supposed to be dead. Some brancardiers soon afterwards passing by, and thinking that he had been wounded in the battle, placed him on a stretcher. It was then discovered that he was still alive. A soldier went up to him to finish him off, but his gun missed fire. He was then handed another, when he blew out the wretched man's brains. From all I can learn from the people connected with the different ambulances, our loss yesterday does not amount to above 2000 killed and wounded. Most of the newspapers estimate it far higher. At Buzenval, where the only really sharp fighting took place, an officer who was in command tells me that there were about 300 killed. For the sake of humanity, it is to be hoped that we shall have no more of these blind sorties.

The French get through the first Prussian lines; they are then arrested by the fire of the batteries in the second line; reinforcements are brought up by the enemy; and the well-known movement to the rear commences. "Our losses," say the official reports the next morning, "are great; those of the enemy enormous. Our troops fought with distinguished valour, but ———"

January 21st.

It was so wet last night that there were but few groups of people on the Boulevards. At the clubs Trochu was universally denounced. Almost every one is now in despair. Of what use, they say, are the victories of Bourbaki; he cannot be here in time. We had pinned our faith on Chanzy, and the news of his defeat, coupled with our own, has almost extinguished every ray of hope in the breasts even of the most hopeful. The Government, it is thought, is preparing the public mind for a capitulation. *La Liberté*, until now its strongest supporter, bitterly complains that it should publish the truth! Chandordy's despatch went first to Jules Favre. He stood over the man who was deciphering it. When he read the opening sentence, "Un grand malheur," he refused to read more, and sent it undeciphered to Trochu. When it reached the Governor, no one on his staff could decipher it, so it had to be returned to the Foreign-office. The moment for the quacks is at hand. A "General" offers to raise the siege if he be given 50,000 men. A magician offers a shell which will destroy the Prussians root and branch. M. Felix Pyat, in his organ, observes that Sparta never was taken, and that the Spartans used to eat in common. He proposes, therefore, as a means to free Paris, that a series of public suppers should be inaugurated. I can only say that I hope that they may be, for I certainly shall attend. Even Spartan broth would be acceptable. The bread is all but uneatable. If you put it in water, straw and bits of hay float about. A man, who ought to know, solemnly assured me this morning that we had only food for six days; but then men who ought to know are precisely those who know nothing. I do not think that we are so badly off as this; but the end is a question no longer of months, but of days, and very soon it will be of hours. Those who desire a speedy capitulation are called *les capitulards*, and they are in a majority of nine to one. There are still many who clamour for a grand sortie, but most of those who do so are persons who by no possibility can themselves share in the sortie. The street orators are still at poor Jonah Trochu, and their hearers seem to agree with them. These sages, however, do not explain who is to replace him. Some of the members of the Government, I hear, suggest an admiral; but what admiral would accept this *damnosa hæreditas?* Among the generals, each has his partisans, and each seems to be of opinion that he himself is a mighty man of war, and all the others fools. Both Vinoy and Ducrot declined to attend the Council of War which sat before the late sortie. They were generals of division, they said, and they would obey orders, but they would accept no further responsibilities. Ducrot, who was the *fidus Achates* of Trochu, is no longer in his good graces. The *Réveil* of this afternoon, which is usually well-informed on all matters which concern our Mayors, gives the following account of the meeting of yesterday: "At three o'clock the meeting took place in the presence of all the members of the Government. M. Trochu declared formally that he would fight no more. M. Favre said that the Government was 'disappearing.' M. Favre proposed that the Government should give up its power to the Mayors. The Mayors refused. The discussion was very violent. Several propositions, one more absurd than another, were brought forward by some of the members of the Government. They were not discussed. As usual, the meeting broke up without any result." The best man they have is Vinoy; he is honest, disinterested, and determined. It is to be hoped that if Trochu resigns, he will take his place.

January 22nd.

So poor Jonah has gone over, and been swallowed up by the whale. He still remains the head of the civil government, but it only is as a figure-head. He is an upright man; but as a military chief he has proved himself a complete failure. He was a man of plans, and never could alter the details of these plans to suit a change of circumstances. What his grand plan was, by which Paris was to be saved, no one now, I presume, ever will know. The plans of his sorties were always elaborately drawn up; each divisional commander was told in the minutest details what he was to do. Unfortunately, General Moltke usually interfered with the proper development of these details—a proceeding which always surprised poor Trochu—and in the account the next day of his operations, he would dwell upon the fact as a reason for his want of success. That batteries should be opened upon his troops, and that reinforcements should be brought up against them, were trifles—probable as they might seem to most persons—which filled him with an indignant astonishment. At the last sortie Ducrot excuses himself for being late at La Malmaison because he found the road by which he had been ordered to advance occupied by a long line of artillery, also there by Trochu's orders. General Vinoy, who has replaced him, is a hale old soldier about seventy years old. He has risen from the ranks, and in the Crimea was a very intimate friend of Lord Clyde. When the latter came, a few years before his death, to Paris, the English Ambassador had prepared a grand breakfast for him, and had gone to the station to meet him. On the platform was also Vinoy, who also had prepared breakfast for his old comrade in arms; and this breakfast, very much to the disgust of the diplomatist, Lord Clyde accepted. General Vinoy has to-day issued a proclamation to the troops, which in its plain, simple, modest language contrasts very favourably with the inflated bombast in which his predecessor was so great an adept.

The newspapers are already commencing to prove to their own satisfaction that the battle of last Thursday was not a defeat, but an "incomplete victory." As for the National Guard, one would suppose that every one of them had been in the action, and that they were only prevented from carrying everything before them by the timidity of their generals. The wonderful feats which many of these heroes have told me they performed would lead one to suppose that Napoleon's old Guard was but a flock of sheep in comparison with them. I cannot help thinking that by a certain indistinctness of recollection they attribute to themselves every exploit, not only that they saw, but that their fertile imaginations have ever dreamt to be possible. In all this nonsense they are supported by the newspapers, who think more of their circulation than of truth. To read the accounts of this battle one would suppose that neither the Line nor the Mobiles had been in it. A caricature now very popular represents a lion in the uniform of a National Guard held back by two donkeys in the uniforms of generals, and vainly endeavouring to rush upon a crowd of terrified Germans. As a matter of fact—about 5,000 National Guards were in the thick of it—the men behaved tolerably well, and many of the officers very well. The great majority of the marching battalions which were in the peninsula "did not give," to use the French phrase; and some of them, notwithstanding the efforts of their officers, were unable to remain steady as soon as the Prussian bombs reached them. This *sic vos non vobis* which is meted out to the Mobiles and the Line makes me indignant. As for the sailors, they are splendid fellows—and how we always manage to beat them afloat increases my admiration of the British tars. They are kept under the strictest discipline by their captains and admirals, one of whom once said to me when I asked him whether his men fraternized with the soldiers, "If I saw one of them associating with such *canaille*, I would put him under arrest for twenty-four hours." In the forts they are perfectly cool under the heaviest fire, and both at Le Bourget and at Chantillon they fought like heroes. "Ten thousand of them," observed a general to me the other day, "are worth more than the whole National Guards."

The bombardment still continues. Bombs fall into the southern part of the town; but habit in this world is everything, and no one troubles himself much about them. At night the Trocadero has become a fashionable lounge for the *cocottes*, who still honour us with their presence. The line of the Prussian batteries and the flash of their guns can be seen. The hissing, too, of the bombs can be heard, when the *cocottes* crouch by their swains in affected dread. It is like Cremorne, with its ladies and its fireworks. Since yesterday morning, too, St. Denis has been bombarded. Most of its inhabitants have taken refuge in Paris, but it will be a pity if the cathedral, with the tombs of all the old French Kings, is damaged. St. Denis is itself a species of fort. Its guns are not, a friend tells me who has just come from there, replying with vigour. The Prussians are firing on it from six separate batteries, and it is feared that it will fall. Our attention to-day has been diverted from the Prussians outside by a little domestic quarrel at home, and we have been shooting each other, as though the Prussian missiles were not enough for our warlike stomachs, and death were not raging around our prison.

Between twelve and one this morning a band of armed patriots appeared before the prison of Mazas, and demanded the release of Flourens and the political prisoners who were shut up there. The director, instead of keeping the gate shut, allowed a deputation to enter. As soon as the gate was opened, not only the deputation, but the patriots rushed in, and bore off Flourens and his friends in triumph. With the Mayor at their head, they then went to the Mairie of the 20th Arrondissement, and pillaged it of all the rations and bread and wine which they found stored up there. Then they separated, having passed a resolution to go at twelve o'clock to the Hôtel de Ville, to assist their "brothers" in turning out the Government. I got myself to the Place of the Hôtel de Ville at about two o'clock. There were then about 5000 persons there. The gates were shut. Inside the rails before them were a few officers; and soldiers could be seen at all the windows. Some few of the 5000 were armed, but most of them were unarmed. Close in by the Hôtel de Ville there seemed to be some sort of military order in the positions occupied by the rioters. I took up my stand at the corner of the Rue de Rivoli. Every moment the crowd increased. It was composed partly of sightseers, for on Sunday every one is out of doors; partly of sympathisers. These sympathisers were not, as on October 31, working men, but mainly what Count Bismarck would call the populace. Their political creed may be summed up by the word "loot;" their personal appearance by the word "hangdog." I found myself in the midst of a group of hangdogs, who were abusing everyone and everything. On one side of me was a lady of expansive figure, whose breath showed that she had partaken lately of ardent spirits, and whose conversation showed that if she was a "matron of Cornelia's mien," her morals were better than her conversation. "The people are slaves," she perpetually yelled, "they will no longer submit to traitors; I say it to you, I, the mother of four children." This maternal vantage ground which she assumed evidently gave her opinions weight, for her neighbours replied, "Oui, elle a raison, la mère." A lean, bilious-looking fellow, who looked as though through life he had not done an honest day's work, and whose personal charms were not heightened by a grizzled beard and a cap of catskin, close by the matron, was bawling out, "The Hôtel de Ville belongs to us, I am a taxpayer;" whilst a youth about fifteen years old, hard by, explained in a shrill treble the military errors which Trochu and the generals had committed. At a little after three o'clock, a fresh band, all armed, with a drum beating the charge, appeared, and as they neared the chief entrance of the Hôtel de Ville, just one shot, and then a number of shots were fired. Everybody who had a gun then shot it off with an eager but general idea of doing something, as he fled, like a Parthian bowman. The stampede soon became general; numbers of persons threw themselves on the ground. I saw the mother of four children sprawling in the mire, and the bilious taxpayer fall over her, and then I followed the youthful strategist into an open door. Inside were about twenty people. The door was shut to, and for about twenty minutes we heard muskets going off. Then, as the fight seemed over, the door was opened and we emerged. The Place had been evacuated by the mob, and was held by the troops. Fresh regiments were marching on it along the quay and the Rue de Rivoli. Wounded people were lying about or crawling towards the houses. Soon some *brancardiers* arrived and picked up the wounded. One boy I saw evidently dying —the blood was streaming out of two wounds. The windows of the Hôtel de Ville were broken, and the façade bore traces of balls, as did some of the houses round the Place. I remained until dusk. Even when I left the streets were full of citizens. Each man who had rolled in the mire, and whose clothes showed traces of it, was the centre of a group of sympathisers and non-sympathisers, to whom he was explaining how the Breton brigands had fired on him, a poor innocent lamb, who had done no harm. The non-sympathisers, however, were in the majority, and "served him right" seemed to be the general verdict on those who had been shot, or who had spoilt their clothes. Every now and then some window would slam or a cart would rumble by, when there would be a general scamper for a few yards. After dinner I again returned to the Hôtel de Ville. The crowd had dispersed, and the Place was militarily occupied; so we may suppose that this little domestic episode is over.

Jaanary 23rd, morning.

The clubs are closed, and the *Réveil* and the *Combat* suppressed. Numbers of people are coming in from St. Denis, where the bombardment is getting very hot. Bombs last night fell in one of the islands on the Seine; so the flood is mounting, and our dry ground is every day diminishing. I see in an extract from a German paper, that it has been telegraphed to England that the village of Issy has been entirely destroyed by the Prussian fire. This is not the case. I was there the other day, and the village is still there. It is not precisely the spot where one would wish one's property to be situated, but most of the houses are, as yet, intact.

CHAPTER XVIII.

January 27th.

I WRITE this, as I hear that the last balloon is to start tonight. How lucky for the English public that just when the siege of Paris ceases the conscript fathers of the nation will still furnish them with reading in their newspapers. The light, airy wit of Professor Fawcett, and the pleasant fancy of Mr. Newdegate, will be served up for them with their hot rolls every morning instead of the bulletins of Count Moltke—lucky public!

Most of us here are much like heirs at a rich man's funeral. We have long faces, we sigh and we groan, but we are not quite so unhappy as we look. The *Journal Officiel* of this morning announces that Paris will not be occupied, and that the National Guard will not go to Germany. This is, we say, very different from a capitulation—it is a political incident; in a few days I expect to hear it called a victory. The editor of the *Liberté*—why is this gentleman still alive? for the last three months he has been making pacts with death—explains that Paris never would have and never will capitulate, but that an armistice is a very different sort of thing. Last night, notwithstanding the cold which has again set in, the Boulevard was blocked up with groups of patriots and wiseacres discussing the state of things, and explaining what Paris would agree to and what she would not agree to. Occasionally some "pure"—a "pure" is an Ultra—threw out that the Parisians themselves were only reaping what they had sown; but the pure, I need hardly say, was soon silenced, and it seemed to be generally agreed that Paris has been sublime and heroic, but that if she has been neither, it has been the fault of the traitors to whom she has confided her destinies. Some said that the admirals had stated that they would blow up their forts rather than surrender them; but if the worthies who vouched for this had been informed by the admirals of their intentions, I can only say that these honest tars had chosen strange confidants.

Paris, as I have already said more than once, has been fighting as much for her own supremacy over the provinces as for victory over the Prussians. The news—whether true or false I know not—that Gambetta, who is regarded as the representative of Paris, has been replaced by a sort of Council of Regency, and that this Council of Regency is treating, has filled everyone here with indignation. Far better, everyone seems to think, that Alsace should be lost to France, than that France should be lost to Paris. The victories of Prussia have been bitter to Frenchmen, because they had each of them individually assumed a vicarious glory in the victories of the First Empire; but the real patriotism of the Parisians does not extend farther than the walls of their own town. If the result of this war is to cause France to undertake the conduct of its own affairs, and not to allow the population of Paris and the journalists of Paris to ride roughshod over her, the country will have gained more than she has lost by her defeats, no matter what may be the indemnity she be called upon to pay. The martial spirit of the National Guard has of course been lauded to the skies by those newspapers which depend for their circulation on these braves. The question what they have done may, however, be reduced to figures. They number above 300,000. According to their own statements they have been fighting for nearly five months, and I venture to say that during the whole campaign they have not lost 500 men. They have occasionally done duty in the trenches, but this duty has been a very brief one, and they have had very long intervals of repose. I do not question that in the National Guard there are many brave men, but one can only judge of the fighting qualities of an army by comparison, and if the losses of the National Guard be statistically compared with those of the Line, of the Mobiles, and of the sailors, it will be shown that—to use an Americanism—their record is a bad one. The soldiers and the sailors have fought, and the women have suffered during the siege. The male population of Paris has done little more than bluster and drink and brag.

To-day there is no firing, and I suppose that the last shell has fallen into Paris. I went out yesterday to St. Denis. Along the road there were a few people coming into Paris with their beds and tables in hand-carts. In the town the bombardment, although not so heavy as it had been, was far too heavy to be pleasant. Most of the people still remaining have established themselves in their cellars, and every moment one came against some chimney emerging from the soil. Some were still on the ground-floor of their houses, and had heaped up mattresses against their windows. The inhabitants occasionally ran from one house to another, like rabbits in a warren from hole to hole. All the doors were open, and whenever one heard the premonitory whistle which announced the arrival of one of the messengers of our psychological friends outside, one had to dodge into some door. I did not see any one hit. The houses were a good deal knocked about; the cathedral, it was said, had been hit, but as shells were falling in the Place before it, I reserved investigations for a more quiet moment. Some of the garrison told me that the forts had been "scratched," but as to how far this scratching process had been carried

I cannot say from personal observation, as I thought I might be scratched myself if I pushed my reconnaissance farther. I am not a military man, and do not profess to know anything about bombs technically, but it seems to me, considering that it is their object to burst, and considering the number of scientific persons who have devoted their time to make them burst, it is very strange how very few do burst. I am told that one reason for this is the following :—when they lose the velocity of the impelling force they turn over in the air, and as the percussion cap is on the lighter end, the heavier one strikes the ground. Many of these, too, which have fallen in the town, and which have burst, have done no mischief, because the lead in which they are enveloped has kept the pieces together. The danger, indeed, to life and limb of a bombardment is very slight. I would at any time prefer to be for 24 hours in the most exposed portion of a bombarded town, than walk 24 times across Oxford Street in the middle of the day. A bomb is a joke in comparison with those great heavy wagons which are hurled at pedestrians by their drivers in the streets of London.

January 28th.

The Government has not yet made up its mind to bell the cat, and to let us know the terms of the armistice or capitulation, whichever it is to be called. We hear that it is expected that trains will run to England on Tuesday or Wednesday, and by the first train I for one shall endeavour to get out of this prison. It will be such a relief to find oneself once more among people who have glimpses of common sense, who are not all in uniform, and who did not insist so very strongly on their sublime attitude. Yesterday evening there were a series of open-air clubs held on the Boulevards and other public places. The orators were in most instances women or aged men. These Joans of Arc and ancient Pistols talked very loudly of making a revolution in order to prevent the capitulation; and it seemed to me that among their hearers, precisely those who whilst they had an opportunity to fight thought it wise not to do so, were most vociferous in their applause. The language of the National Guard is indeed most warlike. Several hundred of their officers have indulged in the cheap patriotism of signing a declaration that they wish to die rather than yield. This morning many battalions of the National Guard are under arms, and are hanging about in the streets with their arms stacked before them. Many of the men, however, have not answered to the rappel, and are remaining at home, as a mode of protesting against what is passing. General Vinoy has a body of troops ready to act, and as he is a man of energy I do not anticipate serious disturbances for the moment. As for the soldiers and the Mobiles, they are wandering about in twos and threes without arms, and do not affect to conceal that they are heartily glad that all is over. Poor fellows, their torn and tattered uniforms contrast with the spick and span military gear of the National Guard. They have had during the siege hard work, and they have done good duty, with but little thanks for it. The newspapers are one and all down on the Government. It is of course held to be their fault that the lines of the besiegers have not been forced. General Trochu is not a military genius, and his colleagues have not proved themselves better administrators than half a dozen lawyers who have got themselves elected to a legislative assembly by the gift of the gab were likely to be; but still this system of sacrificing the leaders whenever any disaster takes place, and accusing them of treachery and incompetence, is one of the worst features in the French character. If it continues, eventually every man of rank will be dubbed by his own countrymen either a knave or a fool.

January 31st.

Finita la Comedia. Let fall the curtain. The siege of Paris is over; the last balloon has carried our letters through the clouds; the last shot has been fired. The Prussians are in the forts, and the Prussian armies are only not in the streets because they prefer to keep watch and guard outside the vanquished city. What will be the verdict of history on the defence? Who knows! On the one hand the Parisians have kept a powerful army at bay far longer than was anticipated; on the other hand, every sortie that they have made has been unsuccessful—every attempt to arrest the approach of the besiegers has failed. Passively and inertly they have allowed their store of provisions to grow less and less, until they have been forced to capitulate, without their defences having been stormed, or the cannon silenced. The General complains of his soldiers, the soldiers complain of their General; and on both sides there is cause of complaint. Trochu is not a Todleben. His best friends describe him as a sort of military Hamlet, wise of speech, but weak and hesitating in action—making plans, and then criticising them instead of accomplishing them. As a commander, his task was a difficult one; when the siege commenced he had no army; when the army was formed, it was encompassed by earthworks and redoubts so strong that even better soldiers would have failed to carry them. As a statesman, he never was the master of the situation. He followed rather than led public opinion, and subordinated everything to the dread of displeasing any section of a population, which, to be ruled—even in quiet times—must be ruled with a rod of iron. Success is the criterion of ability in this country, and poor Trochu is as politically dead as though he never had lived. His enemies call him a traitor; his friends defend him from the charge by saying that he is only a vain fool.

As regards the armed force, the sailors have behaved so

well that I wonder at the ease with which our own tars have always beaten them. They have been kept under a rigid discipline by their naval commanders. The line, composed of depôt battalions, and of the regiments which Vinoy brought back from Mézières, without being equal to old seasoned troops, have fought creditably. Their great defect has been an absence of strict discipline. The Mobiles, raw peasants fresh from their homes, have shown themselves brave in action, and have supported the hardship of lengthy outpost duty without a murmur. Unfortunately they elected their own officers, and this weakened their efficiency for offensive purposes. When the siege commenced, every citizen indiscriminately assumed the uniform of the National Guard. Each battalion of this motley force elected its officers, and both men and officers united in despising discipline as a restraint to natural valour. The National Guard mounted guard occasionally on the ramparts, and the rest of their time they passed in parading the streets, drinking in the pothouses, and discussing the conduct of their military superiors. General Trochu soon discovered that this force was, for all purposes of war, absolutely useless. He called for volunteers, and he anticipated that 100,000 men would answer to the appeal; not 10,000 did so. He then ordered a marching company to be formed from each battalion. Complaints innumerable arose. Instead of a generous emulation to fight, each man sought for an excuse to avoid it. This man had a mother, that man a daughter; one had weak lungs, and another weak legs. At length, by dint of pressure and coaxing, the marching battalions were formed. Farewell suppers were offered them by their comrades. They were given new coats, new trousers, and new saucepans to strap on their havresacks. They have done some duty in the trenches, but they were always kept away from serious fighting, and only gave a "moral support" to those engaged in the conflict, until the fiasco in the Isthmus of Gennevilliers a fortnight ago. Then, near the walls of Buzanval, the few companies which were in action fought fairly if not successfully, whilst in another part of the field of battle, those who formed the reserves broke and fled as soon as the Prussian bombs fell into their ranks. The entire National Guard, sedentary and marching battalions, has not, I imagine, lost 500 men during its four months' campaign. This can hardly be called fighting to the death *pro aris et focis*, and sublimity is hardly the word to apply to these warriors. If the 300 at Thermopylæ had, after exhausting their food, surrendered to the Persian armies, after the loss of less than one per cent. of their number—say of three men, they might have been very worthy fellows, but history would not have embalmed their act. Politically, with the exception of the riot on October 31, the Government of National Defence has met with no opposition since September last. There are several reasons for this. Among the bourgeoisie there was little of either love or confidence felt in Trochu and his colleagues, but they represented the cause of order, and were indeed the only barrier against absolute anarchy. Among the poorer classes everyone who liked was clothed, was fed, and was paid by Government for doing nothing, and consequently many who otherwise would have been ready to join in a revolt, thought it well not to disturb a state of things so eminently to their satisfaction. Among the Ultras, there was a very strong distaste to face the fire either of Prussians or of Frenchmen. They had, too, no leaders worthy of the name, and many of them were determined not to justify Count Bismarck's taunt that the "populace" would aid him by exciting civil discord. The Government of September, consequently, is still the Government of to-day, although its chief has shown himself a poor general, and its members, one and all, have shown themselves wretched administrators. In unblushing mendacity they have equalled, if not surpassed, their immediate predecessor, the virtuous Palikao. The only two of them who would have had a chance of figuring in England, even as vestrymen, are M. Jules Favre and M. Ernest Picard. The former has all the brilliancy and all the faults of an able lawyer—the latter, although a lawyer, is not without a certain modicum of that plain practical common sense, which we are apt to regard as peculiarly an English characteristic.

The sufferings caused by the dearth of provisions and of fuel have fallen almost exclusively on the women and children. Among the well-to-do classes, there has been an absence of many of those luxuries which habit had made almost necessaries, but this is all. The men of the poorer classes, as a rule, preferred to idle away their time on the 1fr. 50c. which they received from the Government, rather than gain 4 or 5fr. a day by working at their trades; consequently if they drank more and ate less than was good for them, they have had only themselves to thank for it. Their wives and children have been very miserable. Scantily clad, ill fed, without fuel, they have been obliged to pass half the day before the bakers' doors, waiting for their pittance of bread. The mortality and the suffering have been very great among them, and yet, it must be said to their credit, they have neither repined nor complained.

Business has, of course, been at a stand-still since last September. At the Bourse the transactions have been of the most trifling description, much to the disgust of the many thousands who live here by peddling gains and doubtful speculations in this temple of filthy lucre. By a series of decrees payment of rent and of bills of exchange has been deferred from month to month. Most of the wholesale exporting houses have been absolutely closed. In the retail shops nothing has been sold except by the grocers, who must have made large profits. Whether the city has a recuperative power strong enough to enable it to recover from this period of stagnation, and to pay its taxation, which henceforward will be enormous, has yet to be seen. The world is the market for *articles de Paris*, but then to preserve this market, the prices of these articles must be low. Foreigners, too, will not come here if the cost of living is too exorbitant, and yet I do not see how it is to be otherwise. The talk of the people now is, that they mean to become serious—no longer to pander to the extravagances of strangers, and no longer to encourage their presence amongst them. If they carry out these intentions, I am afraid that, however their morals may be improved, their material interests will suffer. Gambling tables may not be an advantage to Europe, but without them Homburg and Baden would go to the wall. Paris is a city of pleasure—a cosmopolitan city; it has made its profit out of the follies and the vices of the world. Its prices are too high, its houses are too large, its promenades and its public places have cost too much for it to be able to pay its way as the sober, decent capital of a moderate-sized country, where there are few great fortunes. If the Parisians decide to become poor and respectable, they are to be congratulated upon the resolve, but the present notion seems to be that they are to become rich and respectable—a thing more difficult. Paris—the Paris of the Empire and of Haussmann—is a house of cards. Its prosperity was a forced and artificial one. The war and the siege have knocked down the cards, and it is doubtful whether they will ever serve to build a new house.

As regards public opinion, I cannot see that it has changed one iota for the better since the fall of the Empire, or that common sense has made any headway. There are of course sensible men in Paris, but either they hold their tongues, or their voices are lost in the chorus of blatant nonsense, which is dinned into the public ears. *Mutatis mutandis* the newspapers, with some few exceptions, are much what they were when they worshipped Cæsar, chronicled the doings of the *demi-monde*, clamoured for the Rhine, and invented Imperial victories. Their ignorance respecting everything beyond the frontiers of France is such, that a charity-schoolboy in England or Germany would be deservedly whipped for it. *La Liberté* has, I am told, the largest circulation at present. Every day since the commencement of the siege I have invested two sous in this journal, and I may say, without exaggeration, that never once—except one evening when it was burnt on the boulevard for inadvertently telling the truth—have I been able to discover in its columns one single line of common sense. Its facts are sensational—its articles engross appeals to popular folly, popular ignorance, and popular vanity. Every petty skirmish of the National Guard has been magnified into a stupendous victory; every battalion which visited a tomb, crowned a statue, or signed some manifesto pre-eminent in its absurdity, has been lauded in language which would have been exaggerated if applied to the veterans of the first Napoleon. The editor is, I believe, the author of the "pact with death," which has been so deservedly ridiculed in the German newspapers. The orators of the clubs have not been wiser than the journalists. At the Ultra gatherings, a man who says that he is a republican is regarded as the possessor of every virtue. The remedy for all the ills of France has been held to be, to copy exactly what was done during the First Revolution. "Citizens, we must have a *Commune*, and then we shall drive the Prussians out of France," was always received with a round of sympathetic applause, although I have never yet found two persons to agree in their explanation of what is meant by the word "*Commune.*" At the Moderate clubs, the speeches generally consisted of ignorant abuse of Germany, attempts to disprove well-established facts, and extravagant self-laudation. I have attended many clubs—Ultra and Moderate—and I never heard a speaker at one of them who would have been tolerated for five minutes by an ordinary English political meeting.

The best minister whom the Parisians have, is M. Dorian. He is a manufacturer, and as hard-headed and practical as a Scotsman. Thanks to his energy and business qualities, cannon have been cast, old muskets converted into breech-loaders, and ammunition fabricated. He has had endless difficulties to overcome, and has overcome them. The French are entirely without what New Englanders call shiftiness. As long as all the wheels of an administration work well, the administrative coach moves on, but let the smallest wheel of the machine get out of order, and everything stands still. To move on again takes a month's discussion and a hundred despatches. A redoubt which the Americans during their civil war would have thrown up in a night has taken the Parisians weeks to make. Their advanced batteries usually were without traverses, because they were too idle to form them. Although in modern sieges the spade ought to play as important a part as the cannon, they seem to have considered it beneath their dignity to dig—500 navvies would have done more for the defence of the town than 500,000 National Guards did do. At the commencement of October, ridiculous barricades were made far inside the ramparts, and although the generals have complained ever since that they impeded the movements of their troops, they have never been removed.

I like the Parisians and I like the French. They have much of the old Latin *urbanitas*, many kindly qualities, and most of the minor virtues which do duty as the small change of social intercourse. But for the sake of France, I am glad that Paris has lost its *prestige*, for its rule has been a blight and a curse to the entire country; and for the sake of Europe, I am glad that France has lost her military prestige, for this prestige has been the cause of most of the wars of Europe during the last 150 years. It is impossible so to adapt the equilibrium of power, that every great European Power shall be co-equal in strength. The balance tips now to the side of Germany. That country has attained the unity after which she has so long sighed, and I do not think she will embroil the continent in wars, waged for conquest, for an "idea," or for the dynastic interests of her princes. The Germans are a brave race, but not a war-loving race. Much, therefore, as I regret that French provinces should against the will of their inhabitants become German, and strongly as I sympathise with my poor friends here in the overthrow of all their illusions, I console myself with the thought that the result of the present war will be to consolidate peace. France will no doubt look wistfully after her lost possessions, and talk loudly of her intention to re-conquer them. But the difficulty of the task will prevent the attempt. Until now, to the majority of Frenchmen, a war meant a successful military promenade, a plentiful distribution of decorations, and an inscription on some triumphal arch. Germany was to them the Germany of Jena and Austerlitz. Their surprise at seeing the Prussians victors at the doors of Paris, is much that which the Americans would feel if a war with the Sioux Indians were to bring these savages to the suburbs of New York. The French have now learnt that they are not invincible, and that if war may mean victory, it may also mean defeat, invasion, and ruin. When, therefore, they have paid the bill for their *à Berlin* folly, they will think twice before they open a fresh account with fortune.

I would recommend sightseers to defer their visit to Paris for the present, as during the armistice it will not be a very pleasant residence for foreigners. I doubt whether the elections will go off, and the decisions of the National

Assembly be known without disturbances. The vainest of the vain, irritable to madness by their disasters, the Parisians are in no humour to welcome strangers. The world has held aloof whilst the "capital of civilisation" has been bombarded by the "hordes of Attila," and there is consequently, just now, no very friendly feeling towards the world.

Of news, there is very little. We are in a state of physical and moral collapse. The groups of patriots which invested the Boulevards on the first announcement of the capitulation have disappeared; and the gatherings of National Guards who announced their intention to die rather than submit have discontinued their sittings, owing it, as they said, to their country to live for her. No one hardly now affects to conceal his joy that all is over. Every citizen with whom one speaks, tells you that it will be the lasting shame of Paris that with its numerous army it not only failed to force the Prussians to raise the siege, but also allowed them whenever they pleased to detach corps d'armée against the French generals in the provinces. This, of course, is the fault of the Government of Trochu and of the Republic, and having thus washed his hands of everything that has occurred, the citizen goes on his way rejoicing. The Mobiles make no secret of their delight at the thought of getting back to their homes. Whatever the Parisians may think of them, they do not think much of the Parisians. The army, and more particularly the officers, are very indignant at the terms of the armistice. They bitterly say that they would far rather have preferred to have been made prisoners of war at once, and they feel their anomalous position in Paris, a pledge that peace will be made. M. Jules Ferry was treated so coldly the other day by General Vinoy's staff, when he went upon some business to the head-quarters of the Commander-in-Chief, that he asked the cause, and was told in plain terms that he and his colleagues had trifled with the honour of the army. The armistice was, as you are aware, concluded by M. Jules Favre in person. It was then thought necessary to send a General to confer with Count Moltke on matters of detail. General Trochu seized upon this occasion to assert himself, and requested to be allowed to send a General of his choice, saying that his book which he published in 1867 must be so well known at the German head-quarters, that probably his envoy would meet with peculiar respect. To this General Vinoy acceded, but Count Moltke refused to treat with Trochu's General, and the chief of General Vinoy's staff had to be substituted in his stead. General Ducrot is still here. He resigned his command, not as is generally supposed, because the Prussians insisted upon it in consequence of his evasion from Sédan, but because General Vinoy on assuming the command of the army gave him a very strong hint to do so. "I did not," observed Vinoy, "think your position sufficiently *en règle* to serve under *you*, and so——"

The question of the revictualling is the most important one of the moment. The railroad kings, who had an interview with Count Bismarck at Versailles, seem to be under the impression that this exceedingly wide-awake statesman intends to throw impediments in the way of Paris getting provisions from England, in order that the Germans may turn an honest penny by supplying the requirements of the town. He has thrown out hints that he himself can revictual us for a short time, if it really be a question of life and death. Even when the lines are opened to traffic and passengers, the journey to England, *viâ* Amiens, Rouen, and Dieppe will be a tedious one. The Seine, we learn, has been rendered impassable by the boats which have been sunk in it.

We have as yet had no news from outside. The English here find the want of a consul more than ever. The Foreign

Office has sent in an acting commission to Mr. Blount, a gentleman who may be an excellent banker, but knows nothing of consular business, notwithstanding his courtesy. As whenever any negotiation is to take place at a foreign court a Special Envoy is sent, and, as it now appears, whenever a Consul is particularly wanted in a town a Special Consul is appointed, would it not be as well at once to suppress the large staff of permanent ambassadors, ministers, and consuls who eat their heads off at a heavy cost to the country. I should be curious to know how many years it would take to reduce the intelligence of an ordinary banker's clerk to the level of a Foreign Office bureaucrat. How the long-suffering English public can continue to support the incompetency and the supercilious contempt with which these gentry treat their employers is to me a mystery. Bureaucrats are bad enough in all conscience, but a nest of fine gentleman bureaucrats is a public curse, when thousands are subjected to their whims, their ignorance, and their airs.

The Republic is in very bad odour just now. It has failed to save France, and it is rendered responsible for this failure. Were the Comte de Paris a man of any mark, he would probably be made King. As it is, there is a strong feeling in favour of his family, and more particularly in favour of the Duc d'Aumale. Some talk of him as President of the Republic, others suggest that he should be elected King. The Bonapartists are very busy, but as regards Paris there is no chance either for the Emperor or the Empress Regent. As for Henri V., he is, in sporting phraseology, out of the betting. Among politicians, the general opinion is that a moderate Republic will be tried for a short time, and that then we shall gravitate into a Constitutional Monarchy.

Little heed is taken of the elections which are so close at hand. No one seems to care who is elected. As it is not known whether the National Assembly will simply register the terms of peace proposed by Germany, and then dissolve itself, or whether it will constitute itself into an *Assemblée Constituante*, and decide upon the future form of government, there is no very great desire among politicians to be elected to it. Several Electoral Committees have been formed, each of which puts forward its own list—that which sits under the Presidency of M. Dufaure, an Orleanist, at the Grand Hotel, is the most important of them. Its list is intended to include the most practical men of all parties; the rallying cry is to be France, and in theory its chiefs are supposed to be moderate Republicans.

The ceremony of the giving up of the forts has passed over very quietly. The Prussians entered them without noise or parade. At St. Denis, the mayor of which said that no Prussian would be safe in it, friends and foes, I am told by a person who has just returned, have fraternised, and are pledging each other in every species of liquor. The ramparts are being dismantled of their guns; the National Guard no longer does duty on them, and crowds assemble and stare vaguely into the country outside. During the whole siege Paris has not been so dismal and so dreary as it is now. There is no longer the excitement of the contest, and yet we are prisoners. The only consolation is that a few weeks will put an end to this state of things.

CHAPTER XIX.

February 1st.

THE Government of National Defence has almost disappeared from notice. It has become a Committee to preside over public order. The world may calumniate us, they said in a proclamation the other day. It would be impossible, replied the newspapers. Trochu and Gambetta, once the idols of the Parisians, are now the best abused men in France. Trochu (a friend of his told me to-day) deserted by all, makes speeches in the bosom of his family. No more speeches, no more lawyers; is the cry of the journals. And then they spin out phrases of exaggerated Spartanism by the yard, and suggest some lawyer as the rising hope of the country.

The cannon have been taken from the ramparts. The soldiers—Line and Mobile—wander about unarmed, with their hands in their pockets, staring at the shop-windows. They are very undemonstrative, and more like peaceful villagers than rough troopers. They pass most of their time losing their way and trying to find it again; the Mobiles all longing to get back to their homes. It appears now that there was an error in the statistics published by the Government respecting the stock of grain in hand. Two accounts, which were one and the same, were added together. The bread is getting less like bread every day. Besides peas, rice, and hay, starch is now ground up with it. In the eighth arrondissement yesterday, there were no rations. The Northern Company do not expect a provision train from Dieppe before Friday, and do not think they will be able to carry passengers before Saturday. We are in want of fuel as much as of food. A very good thing is to be made by any speculator who can manage to send us coal or charcoal.

More than 23,000 persons have applied for permits to quit Paris, on the ground that they are provincial candidates for the Assembly. Of course this is a mere pretext. A commission, as acting British Consul, has been sent to Mr. Blount, a banker. Will some M.P. move that the Estimates be reduced by the invisible Consul, who seems to consider Paris *in partibus infidelium?*

The only outsider who has penetrated through the double cordon of Prussians and French, is your Correspondent at the Headquarters of the Crown Prince of Saxony. He startled us quite as much as Friday did Robinson Crusoe. He was enthusiastically welcomed, for he had English newspapers in one pocket, and some slices of ham in the other.

VERSAILLES, *February 6th.*

I am not intoxicated, but I feel so heavy from having imbibed during the last twenty-four hours more milk than I did during the first six months which I passed in this planet, that I have some difficulty in collecting my thoughts in order to write a letter. Yesterday I arrived here in order to breathe for a moment the air of freedom. In vain my hospitable friends, who have put me up, have offered me wine to drink, and this and that delicacy to eat—I have stuck to eggs, butter, and milk. Pats of butter I have bolted with a greasy greediness which would have done honour to Pickwick's fat boy; and quarts of milk I have drunk with the eagerness of a calf long separated from its maternal parent.

Although during the last few months I have seen but two or three numbers of English papers, I make no doubt that so many good, bad, and indifferent descriptions of every corner and every alley in this town have appeared in print, that Londoners are by this time as well acquainted with it as they are with Richmond or Clapham. Versailles must, indeed, be a household word—not to say a household nuisance—in England. It has been a dull, stupid place, haunted by its ancient grandeurs; with too large a palace, too large streets, and too large houses, for many a year; and while the presence of a Prussian army and a Prussian Emperor may render it more interesting, they fail to make it more lively. Of the English correspondents, some have gone into Paris in quest of "phases" and impressions; many, however, still remain here, battening upon the fat of the land, in the midst of kings and princes, counts and what not. I myself have seldom got beyond a distant view of such grand beings. What I know even of the nobility of my native land, is derived from perusing the accounts of their journeys in the fashionable newspapers, and from the whispered confidences of their third cousins. To find myself in familiar intercourse with people who habitually hobnob at Royal tables, and who invite Royal Highnesses to drop in promiscuously and smoke a cigar, almost turns my head. To-morrow I shall return to Paris, because I feel, were I to remain long in such grand company, I should become proud and haughty; and, perhaps, give myself airs when restored to the society of my relatives, who are honest but humble. There is at present no difficulty in leaving Paris. A pass is given at the Prefecture to all who ask for one, and it is an "open sesame" to the Prussian lines. I came by way of Issy, dragged along by an aged Rosinante, so weak from low living that I was obliged to get out and walk the greater part of the way, as he positively declined to draw me and the chaise.

This beast I have only been allowed to bring out of Paris after having given my word of honour that I would bring him back, in order, if necessary, to be slain and eaten, though I very much doubt whether a tolerably hungry rat would find meat enough on his bones for a dinner.

I have been this morning sitting with a friend who, under the promise of the strictest secrecy, has given me an account of the condition of affairs here. I trust, therefore, that no one will mention anything that may be found in this letter, directly or indirectly relating to the Prussians. The old King, it appears, is by no means happy as an Emperor. He was only persuaded to accept this title for the sake of his son, "Our Fritz," and he goes about much like some English squire of long descent, who has been induced to allow himself to be converted into a bran new peer, over-persuaded by his ambitious progeny. William is one of that numerous class of persons endowed with more heart than brains. Putting aside, or regarding rather as the delusion of a diseased brain, his notion that he is an instrument of Heaven, and that he is born to rule over Prussian souls by right divine, the old man is by no means a bad specimen of a good-natured, well-meaning, narrow-minded soldier of the S. U. S. C. type; and between Bismarck and Moltke he has of late had by no means an easy time. These two worthies, instead of being, as we imagined in Paris, the best of friends, abominate each other. During the siege Moltke would not allow Bismarck to have a seat at any council of war; and in order to return the compliment, Bismarck has not allowed Moltke to take any part in the negotiations respecting the armistice, except on the points which were exclusively military. Bismarck tells the French that had it not been for him, Paris would have been utterly destroyed, while Moltke grumbles because it has not been destroyed; an achievement which this talented captain somewhat singularly imagines would fittingly crown his military career. But this is not the only domestic jar which destroys the harmony of the happy German family at Versailles. In Prussia it has been the habit, from time immemorial, for the heir to the throne to coquet with the Liberals, and to be supposed to entertain progressive opinions. The Crown Prince pursues this hereditary policy of his family. He has surrounded himself with intelligent men, hostile to the present state of things, and who understand that in the present age no country can be great and powerful, where all who are not country gentlemen, chamberlains, or officers, are excluded from all share in its government. Bismarck, on the other hand, is the representative, or rather the business man, of the squirearchy and of the Vons—much in the same way as Mr. Disraeli is of the Conservatives in England; and, like the latter, he despises his own friends, and scoffs at the prejudices, a pretended belief in which has served them as a stepping-stone to power. The consequence of this divergency of opinion is, that Bismarck and "Our Fritz" are very nearly what school-boys call "cuts," and consequently when the old King dies, Bismarck's power will die with him, unless he is wise enough to withdraw beforehand from public life. "Our Fritz," I hear, has done his best to prevent the Prussian batteries from doing any serious damage to Paris, and has not concealed from his friends that he considers that the bombardment was, in the words of Fouché, worse than a crime—an error.

I find many of the Prussian officers improved by success. Those with whom I have come in personal contact have been remarkably civil and polite, but I confess that—speaking of course generally—the sight of these mechanical instruments of war, brought to the highest state of perfection in the trade of butchery, lording it in France, is to me most offensive. I abhor everything which they admire. They are proud of walking about in uniform with a knife by their side. I prefer the man without the uniform and without the knife. They despise all who are engaged in commercial pursuits. I regard merchants and traders as the best citizens of a free country. They imagine that the man whose ancestors have from generation to generation obscurely vegetated upon some dozen acres, is the superior of the man who has made himself great without the adventitious aid of birth; I do not. When Jules Favre met Bismarck over here the other day, the latter spoke of Bourbaki as a traitor, because he had been untrue to his oath to Napoleon. "And was his country to count for nothing?" answered Favre. "In Germany king and country are one and the same," replied Bismarck. This is the abominable creed which is inculcated by the military squires who now hold the destinies of France and of Germany in their hands; and on this detestable heresy they dream of building up a new code of political ethics in Europe. Liberalism and common sense are spreading even in the army; but take a Tory squire, a Groom of the Chamber, and a Life-guardsman, boil them down, and you will obtain the ordinary type of the Prussian officer. For my part, I look with grim satisfaction to the future. The unity of Germany has been brought about by the union of Prussian Feudalists and German Radicals. The object is now attained, and I sincerely hope that the former will find themselves in the position of cats who have drawn the chestnuts out of the fire for others to eat. If "Our Fritz," still following in the steps of his ancestors, throws off his Liberalism with his Crown Princedom, his throne will not be a bed of roses; it is fortunate, therefore, for him, that he is a man of good sense. I am greatly mistaken if the Germans will long submit to the horde of squires, of princes, of officers, and of court flunkeys, who together, at present, form the ruling class. Among the politicians here there is a strong feeling of dislike to the establishment of a Republic in France. If they could have their own way they would re-establish the Empire. But those who imagine that this is possible understand very little of the French character. The Napoleonic legend was the result of an epoch of military glory; the capitulation of Sedan not only scotched it, but killed it. A Frenchman still believes in the military superiority of his race over every other race, as firmly as he believes in his own existence. If a French army is defeated, it is owing to the treachery or the incapacity of the commander. If a battle be lost, the General must pay the penalty for it; for his soldiers are invincible. It is Napoleon, according to the received theory, who has succumbed in the present war; not the French nation. If Napoleon be restored to power, the nation will accept the responsibility which they now lay to his door. The pride and vanity of every Frenchman are consequently the strongest securities against an Imperial Restoration. Were I a betting man, I would bet twenty to one against the Bonapartes; even against a Republic lasting for two years; and I would take five to one against the Comte de Paris becoming King of the French, and three to one against the Duc d'Aumale being elected President of the Republic. This would be my "book" upon the political French Derby.

The Prussians are making diligent use of the armistice to complete their engineering work round Paris, and they appear to consider it possible that they may yet have trouble with the city. If this be their opinion I can only say that they are badly served by their spies. The resistance *à outrance* men in Paris, who never did anything but talk, will very possibly still threaten to continue the struggle; but they will not fight themselves, and most assuredly they will not find others to fight for them. If the preliminaries of peace be signed at Bordeaux, Paris will not protest; if they are rejected, Paris will not expose itself to certain destruction by any attempt at further resistance, but will capitulate, not as the capital of France, but as a besieged French town. General Vinoy is absolute master of the situation; he is a calm, sensible man, and will listen to no nonsense either from the "patriots," or his predecessors, or from Gambetta. From the tone of the decree of the latter of the 3rd instant, he seems to be under the impression that he is still the idol of the Parisians. Never did a man labour under so complete a delusion. Before by a lucky speech he was pitchforked into the Corps Législatif, he was a briefless lawyer, who used to talk very loudly and with vast emphasis at the Café de Madrid. He is now regarded as a pot-house politician, who ought never to have been allowed to get beyond the pot-house.

The Germans appear to be carrying on the war upon the same principles of international law which formed many thousand years ago the rule of conquest among the Israelites. They are spoiling the Egyptians with a vengeance. Even in this town, under the very eyes of the King, there is one street — the Boulevard de la Reine — in which almost every house is absolutely gutted. This, I hear, was done by the Bavarians. The German army may have many excellent qualities, but chivalry is not among them. War with them is a business. When a nation is conquered, there is no sentimental pity for it, but as much is to be made out of it as possible. Like the elephants, which can crush a tree or pick up a needle, they conquer a province and they pick a pocket. As soon as a German is quartered in a room he sends for a box and some straw; then carefully and methodically packs up the clock on the mantelpiece, and all the stray ornaments which he can lay his hands on; and then, with a tear glistening in his eye for his absent family, directs them either to his mother, his wife, or his lady-love. In vain the proprietor protests; the philosophical warrior utters the most noble sentiments respecting the horrors of war; ponderously explains that the French do not sufficiently appreciate the blessings of peace ; and that he is one of the humble instruments whose mission it is to make these blessings clear to them. Then he rings the bell, and in a mild and gentle voice, orders his box of loot to be carried off by his military servant. Ben Butler and his New Englanders in New Orleans might have profitably taken lessons from these all-devouring locusts. Nothing escapes them. They have long rods which they thrust into the ground to see whether anything of value has been buried in the gardens. Sometimes they confiscate a house, and then re-sell it to the proprietor. Sometimes they cart off the furniture. Pianos they are very fond of. When they see one, they first sit down and play a few sentimental ditties, then they go away, requisition a cart, and minstrel and instrument disappear together. They are a singular mixture of bravery and meanness. No one can deny that they possess the former quality, but they are courageous without one spark of heroism. After fighting all day, they will rifle the corpses of their fallen foes of every article they can lay their hands on, and will return to their camp equally happy because they have won a great victory for Fatherland, and stolen a watch from one of the enemies of Fatherland. They have got now into such a habit of appropriating other people's property, that I confess I tremble when one of them fixes his cold glassy eye upon me. I see that he is meditating some new philosophical doctrine, which, some way or other, will transfer what is in my pocket into his. His mind, however, fortunately, works but slowly, and I am far away from him before he has elaborated to his own satisfaction a system of confiscation applicable to my watch or purse.*

---

* Several complaints having been received from Germans respecting these charges against the German armies, the following extract from an Article—quoted by the *Pall Mall Gazette*—in his new paper *Im Neuen Reich*, by the well-known German author, Herr Gustav Freytag, will prove that they are not unfounded:—
" Officers and soldiers," he says, " have been living for months under the bronze

Paris, *February 7th.*

Rosinante has brought me back with much wheezing from Versailles to Paris; and with me he brought General Duff, U.S.A., and a leg of mutton. At the gate of Versailles we were stopped by the sentinels, who told us that no meat could be allowed to leave the town. I protested; but in vain. Mild blue-eyed Teutons with porcelain pipes in their mouths bore off my mutton. The General protested too, but the protest of the citizen of the Free Republic fared like mine. I followed my mutton into the guard-house, where I found a youthful officer, who looked so pleasant that I determined to appeal to the heart which beat beneath his uniform. I attacked the heart on its weak side. I explained to him that it was the fate of all to love. The warrior assented, and heaved a great sigh to his absent Gretchen. I pursued my advantage, and passed from generalities to particulars. "My lady love," I said, "is in Paris. Long have I sighed in vain. I am taking her now a leg of mutton. On this leg hang all my hopes of bliss. If I present myself to her with this token of my affection, she may yield to my suit. Oh, full-of-feeling, loved-of-

clocks, marble tables, damask hangings, artistic furniture, oil-paintings, and costly engravings of Parisian industry. The musketeers of Posen] and Silesia broke up the velvet sofas to make soft beds, destroyed the richly inlaid tables, and took the books out of the book-cases for fuel in the cold winter evenings. . . . . It was lamentable to see the beautiful picture of a celebrated painter smeared over by our soldiers with coal dust, a Hebe with her arms knocked off, a priceless Buddhist manuscript lying torn in the chimney grate. . . . . Then people began to think it would be a good thing to obtain such beautiful and tasteful articles for one's friends. A system of 'salvage' was thus introduced, which it is said even eminent and distinguished men in the army winked at. Soldiers bargained for them with the Jews and hucksters who swarm at Versailles; officers thought of the adornment of their own houses; and such things as could be easily packed, such as engravings and oil-paintings, were in danger of being cut out of their frames and rolled up for home consumption." Herr Freytag then points out that these articles are private property, and that the officers and soldiers had no right to appropriate them to their own use. "We are proud and happy," he concludes, addressing them, "at your warlike deeds; behave worthily and honourably also as men. Come back to us from this terrible war with pure consciences and clean hands."

beauteous-women, German warrior, can you refuse me?" He "gazed on the joint that caused his shame; gazed and looked, then looked again." The battle was won; the vanquished victor stalked forth, forgetting the soldier in the man, and gave order that the General, the Englishman, and the leg of mutton should be allowed to go forth in peace. Rosinante toiled along towards Paris; we passed through St. Cloud, now a heap of ruins, and we arrived at the Bridge of Neuilly. Here our passes were examined by a German official, who was explaining every moment to a French crowd in his native language that they could not be allowed to pass into Paris without permits. The crowd was mainly made up of women, who were carrying in bags, pocket handkerchiefs, and baskets of loaves, eggs, and butter to their beleaguered friends. "Is it not too bad of him that he will pretend not to understand French?" said an old lady to me. "He looks like a fiend," said another lady, looking up at the good-natured face of the stolid military gaoler. The contrast between the shrieking, gesticulating, excited French, and the calm, cool, indifferent air of the German, was a curious one. It was typical of that between the two races. Having reached Paris, I consigned poor old long Rosinante to his fate—the knackers, and, with my leg of mutton under my arm, walked down the Boulevard. I was mobbed, positively mobbed. "Sir," said one man, "allow me to smell it." With my usual generosity I did so. How I reached my hotel with my precious burthen in safety is a perfect mystery. N.B. The mutton was for a friend of mine; Gretchen was a pious fraud; all being fair in love and war.

In the quarter in which I live I find that the rations have neither been increased nor diminished. They still re-remain at 3-5ths lb. of bread, and 1-25th lb. of meat per diem. In some other districts a little beef has been distributed. Some flour has come in from Orleans, and it is expected that in the course of a few days the bread will cease to be made of the peas, potatoes, and oats which we now eat. In the restaurants, beef—real beef—is to be obtained for little more than three times its normal price. Fish, too, in considerable quantities has been introduced by some enterprising speculator. The two delegates, also, of the Lord Mayor's Relief Fund have arrived with provisions, &c. This evening they are to telegraph to London for more. These gentlemen are somewhat at sea with respect to what is wanted, and by what means it is to be distributed. One of them did me the honour to consult me this afternoon on these two points. With respect to the first, I recommended him to take the advice of Mr. Herbert—to whose energy it is due that during the siege above one thousand English have not been starved—and the Archbishop of Paris, who is a man of sterling benevolence, with a minimum of sectarianism. With respect to the latter, I recommended Liebig, milk, and bacon. The great point appears to me to be that the relief should be bestowed on the right persons. The women and children have been the greatest sufferers of late. The mortality is still very great among them; not because they are absolutely without food, for the rations are distributed to all; but because they are in want of something more strengthening than the rations. Coal is wanted here as much as food. The poorer classes are without the means of cooking whatever meat they may obtain, and it is almost impossible for them, on account of the same reason, to make soup. If I might venture a suggestion to the charitable in England, it would be to send over a supply of fuel.

I had some conversation with a gentleman connected with the Government this evening respecting the political situation. He tells me that Arago, Pelletan, and Garnier Pagès were delighted to leave Paris, and that it was only the absolute necessity of their being as soon as possible at Bordeaux, that induced General Vinoy to consent to their departure. As for Gambetta, he says, it is not probable that he has now many adherents in the provinces; and it is certain that he has very few here. When a patient is given up by the faculty a quack is called in; if the quack effects a cure he is lauded to the skies; if he fails, he is regarded as a *charlatan*, and this is now the case with M. Gambetta. My informant is of opinion that a large number of Ultra-Radicals will be elected in Paris; this will be because the Moderates are split up into small cliques, and each clique insists upon its own candidates being supported, whereas the *Internationale* commands 60,000 votes, which will all be cast for the list adopted by the heads of that society, and because the National Guard are averse to all real work, and hope that the Ultras will force the National Assembly to continue to pay them the 1f. 50c. which they now receive, for an indefinite period. Gambetta, in his desire to exclude from political power a numerous category of his fellow-citizens, has many imitators here. Some of the journals insist that not only the Bonapartists, but also the Legitimists and the Orleanists should be disfranchised. They consider that as a preliminary step to electing a National Assembly to decide whether a Republic is henceforward to be the form of government of the country, it is desirable, as well as just, to oblige all candidates to swear that it shall be. The fact is, the French, no matter what their opinions may be, seem to have no idea of political questions being decided by a majority; or of a minority submitting to the fiat of this majority. Each citizen belongs to a party; to the creed of this party, either through conviction or personal motives, he adheres, and regards every one who ventures to entertain other views as a scoundrel, an idiot, or a traitor. I confess that I have always regarded a Republican form of government as the best, wherever it is possible. But in France it is not possible. The people are not sufficiently educated, and have not sufficient common sense for it. Were I a Frenchman a Republic would be my dream of the future; for the present I should be in favour of a Constitutional Monarchy. A Republic would soon result in anarchy or in despotism; and without any great love for Kings of any kind, I prefer a Constitutional Monarch to either Anarchy or a Cæsar. One must take a practical view of things in this world, and not sacrifice what is good by a vain attempt to attain at once what is better.

Will the Prussians enter Paris? is the question which I have been asked by every Frenchman to whom I have mentioned that I have been at Versailles. This question overshadows every other; and I am fully convinced that this vain, silly population would rather that King William should double the indemnity which he demands from France than march with his troops down the Rue Rivoli. The fact that they have been conquered is not so bitter to the Parisians as the idea of that fact being brought home to them by the presence of their conquerors even for half-an-hour within the walls of the sacred city. I have no very great sympathy with the desire of the Prussians to march through Paris; and I have no great sympathy with the horror which is felt by the Parisians at their intention to do so. The Prussian flag waves over the forts, and consequently to all intents and purposes Paris has capitulated. A triumphal march along the main streets will not mend matters, nor mar matters. " Attilla without" stands before vanquished Paris, as the Cimbrian slave did before Marius. The sword drops from his hand; " awed by the majesty of the past, he flees and dares not strike," is the way in which a newspaper I have just bought deals with the question. It is precisely this sort of nonsense which makes the Prussians determined that the Parisians shall drink the cup of humiliation to its last dregs.

I was told at Versailles that St. Cloud had been set on

fire on the morning after the last sortie, and that although many houses were still burning when the armistice was signed, none had subsequently been either pillaged or burnt. This act of vandalism has greatly incensed the French, and I understand that the King of Prussia himself regrets it, and throws the blame of it on one of his generals, who acted without orders. A lady who was to-day at St. Cloud tells me that she found Germans eating in every room of her house. Both officers and men were very civil to her. They told her that she might take away anything that belonged to her, and helped to carry to her carriage some valuable china; which, by good luck, had not been smashed. With respect to the charge of looting private property, which is brought by the French against their invaders, no unprejudiced person can, after looking into the evidence, doubt that whilst in the German Army there are many officers, and even privates, who have done their best to prevent pillage, many articles of value have disappeared from houses which have been occupied by the German troops, and much wanton damage has been committed in them. I assert the fact, without raising the question whether or not these are the necessary consequences of war. It is absurd for the Germans to pretend that the French Francs-tireurs are the culprits and not they. Francs-tireurs were never in the Boulevard de la Reine at Versailles, and yet the houses in this street have been gutted of everything available.

I venture to repeat a question which I have already frequently asked—Where is the gentleman who enjoys an annual salary as British Consul at Paris? Why was he absent during the siege? Why is he absent now? Why is a banker, who has other matters to attend to, discharging his duties? I am a tax-payer and an elector; if "my member" does not obtain a reply to these queries from the official representative of the Foreign Office in the House of Commons, I give him fair notice that he will shake me by the hand, ask after my health, and affect a deep interest in my reply, in vain at the next general election; he will not have my vote.

The *Electeur Libre*, the journal of M. Picard, has put forth a species of political programme, or rather a political defence of the wing of the Government of National Defence to which that gentleman belongs. For a French politician to praise himself in his own organ, and to say under the editorial " we " that he intends to vote for himself, and that he has the greatest confidence in his own wisdom, is regarded here as nothing but natural.

PARIS, *February 9th.*

" We have been conquered in the field, but we have gained a moral victory." What this phrase means I have not the remotest idea; but as it consoles those who utter it, they are quite right to do so. For the last two days long lines of cannon have issued from the city gates, and have been, without noise or parade, handed over to the Prussians at Issy and Sevran. Few are aware of what has taken place, or know that their surrender had been agreed to by M. Jules Favre. Representations having been made to Count Bismarck that 10,000 armed soldiers were insufficient for the maintenance of the peace of the capital, by an additional secret clause added to the armistice the number has been increased to 25,000. The greatest ill-feeling exists between the Army and the National Guards in the most populous quarters. A general quartered in one of the outer faubourgs went yesterday to General Vinoy, and told him that if he and his men were to be subjected to insults whenever they showed themselves in the streets, he could not continue to be responsible for either his or their conduct. Most persons of sense appear to consider that the armistice was an error, and that the wiser policy would have been to have surrendered without conditions. M. Jules Favre is blamed for not having agreed, upon the occasion, to disarm the National Guards. Many of their battalions, as long as they have arms, and receive pay for doing nothing, will be a standing danger to order. The sailors have been paid off; and the fears that were entertained of their getting drunk and uproarious have not been confirmed. They are peaceably and sentimentally spending their money with the "black-eyed Susans" of their affections. The principal journalists are formally agitating the plan of a combined movement to urge the population to protest against the Prussian triumphal march through the city, by absence from the streets through which the invading army is to defile. Several are, however, opposed to any action, as they fear that their advice will not be followed. Curiosity is one of the strongest passions of the Parisians, and it will be almost impossible for them to keep away from the "sight." Even in Coventry one Peeping Tom was found, and here there are many Peeping Toms. Mr. Moore and Colonel Stuart Wortley, the delegates of the London Relief Fund, have handed over 5,000*l.* of provisions to the Mayors to be distributed. They could scarcely have found worse agents. The Mayors have proved themselves thoroughly inefficient administrators, and most of them are noisy, unpractical humbugs. Colonel Stuart Wortley and Mr. Moore are very anxious to find means to approach what are called here *les pauvres honteuses;* that is to say, persons who are in want of assistance, but who are ashamed to ask for it. From what they told me yesterday evening, they are going to obtain two or three names of well-known charitable persons in each arrondissement, and ask them to make the distribution of the rest of their provisions in store here, and of those which are expected shortly to arrive. Many families from the villages in the neighbourhood of Paris have been driven within its walls by the invaders, and are utterly destitute. In the opinion of these gentlemen they are fitting objects for charity. The fact is, the difficulty is not so much to find people in want of relief, but to find relief for the thousands who require it. Ten, twenty, or thirty thousand pounds are a mere drop in the ocean, so wide-spread is the distress. "I have committed many sins," said a Bishop of the Church of England, "but when I appear before my Maker, and say that I never gave to one single beggar in the streets they will be forgiven." There are many persons in England who, like this prelate, are afraid to give to beggars, lest their charity should be ill applied. No money, no food, no clothes, and no fuel, if distributed with ordinary discretion, can be misapplied at present in Paris. The French complain that all they ever get from England is good advice and sterile sympathy. Now is the moment for us to prove to them that, if we were not prepared to go to war in order to protect them from the consequences of their own folly, we pity them in their distress; and that our pity means something more than words and phrases which feed no one, clothe no one, and warm no one.

The Prussian authorities appear to be deliberately setting to work to render the armistice as unpleasant to the Parisians as possible, in order to force them to consent to no matter what terms of peace in order to get rid of them; and I must congratulate them upon the success of their efforts. They refuse now to recognise passes signed by the Prefect of the Police, and only recognise those bearing the name of General Valdau, the chief of the Staff. To-morrow very likely they will require some fresh signature. Whenever a French railroad company advertises the departure of a train at a particular hour, comes an order from the Prussians to alter that hour. Every Frenchman who quits Paris is subjected to a hundred small, teasing vexations from these military bureaucrats, and made to feel at every step he takes that he is a prisoner on leave of absence, and only breathes the air of his native land by the good-will of his conquerors. The English public must not forget that direct postal communications between Paris and foreign countries are not re-established. Letters from and to England must be addressed to some agent at Versailles or elsewhere, and from thence re-addressed to Paris. As in a day or two trains will run pretty regularly between Paris and London, had our diplomatic wiseacres been worth in pence what they cost us in pounds, by this time they would have made some arrangement to ensure a daily mail-bag to England leaving Paris.

News was received yesterday that Gambetta had resigned, and it has been published this morning in the *Journal Officiel*. A witness of the Council at which it was agreed to send the three old women of the Government to Bordeaux to replace him, tells me that everybody kissed and hugged everybody for half an hour. The old women were ordered to arrest Gambetta if he attempted resistance. It was much like telling a street-sweeper to arrest a stalwart Guardsman. "Do not be rash," cried Trochu. "We will not," replied the old women; "we will remain in one of the suburbs of Bordeaux, until we learn that we can enter it with safety." This reply removed from the minds of their friends any fear that they would incur unnecesary risks in carrying out their mission.

Provisions are arriving pretty freely. All fear of absolute famine has disappeared. To-day the bread is far better than any we have had of late. Some sheep and oxen were seen yesterday in the streets.

The walls are covered with the professions of faith of citizens who aspire to the honour of a seat in the National Assembly. We have the candidate averse to public affairs, but yielding to the request of a large number of supporters; the candidate who feels within himself the power to save the country, and comes forward to do so; the candidate who is young and vigorous, although as yet untried; the candidate who is old and wise, but still vigorous; the man of business candidate; the man of leisure candidate, who will devote his days and nights to the service of the country; then there is the military candidate, whose name, he modestly flatters himself, has been heard above the din of battle, and typifies armed France. I recommend to would-be M.P.'s at home, the plan of M. Maronini. He has as yet done nothing to entitle him to the suffrages of the electors beyond making printing presses, which are excellent and very cheap; so he heads his posters with a likeness of himself. Why an elector should vote for a man because he has an ugly face, I am not aware; but the Citizen Maronini seems to be under the impression that, from a fellow-feeling at least, all ugly men will do so ; and perhaps he is right. Another candidate commences his address : " *Citoyens, je suis le representant du* go ahead." In the clubs last night everyone was talking, and no one was listening. Even the Citizen Sans, with his eternal scarlet shawl girt round his waist, could not obtain a hearing. The Citizen Beaurepaire in vain shouted that, if elected, he would rather hew off his own arm than sign away Alsace and Lorraine. This noble figure of rhetoric, which has never been uttered by a club orator during the siege without eliciting shouts of applause, was received with jeers. The absurdity of the proceedings at this electoral gathering is, that a candidate considers himself insulted if any elector ventures to ask him a question. The president, too, loses his temper half a dozen times every hour, and shakes his fist, screams and jabbers, like an irate chimpanzee, at the audience. If the preliminary electoral meetings are ridiculous, the system of voting, on the other hand, is perfect in comparison with ours. Paris to-day in the midst of a general election is by far more orderly than any English rotten village on the polling-day. Three days ago each elector received at his own house a card, telling him where he was to vote. Those who were entitled to the suffrage, and by accident did not get one of these cards, went the next day to their respective mairies to obtain one. I have just come from one of the rooms in which the votes are taken. I say rooms; for the Parisians do not follow our silly example, and build up sheds at the cost of the candidate. At one end of this room was a long table. A box was in the middle of it, and behind the box sat an employé. To his right sat another. The elector went up to this latter, gave in his electoral card, and wrote his name; he then handed to the central employé his list of names, folded up. This the employé put into the box. About thirty National Guards were on duty in or about the room. The box will remain on the table until to-night, and the National Guards during this time will not lose sight of it; they will then carry it to the Hotel de Ville, where it, and all other voting boxes, will be publicly opened, the votes counted up, and the result, as soon as it is ascertained, announced. How very un-English, some Briton will observe. I can only say that I regret it is un-English. Our elections are a disgrace to our civilisation, and to that common-sense of which we are for ever boasting that we possess so large a share. Last year I was in New York during a general election; this year I am in Paris during one; and both New York and Paris are far ahead of us in their mode of registering the votes of electors.

CHAPTER XX.

CALAIS, *February 10th.*

AT 4 o'clock p.m. on Wednesday I took my departure from Paris, leaving, much with the feelings of Daniel when he emerged from the lions' den, its inhabitants wending their way to the electoral "urns;" the many revolving in their minds how France and Paris were to manage to pay the little bill which their creditor outside is making up against them; the few—the very few—still determined to die rather than yield, sitting in the cafés on the boulevard, which is to be, I presume, their "last ditch." Many correspondents, "special," "our own," and "occasional," had arrived, and were girding up their loins for the benefit of the British public. Baron Rothschild had been kind enough to give me a pass which enabled me to take the Amiens train at the goods station within the walls of the city, instead of driving, as those less fortunate were obliged to do, to Gonesse. My pass had been signed by the proper authorities, and the proper authorities, for reasons best known to themselves—I presume because they had elections on the brain—had dubbed me "Member of the House of Commons, rendering himself to England to assist at the conferences of the Parliament." I have serious thoughts of tendering this document to the doorkeeper of the august sanctuary of the collective wisdom of my country, to discover whether he will recognise its validity.

The train was drawn up before a shed in the midst of an ocean of mud. It consisted of one passenger carriage, and of about half a mile of empty bullock vans. The former was already filled; so, as a bullock, I embarked—I may add, as an ill-used bullock; for I had no straw to sit on. At St. Denis, a Prussian official inspected our passes, and at Gonesse about 200 passengers struggled into the bullock vans. We reached Creil, a distance of thirty miles, at 11.30. I and my fellow-bullocks here made a rush at the buffet. But it was closed. So we had to return to our vans, very hungry, very thirsty, very sulky, and very wet; for it was raining hard. In this pleasant condition we remained until 9 o'clock on Thursday; occasionally slowly progressing for a few miles; then making a halt of an hour or two. Why? No one—not even the guard—could tell. All he knew was, that the Prussians had hung out a signal ordering us, their slaves, to halt, and therefore halt we must. We did the forty miles between Creil and Breteuil in ten hours. There, in a small inn, we found some eggs and bread, which we devoured like a flight of famished locusts. It was very cold, and several of us sought shelter in a room at the station, where there was a fire. In the middle of this room there were two chairs, on one of them sat a Prussian soldier, on the other reposed his legs. He was a big red-haired fellow, and evidently in some corner of his Fatherland passed as a man of wit and humour. He was good enough to explain to us, with a pleasant smile, that in his eyes we were a very contemptible sort of people, and that if we did not consent to all the terms of peace which were proposed by "the Bismarck," he and his fellow warriors would burn our houses over our heads, and in many other ways make things generally uncomfortable to us. "Ah! speak to me of Manteuffel," he occasionally said: and as no one did speak to him of Manteuffel, he did so himself, and narrated to us many tales of the wondrous skill and intelligence of that eminent general. As he called, after the manner of his nation, a *batterie* a *paderie,* and otherwise Germanized the French language, much of his interesting conversation was unintelligible.

We had been at Breteuil about an hour when a Prussian train came puffing up. I managed to induce an official to allow me to get into the luggage van; and thus, having started from Paris as a bullock, I reached Amiens at twelve o'clock as a carpet-bag. The Amiens station, a very large one covered in with glass, was crowded with Prussian soldiers; and for one hour I stood there the witness of and sufferer from unmitigated ruffianism. The French were knocked about, and pushed about. Never were negro slaves treated with more contempt and brutality than they were by their conquerors. I could not stand on any spot for two minutes without being gruffly ordered to stand on another by some officer. Twice two soldiers raised their muskets with a general notion of staving in my skull "pour passer le temps." Frenchmen, whatever may be their faults, are always extremely courteous in all their relations with each other, and with strangers. In their wildest moments of excitement they are civil. They may poison you, or run a hook through you; but they will do it, as Isaac Walton did with the worm, "as though they loved" you. They were perfectly cowed with the rough bullying of their masters. It is most astonishing—considering how good-natured Germans are when at home, that they should make themselves so offensive in France, even during a truce. At one o'clock I left this orgie of German terrorism in a train, and from thence to Calais all was straight sailing. At Abbeville we passed from the Prussian into the French lines. Calais we reached at seven p.m., and right glad was I to eat a Calais supper and to sleep in a Calais bed.

THE END.

www.ingramcontent.com/pod-product-compliance
Lightning Source LLC
Chambersburg PA
CBHW030427300426
44112CB00009B/886